Shylock and the Jewish Question

JOHNS HOPKINS JEWISH STUDIES

Sander Gilman and Steven T. Katz
Series Editors

Shylock

and the

Jewish Question

୬ ୬ ୬

Martin D. Yaffe

The Johns Hopkins University Press
Baltimore & London

This book has been brought to publication with the generous
assistance of Dr. Robert Fine and Nina Cortell and family,
and of Norman and Carol Miller and family.

Johns Hopkins Paperbacks edition, 1999
2   4   6   8   9   7   5   1

The Johns Hopkins University Press
2715 North Charles Street
Baltimore, Maryland 21218-4363
www.press.jhu.edu

Library of Congress Cataloging-in-Publication Data will be found
at the end of this book.
A catalog record for this book is available from the British Library.

ISBN 0-8018-6261-2 (pbk.)

For Ellis Rivkin

עינים הייתי לעור ורגלים לפסח אני,

אב אנכי לאביונים וריב לא ידעתי אחקרהו.

(Job 29:15–16)

Contents

Acknowledgments

IT IS HARD TO SAY EXACTLY WHEN MY THOUGHTS ON SHYLOCK and the Jewish question first began to jell in the form of a book, or just whom I should then include in a short list of benefactors. The first glimmer of a suggestion that the authors under consideration here might be intimately connected probably came during conversations with Ellis Rivkin, to whom this book is dedicated. Yet it was Harry Jaffa who first alerted me to the pertinent philosophical dimensions of Shakespeare's plays, and Michael Platt encouraged my ongoing study of them. Robert Eden read each draft of my chapters-in-progress, and his probing questions were often the cause of the next draft. David Lowenthal was kind enough to send me his engaging chapter on *The Merchant of Venice* from his forthcoming *Shakespeare for the Study*. Helpful remarks at one or another stage of my writing came from George Anastaplo, Gisela and Laurence Berns, Tony Brennan, Robert Faulkner, Robert Grudin, Grant Mindle, Helen Yaffe Ostovich, Richard Owsley, Barbara Tovey, and Gene Wright. Alan Udoff has been generous with sound practical advice about the book. And I am very grateful for the comments of two anonymous readers for the Johns Hopkins University Press.

I owe much to Irma Garlick for her instructive stylistic suggestions and to Rafe Major for his judicious help in compiling the index.

An earlier version of chapter 4 was presented to the Academy for Jewish Philosophy in 1991, and an earlier version of chapter 5 is part of a longer piece published in *Political Science Reviewer* 23 (1994). Parts of chapter 5 are also adapted from an article in *Il cannocchiale* (1994). Thanks to Norbert Samuelson, George Carey, and Brunella Antomarini, respectively, for permission to recycle.

Much of the leisure for writing this book is owed to grants from the Lynde and Harry Bradley Foundation and from University of North Texas. All of the labor in transferring my manuscript to the university's mainframe computer, and in revising and reformating it unstintingly and uncomplainingly on request, came from several pairs of skilled hands animated by congenial souls: Kathy Copeland, Rachel Dowdy, Judy Evans, Jo Ann Luksich, Glenda Lynch, Angela Mahle, Patricia Parham, Kay Prewitt, and Bertha Williams.

Finally, my ongoing debt to my wife, Connie, and to our sons, Michael and David, goes beyond words.

Shylock and the Jewish Question

I
✥ ✥

The Mistreatment of Shakespeare's Shylock

The figure of Shylock is like some secondary figure in a Rembrandt painting. To look sometimes with absorption at the suffering, aging Jew alone is irresistible. But the more one is aware of what the play's whole design is expressing through Shylock, of the comedy's high seriousness in its concern for the grace of the community, the less one wants to lose the play Shakespeare wrote for one he merely suggested.

— C. L. Barber, *Shakespeare's Festive Comedy*

✥ I ✥

IN THIS BOOK I ANALYZE THE FIGURE OF SHYLOCK, the unfortunate Jewish villain in Shakespeare's *Merchant of Venice.* My immediate aim is to challenge the widespread presumption that Shakespeare is, in the last analysis, unfriendly to Jews. In so doing, my larger hope is to rescue Shakespeare's play as a helpful guide for the self-understanding of the modern Jew.

What modern Jewish readers find most unpalatable and upsetting about the dramatic fate of Shylock is his forced conversion to Christianity. Shylock, a wealthy moneylender, is made to convert to Christianity as part of the surprising outcome of his personal lawsuit in retaliation against a Christian merchant, the play's title character. The merchant has been waging a vehement one-man crusade on the Rialto against him for his putatively un-Christian business practices. Shylock's harsh and humiliating punishment might be more merited, one suspects, if the moral and legal circumstances surrounding it were more clearcut. But they do not seem to be. Despite its otherwise happy ending or perhaps because of it, Shakespeare's Venetian comedy leaves us unsettled and perplexed over the place of the Jew in the modern city.

Shylock's offense in the eyes of the city is in the end not just civil or even religious. It is criminal. He has granted the merchant an emergency loan of three thousand ducats, interest free but with a sinister, life-threatening penalty clause for late payment. The penalty, for which Shylock eagerly sues, is a pound of the merchant's flesh. Yet his suit proves in court to be treasonous. It is tantamount to the seeking of a Venetian citizen's life by a resident alien — and is therefore punishable by death and by forfeiture of the offender's estate, half to his intended victim and half to the city. Nor is this all. Although the court mercifully waives the death penalty and offers to reduce the claim on its half of Shylock's estate, it soon withholds the waiver pending Shylock's agreement to a counterproposal by the merchant. The latter recommends extending the court's mercy even further. But he adds three constraints. In return for the city's forgiving all penalties, Shylock must now allow the merchant trusteeship over half his estate so long as Shylock lives, must immediately convert, and must designate the Christian bridegroom of his recently converted and eloped daughter as his sole heir. Even so, questions here arise.

To begin with, why does the court ignore Shylock's repeated subjection to publicly tolerated harassment concerning both his religion and his means of livelihood (personal lending, we might call it; loansharking, as Shakespeare's Venetians seem to regard it)? During the trial, moreover, why do spontaneous Jew-baiting outbursts from one of the merchant's friends go uncensured? And why does the court fail to forewarn Shylock about the imminent likelihood of self-incrimination, into which it eventually entraps him? Finally, why has the merchant, admittedly prominent and well liked in Venice, been allowed the final say to determine Shylock's punishment in accord with his own biblically inspired anti-usuriousness? In short, is not Christian Venice itself party to the abusive conduct of its citizens toward Shylock? Shakespeare's play makes us wonder: why can't the city just let Shylock be?

In order to know from the foregoing circumstances whether Shakespeare's play deserves its anti-Jewish reputation, we must face such questions and try to answer them squarely. Our task first and foremost is therefore to look in a scholarly way at the answers, if any, the play itself provides. In my view, the play's own remarkable answers have not been well understood or appreciated by modern scholars. Although it is reasonable to expect some help from the accumulated scholarly literature about the play, when we turn to it with our questions, we find that it has not succeeded very well in answering or even in facing them. A few recent examples will serve to illustrate.

Harold Bloom, in his introduction to an anthology of critical essays on Shakespeare's Shylock, castigates the playwright severely.[1] He calls the play "both a superb romantic comedy, and a marvelously adequate version of a perfectly Christian, altogether murderous anti-Semitism" (1). He is particularly incensed by Shakespeare's having inflicted on his antagonist a "false conversion," an imposed acceptance of Christianity without any word of defiance or complaint (1f.). He finds Shylock's quiet acquiescence here dramatically implausible, on the grounds that Shylock is a "proud and fierce Jew" for whom conversion is entirely out of character. "We sooner could see Falstaff as a monk, than we can contemplate Shylock as a Christian" (2). Where Shylock's character lacks consistency, Shakespeare's art fails. Bloom the critic therefore turns to *ad hominem* speculation about the playwright's "agonistic context" and infers a "need to compete with and overgo Marlowe's superb villain, Barabas, the Jew of Malta" (5). Shakespeare, we are told, chiefly meant to outdo his literary rival in fashioning a vivid and memorable portrait of (what he took to be) a Jew. Yet in so doing, and especially in succeeding as well as he did, he could not help appealing to the ruling anti-Jewish prejudices of his Christian contemporaries. "In this one play alone," Bloom concludes, "Shakespeare was very much of his age, and not for all time" (6).

Leaving aside the suggestive comparison with Christopher Marlowe's *Jew of Malta* for a separate chapter, I limit myself here to noting a significant omission in Bloom's summary description of Shylock as a "proud and fierce Jew." How, we must ask, are we meant to understand Shylock's Jewishness? Neither Bloom in his introduction nor anyone he selects for his anthology has pursued this question very far — though it is central to Shakespeare's play.

Shylock's Jewishness first comes up in act I, scene iii, during his preliminary encounter on the Rialto with Bassanio, the young man for whose sake the merchant, Antonio, needs the emergency loan. When Shylock asks whether he might speak with Antonio directly, Bassanio at once invites him to dinner for that purpose. Evidently the young man does not expect what Bloom would undoubtedly characterize as Shylock's "proud and fierce" reply:

> *Bassanio: If it please you to dine with us.*
> *Shylock: Yes, to smell pork, to eat of the habitation which your*
> *prophet the Nazarite conjured the devil into! I will buy*
> *with you, sell with you talk with you, walk with you,*
> *and so following; but I will not eat with you, drink with*
> *you, nor pray with you.* (I.iii.29–34)[2]

Yet from Shylock's point of view, his insistence that he will do business and otherwise associate with Venice's Christians but will not eat or drink or pray with them implies, in the first instance, not pride and ferocity so much as a strict loyalty to Jewish law, which among other things forbids eating pork (evidently a staple in Shakespeare's Venice)[3] and prescribes the prayers that Jews in particular must recite before eating and drinking. Shakespeare identifies Shylock's Jewishness here with his law-abidingness, that is, with his pious deference to the legal demands of Jewish orthodoxy.[4] Even so, in act II, scene v, when Shylock next appears, we are given occasion to question the steadfastness of Shylock's piety.

Once the terms of the loan have been agreed on and sealed, Shylock returns home to tell his daughter that he has decided to accept an invitation to eat at Bassanio's after all, albeit "in hate" and for an ulterior motive:

> *I am bid forth to supper, Jessica.*
> *These are my keys. But wherefore should I go?*
> *I am not bid for love; they flatter me.*
> *But yet I'll go in hate, to feed upon*
> *The prodigal Christian.*   (II.v.11–15)

Shylock's ulterior motive, "to feed upon / The prodigal Christian," is connected as well with a second reason for having returned home, namely, to announce to his household servant that he will gladly let him switch to the "prodigal" Bassanio's employment:

> *The patch is kind enough, but a huge feeder,*
> *Snail-slow in profit, and he sleeps by day*
> *More than the wildcat. Drones hive not with me;*
> *Therefore I part with him, and part with him*
> *To one that I would have him help to waste*
> *His borrowed purse.*   (II.v.44–49)

Shockingly enough, the motive for which Shylock is prepared to give over his household servant and which is, at least in part, a further extension of that for which he is prepared to suspend his observance of the dietary laws is that of "help[ing] to waste / [Bassanio's] borrowed purse." Shylock's intent to add to Bassanio's overhead in these ways would have the net effect of increasing the likelihood, however slim, of Shylock's extending yet another loan for Bassanio, this time interest bearing, or even under certain conditions (which almost do transpire) of his collecting on his sinister penalty clause with Bassanio's benefactor. At this point, Bloom might well wish to raise the larger question of whether Shakespeare means to imply that Jewish orthodoxy sanctions hatred or revenge against non-Jews; yet as we shall soon see, it is a question the play answers sufficiently clearly in the negative. Meanwhile, contrary to Bloom, we must say that far from simply succumbing to putative Elizabethan stereotypes concerning Jews, Shakespeare evidently understands both Shylock's piety and his departure from it (which appears to begin well before the forced conversion) by the standards of Jewish orthodoxy itself.

But Bloom notwithstanding, whether or not Shakespeare's play is anti-Jewish cannot be decided by a single argument. Controversy over the treatment of Shylock is not confined to questions of character but permeates the entire fabric of the play. With an eye to the considerable range of disagreement about the play among scholarly critics, John Lyon, in his monograph on *The Merchant of Venice* in Twayne's New Critical Introductions to Shakespeare, sounds a timely warning against one-sided readings.[5]

> The play has suffered from the aggressive justifications of its champions no less than the dismissals of its detractors. It seems a rich play where the potential multiplicity of meanings is in excess of any full realization. And to actualize any single interpretation of the play is to stress, and perhaps overstress, one of its parts at the cost of ignoring or doing violence to parts of the play developing in other, equally interesting ways. (5)

Lyon's book calls attention, in general, to the rich mix of particulars as the playwright meant us to savor them. He is properly averse to scholarly arguments that would, in effect, dissolve those particulars into thick generalities for the sake of some bland unifying gloss that looks good from a distance. At the same time, we are admonished that the particulars of the play themselves solicit our subsequent wonderment and inference: "*The Merchant of Venice* is no piece of theatrical ephemera: the play is of a substance to merit and require the kinds of sustained recollection and speculation which occur subsequent to our enjoyment of the play in the theatre" (105). Lyon therefore proposes to "characterize, rather than resolve, the play's puzzles" and to "raise questions about the limits of plausible interpretation" (5). Proceeding somewhat idiosyncratically, the central chapters of his book may be described as a freewheeling tour of Shakespeare's plot, which sometimes fends off, sometimes embraces the views of scholarly critics, depending on whether they block or widen a scenic path through the play's main contours. Lyon justifies his procedure by the assertion that the play is "not *finished*" (8). He finds its dramatic action un-polished and its philosophical perplexities left unresolved. Hence, he infers, it is best approached tentatively, as a play-in-progress, whose chief merit is to testify to the creative and provocative genius of its author.

The practical result of Lyon's argument, however, would seem to be the opposite of the full openness to the dramatic and philosophical richness of the play which he has intended. Instead of encouraging us to venture wide eyed and alert into the play's "puzzles," guided above all by Shakespeare's many-layered text, Lyon effectively discourages us from making the necessary effort to explore whether any one spec-ulation is better than another so far as an understanding of the play as a whole (at least as we have it) is concerned. By simply denying that the play is a finished whole, he denies to us from the outset any standard for judging which interpretations are good or better or best beyond our private fancies. And yet that same denial scarcely prevents him (or anyone else) from interposing judgments that may well block our view of the richness of what Shakespeare has left us.

A single example must suffice. Lyon rightly disputes the answer offered by Harold C. Goddard to one of the questions I began by raising, about the propriety of the Venetian court's legal entrapment of Shylock — at the hands, moreover, of a surprise amicus curiae (se-cretly Bassanio's newly wedded wife, Portia, in disguise): why "didn't she invoke immediately the law prescribing a penalty for any alien plotting against the life of any citizen of Venice instead of waiting until she had put those she supposedly loved [namely, Bassanio and, by extension, his benefactor] on the rack?"[6] To Goddard's hastily advanced claim that "the only possible answer is that she wanted a spectacle, a dramatic triumph with herself at the center," Lyon fit-tingly adds that there may be forensic reasons as well: "With an oppo-nent as legalistically precise as Shylock, Portia needs as much evidence of the reality of Shylock's malevolent intent as he can be brought to give, and it is perhaps only *at* the last moment that the last-moment solution can be safely and effectively revealed" (105).

Nevertheless, faithful to his general caveat that any solution to a given "puzzle" in the play can be only tentative, Lyon immediately expresses his misgivings about what he has just said and meanwhile drops the issue — except to salvage what he takes to be one incontrovertible point. "Certainly," he assures us, "Portia suffers when considered with hindsight" (ibid.). Yet the assurance Lyon offers follows not from the particulars of Portia's actions during the trial but rather from the doubtful premise that he accepts without argument from Goddard, that Portia's actions are largely self-centered. In her admonitory speech to Shylock about the "quality of mercy" (IV.i.182–203), however, Portia emphasizes that her actions are guided not only by the legalities of the case, of which she is evidently the master, but also by justice seasoned with mercy (cf. IV.i.200f.). Contra Goddard, the prospect therefore opens up that Portia's cross-examination of Shylock, while fulfilling the obvious requirements of justice, is at the same time a high-minded act of mercy on the part of someone, indeed the only one in the courtroom, who knows the law. As I argue later, Portia's words give Shylock himself every opportunity to render a spectacular act of mercy so as to render nugatory the law under which she alone knows he stands guilty. Recalling Lyon's previous words (105), we cannot help wondering whether his offhand suppression of this possibility is a consequence of his unsupported insistence that our receptiveness to the play's details and our thinking about them are two separate things — an assumption belied by anyone whose attention is drawn to the thoughtful details of Portia's speech to begin with.

Lyon does not mention the only other full-fledged monograph on the play, Lawrence Danson's, which might have provided him with a direct challenge to the view that *The Merchant of Venice* lacks a dramatic unity.[7] Danson argues for its unity on the basis of "the fact that the play was written by a Christian for a Christian audience, and that it is about Christian issues" (13). According to Danson, Shakespeare's Christianity does not narrow but broadens his understanding of things; it is "an amplifier, not a deadener of conceivable meanings" (15). Nor need we then presume that Shakespeare's thought is a prisoner of (the Christianity of) his time, for as in those plays that consider issues of kingship, "he is drawing upon ideas common to his time. But that is very different from saying that Shakespeare's ideas are common" (16). Against critics who would impute to Shakespeare a Christian teaching that sets itself in opposition to Judaism and seeks to triumph over it, as mercy over justice or the New Law over the Old, he looks instead to the teaching of *"completion* or *fulfillment"* (17f.), that is, of the reconciliation or harmony of souls among themselves and with the divinely ordered cosmos. The main evidence, so far as Portia's aforementioned "quality of mercy" speech is concerned, is that the warrant for her appeal to the need for mercy to temper justice is the Lord's Prayer (66f.), whose theme as she understands it is common to both Jewish and Christian worship, as her words imply:

> *That, in the course of justice, none of us*
> *Should see salvation. We do pray for mercy,*
> *And that same prayer doth teach us all* [sic] *to render*
> *The deeds of mercy.*   (IV.i.197–200)

Danson's argument has the further merit of indicating why the play cannot end with Shylock's defeat in the trial scene of act IV but must conclude in the pastoral setting of act V, at the wealthy Portia's estate in Belmont. There the three newlywed couples — Portia and Bassanio, Portia's maid, Nerissa, and Bassanio's companion Gratiano, and Shylock's eloped daughter, Jessica, and her poet husband, Lorenzo — each for the moment at odds, soon become reconciled. In a moonlit setting under the stars, Lorenzo woos Jessica with a speech about cosmic harmony that prepares us for that reconciliation:

> *Look how the floor of heaven*
> *Is thick inlaid with patens of bright gold.*
> *There's not the smallest orb which thou behold'st*
> *But in his motion like an angel sings,*
> *Still quiring to the young-eyed cherubins;*
> *Such harmony is in immortal souls;*
> *But whilst this muddy vesture of decay*
> *Doth grossly close it in, we cannot hear it.*   (V.i.58–65)

The Christian overtones of Lorenzo's words are undeniable, as Danson points out (186f.): the stars are "patens" (or communion dishes); the harmonics of their geometrically ordered motions are angels' songs; and the reason we hear only intimations of those sounds is our "fallen" earthly condition.[8]

Nevertheless Danson does not take into account the chief evidence against his view, namely, that the play contains at least as many allusions to classical mythology and philosophy as to Christian doctrine. Lorenzo's speech about the harmony of the stars is a case in point, for the notion in terms of which that speech becomes intelligible — that the stars are embedded in invisible concentric spheres surrounding the earth — is ultimately of pre-Christian, Pythagorean origin. To be sure, Danson might easily reply that those same Pythagorean allusions are also found in certain Christian authors who have appropriated them, such as Boethius, to whom he refers briefly (187f.). Still, to the claim that Shakespeare's Christianity is the play's final word there is a further objection from the play itself.

During the tense moments of the trial, when Shylock's insistence on the letter of the law seems to be holding sway, an outraged and frustrated Gratiano exclaims against what he takes to be Shylock's inhuman inflexibility:

> *O, be thou damn'd, inexecrable dog,*
> *And for thy life let justice be accus'd!*
> *Thou almost mak'st me waver in my faith,*
> *To hold opinion with Pythagoras,*
> *That souls of animals infuse themselves*
> *Into the trunks of men. Thy currish spirit*
> *Govern'd a wolf, who, hang'd for human slaughter,*
> *Even from the gallows did his fell soul fleet,*
> *And, whilst thou layest in thy unhallowed dam,*
> *Infus'd itself in thee; for thy desires*
> *Are wolvish, bloody, starv'd, and ravenous.* (IV.i.128–38)

It strikes Gratiano that Shylock's "currish spirit" is evidence for the pagan Pythagoras's view of the transmigration of souls between animals (in this case wolves) and humans. Exasperated, he is on the point of "waver[ing] in [his] faith" to accommodate that view. To Gratiano, at least, Christianity and Pythagoreanism are not simply compatible. Indeed, if Lorenzo is Gratiano's erstwhile teacher in these matters, as the play's description of their close companionship suggests (see I.i.69–71, 106ff.), the same may need to be said of Lorenzo's moonlit speech about harmony and perhaps other Christian-sounding speeches as well. Pace Danson, we shall have to explore how Shakespeare faces and seeks to resolve the evident tension between Christianity and philosophy in the play before we can determine to what extent or in what way its teaching may be said to be Christian.

This last would seem in part to be the aim of Edward Andrew, a political scientist, who also reads the play in the light of what he takes to be its implicit Christian teaching, though unlike Danson he finds that teaching one-sided and faulty.[9] It is the teaching of Christian charity, which Andrew understands to mean the doing of acts of kindness or mercy to others with or without their consent. He follows the literary critic Harry Berger Jr., who adduces the term *mercifixion* to describe Shylock's forced conversion insofar as it is meant for his own good.[10] Shakespeare's scriptural precedent here is said to be Luke 14:23: "Go out into the highways and hedges, and compel them to come in, that my house may be filled." Andrew's interpretation is guided by an appeal to the authority of St. Thomas Aquinas, who appears to him to cite this verse in support of the church's position that it is just to compel unbelievers into the Christian communion. Meanwhile, Andrew also notices an opposing view in the play, which he finds spelled out only incompletely. It is the "possessive individualism" personified by Shylock.[11] As usurer, Shylock embodies the "heartless greed" and "limitless acquisitiveness" at the root of modern entrepreneurial capitalism (4). At the same time, in Shylock's attempts to justify his retaliation against his Christian tormentor, he anticipates the philosophical arguments for religious toleration later articulated in Benedict Spinoza's *Theologico-Political Treatise* (1670) and John Locke's *Letter on Toleration* (1689). Throughout, however, Shylock also shares in his own way the old-fashioned charitableness of his Christian persecutors. According to Andrew's admittedly unconventional analysis of the play, Shylock would like nothing better than to marry his daughter Jessica to a nice Jewish husband. Andrew's Shylock is therefore driven at bottom by a charitable wish to befriend the merchant in order to convert him to Judaism for that purpose.

But Andrew's attributing the merchant's own conversion-seeking zeal to traditional Christian teaching is overly hasty and seriously misleading. In the very passage that Andrew cites in support of his contention that Christianity authorizes the compulsory conversion of Jews, Thomas Aquinas emphasizes exactly the opposite. Here are Thomas's words in response to the question, "Whether the faithless are to be compelled to the faith?"

> I respond that it should be said that certain of the faithless are those who have never taken up the faith, such as gentiles [i.e., pagans] and *Jews*. And such people *are in no way to be compelled to the faith,* in order that they might believe for themselves — since believing is a matter of the will. Nevertheless they are to be compelled by the faithful, if the means are there, in order that they not impede the faith, whether by blasphemies or by bad arguments or even by open persecutions. And on this account faithful Christians frequently make war against the faithless, not in order to compel them to believe (since even if they were to conquer them and hold them captive, they would *leave them at their liberty* concerning whether they wished to believe) but in order to compel them not to impede the Christian faith.[12]

According to Thomas, Jews and pagans alike are exempt from forcible conversion at the hands of Christians, though not from acts of force if they impede the Christian faith by means of slanders, dubious propaganda, or overt harassments. Even so, they are to be left "at their liberty" so far as matters of belief are concerned, if only that they might eventually come to Christian belief on their own. Because belief as such is voluntary, Thomas insists, neither Jews nor pagans can be forced into it.

True, immediately following the passage just quoted, Thomas goes on to justify the punishment of heretics and apostates. But these differ from non-Christians by being deviant and lapsed Christians, who have already put themselves under the authority of the church. In any case, Andrew overlooks Thomas's indication that "liberty" or tolerance is in some sense part of traditional Christian teaching. Despite what Andrew suggests, then, tolerance of Jews can hardly be said to receive its first, to say nothing of its best, philosophical treatment in the theologico-political arguments of Spinoza and Locke. Indeed, in looking later on at the speeches of Shylock to which he calls our attention, we shall have occasion to wonder how well such intimations of the case for religious toleration as Andrew rightly discerns in *The Merchant of Venice* can be understood in terms of the political and religious liberalism of those modern thinkers (as instructive as their arguments might otherwise prove to be). As the example of Pythagoras has already indicated, we shall have to weigh in addition the considerable merits of certain premodern philosophical and theological views that Shakespeare has evidently inherited from thinkers such as Thomas.

It is admittedly possible to read *The Merchant of Venice* as a Christian or quasi-Christian play and yet to defend Shakespeare's presentation of Shylock as being not quite so derogatory toward Jews as it might have been in the hands of another at that time — Marlowe, for example. Such is the approach of the literary journalist John Gross.[13] Shakespeare, he writes, "simply tried to imagine, within the confines of his plot, and within the limits that his culture set him, what it would be like to be a Jew" (349). What is chiefly missing from Shakespeare's Shylock is any "hint . . . of an inner faith, or of religion as a way of life, as opposed to a set of rules" (45). In contrast, the Christian characters in the play are said to "have admirable ideals, and on the whole — in their dealings among themselves, as opposed to their dealings with Shylock — they live up to them" (350). However that may be, the result, to Gross at least, is "tragic," inasmuch as the "anti-Semitism" shown by the other characters "coexists with so many admirable or attractive qualities" (351).

Thankfully, Shakespeare's Shylock is cut somewhat larger than his stereotype. Gross makes much of the playwright's investing his

Jewish character with unforgettable habits of speech, including the staccato repetitions and symmetrical constructions of the money-lender's angry outburst promising revenge against the merchant:

> *— and what's his reason?*
> *I am a Jew. Hath not a Jew eyes? Hath not a Jew hands,*
> *organs, dimensions, senses, affections, passions? fed with*
> *the same food, hurt with the same weapons, subject to*
> *the same diseases, healed by the same means, warmed*
> *and cooled by the same winter and summer as a Chris-*
> *tian is? If you prick us, do we not bleed? If you tickle*
> *us, do we not laugh? If you poison us, do we not die?*
> *And if you wrong us, shall we not revenge? If we are*
> *like you in the rest, we will resemble you in that.* (III.i.50–59)

Gross comments: "Where else, in Shakespeare's time, can you find such sentiments?" (66). True, they are uttered in the service of an "inhuman purpose" (67). And they are followed by an ugly conversation with Shylock's own banker and fellow Jew, Tubal, who presses Shylock mercilessly with reports of looming financial disasters stemming from his eloped daughter's free spending and from the merchant's losses at sea. "Yet," Gross insists, "nothing that happens in the rest of the play cancels out 'Hath not a Jew?' The words have been spoken; the stereotype will never be the same again" (ibid).

Unfortunately, the conclusion Gross would have us reach — that Shakespeare perhaps couldn't help being just a bit anti-Jewish — becomes plausible only if we overlook much of the detailed content of the play. Among Gross's dubious factual claims are that Shylock lacks any "inner faith" (here Harold Bloom seems on stronger ground) and that the Christian characters are by comparison meant to be admirable. (I shall have much to say on the latter point about Gratiano in particular, as well as about the merchant himself, later on.)

Most egregious, because most decisive for his argument, appears to be Gross's erroneous assertion that "at no point [in the play] does anyone suggest that there might be a distinction to be drawn between [Shylock's] being a Jew and his being an obnoxious individual"

(351). Portia aside, to whom I have already referred, it is enough for the moment to quote the highest ranking authority of the court, the Duke himself, in his introductory plea for Shylock to show mercy to the merchant:

> *Shylock, the world thinks, and I think so too,*
> *That thou but leadest this fashion of thy malice*
> *To the last hour of act; and then 'tis thought*
> *Thou'lt show thy mercy and remorse more strange*
> *Than is thy strange apparent cruelty;*
> *And where thou now exacts the penalty,*
> *Which is a pound of this poor merchant's flesh,*
> *Thou wilt not only loose the forfeiture,*
> *But, touch'd with humane gentleness and love,*
> *Forgive a moiety of the principal,*
> *Glancing an eye of pity on his losses,*
> *That have of late so huddled on his back —*
> *Enow to press a royal merchant down*
> *And pluck commiseration of his state*
> *From brassy bosoms and rough hearts of flint,*
> *From stubborn Turks and Tartars never train'd*
> *To offices of tender courtesy.*
> *We all expect a gentle answer, Jew.* (IV.i.17–34)

Here Antonio is said to deserve Shylock's "pity" in light of his overwhelming shipping losses, the putative cause of his failure to repay on time. In the circumstances, the Duke adds, Shylock ought to forgive not only Antonio's penalty but some of his principal too.

What are important here are the Duke's announced reasons for expecting some last-minute, out-of-court refinancing from Shylock. First, he says, everyone including himself believes that Shylock is merely stalling so as to make his eventual show of compassion more spectacular. That is, the Duke attributes to Shylock a sense of theatrics. Second, there is also the depressing magnitude of Antonio's reported losses — enough, as he says, to make even hardboiled, crudely raised observers act compassionately (Turks and Tartars come to the

Duke's mind). Hence, he concludes, "We all expect a gentle answer, Jew." The pertinent question is whether the Duke's concluding reminder that Shylock is a Jew means that he manifestly includes Jews among those who are by nature or upbringing ungentle. Two reasons suggest he does, but then again a third seems to override these. First, a pun on "gentle" yields "gentile," implying that the Duke is seeking a gentile or un-Jewish answer from Shylock.[14] Second, the Duke has already confided to Antonio privately that he considers Shylock incorrigible (IV.i.3–6). Still, third, the Duke, whatever his private opinion, cannot admit publicly that Shylock *as Jew* was "never trained" to be gentle, that is, by Jewish law, without weakening his earlier argument that Shylock's apparent lack of compassion was a deliberate theatrical delay. The inescapable conclusion, then, is that the Duke is forced to give the public impression to Shylock and everyone else that Jewish law does after all teach moral decency, including compassion, and that Shylock, being uncompassionate, is simply being a bad Jew. Evidently Gross's approach, which (in contrast to, say, Danson's) looks not much further than the putative stereotypes Shakespeare is said to share with his contemporaries, blurs just that point in the Duke's speech which goes contrary to stereotype.

In other words, the Duke makes a public effort to compliment Shylock's Jewishness and pleads with him simply to live up to it. As with Portia's subsequent speeches in court, a possibility here emerges that is entirely different from any that Gross seems willing or able to acknowledge. Perhaps the possibility is best put by way of our denial of a remark made in passing by an articulate but overly sympathetic reviewer of Gross's book: "It was clearly not part of Shakespeare's conscious design," writes Robert Alter, "to question the received wisdom of Christian hostility toward the Jews."[15] But the facts we adduce, and which Gross and others ignore, suggest just the opposite.

Even so, the question remains today of Shakespeare's apparent moral obtuseness, his lack of sensitivity (as we say) about Jews and Judaism, whether we ultimately ascribe to him a reformer's intention or not. Once the most obvious incidents of the play, such as we first take note of them, are seen for what they are morally, it is hard to resist interpreting *The Merchant of Venice* as a whole simply in their terms — that is, moralistically. How could anyone who writes such stuff, we tend to ask, have been very nice to Jews? The play undeniably draws from an appalling legacy of Jew-hatred in England from, say, 1290, when Jews were officially expelled, till at least 1753, when the ill-fated Jew Bill, as it was called, momentarily dropped professing the sacraments as a naturalization requirement and so opened citizenship to Jews, who had begun to be formally readmitted under Cromwell a century earlier. Perhaps the most convenient place to begin to acknowledge the bearing of that legacy here is James Shapiro's recent *Shakespeare and the Jews*.[16] Shapiro draws from abundant references to Jews in chronicles, sermons, stories, plays, legal opinions, political tracts, and the like surrounding what he calls the "cultural moment" of the play's first staging (10). He disclaims any overall interpretation of the play, or of Shakespeare's private intentions, for that matter. Still, his comments on passages seen to dovetail with the historical evidence he adduces suggest much by way of innuendo which is morally damaging. Although the passages he cites are few and far between, they are worth listing, so that one can see both the force of the argument to which he contributes and its limitations.

That Jews sometimes suffered brutal reprisals for alleged ritual murders of Christians around Easter time, for example, serves to explain a report in the play of an ominous predawn nosebleed on "Black Monday," or Easter Monday, by Shylock's clownish ex-servant, Launcelot, in his chatterbox cover-up of an impending elopement of Shylock's daughter, Jessica, and her Christian lover, Lorenzo (II.v.22–26) (258 n. 71). Launcelot's report resonates a few lines later during his coded message to Jessica, "There will come a Christian by / Will be worth a Jewess' eye" (II.v.40–41) — the "worth" here alluding less, Shapiro argues, to "the value of a lover than the revenge exacted upon the Jewish community for its crimes" (109). That Shakespeare's contemporaries were generally aware that there was no strictly female counterpart to male circumcision as the sign of Jews' covenant with God, moreover, explains the relative ease with which Jessica could break that covenant in marrying Lorenzo (120). And yet the short-lived contemporary belief that women's earrings could somehow substitute for ritual circumcision, Shapiro thinks, might explain Jessica's absconding with Shylock's jewels and Shylock's afterward lamenting that he would rather see her dead at his feet with the jewels in her ear (III.i.77–79) (ibid.). In any case, the further suspicion that a Jewess who could easily convert might just as easily revert to the old covenant seems to Shapiro to underlie the disturbing exchange between Jessica and Lorenzo comparing their hasty marriage to several thwarted love affairs of classical antiquity (V.i.1–24) (58f.). Finally, contemporary theological discussion over the meaning of "circumcision of the heart" in Paul's Letter to the Romans leads Shapiro to speculate that Shylock's insistence on a pound of Antonio's flesh might be a metonym for genital circumcision or even castration (114–21).

The historical import of these and other derogatory images of Jews, according to Shapiro, was to cast doubt over whether Jews could ever be trusted as fellow denizens, much less citizens, alongside Englishmen. To the extent that Shakespeare may be said to have given further currency to such images, he also seems to have lent them further credibility as his national stature rose. Or so Shapiro finds when looking at the public debate over the Jew Bill more than a century and a half later (195–224). The same images continued to be invoked by opponents of the bill, Shapiro notes, and led to its repeal barely two years after its passage, despite arguments in its favor drawn from more enlightened thinkers such as John Toland, Daniel Defoe, and John Locke. Shapiro leads us to infer, though he does not put it in so many words, that the bill might have had an easier time of it had Shakespeare thought better than to write *The Merchant of Venice* in the first place. For these and other moral reasons, he has no hesitation about calling the play "anti-Jewish" (216).

Here is where the limitations of Shapiro's argument become apparent. Assuming that the popular images as Shapiro describes them were as decisive politically as he suggests, there seems a further need to explain why Parliament itself was not altogether dazzled by them, at least for a time. Why, in short, did public life become as receptive as it was to the position in favor of tolerance of Jews as articulated by Toland, Defoe, Locke, and others? Here Shapiro is comparatively silent. It is testimony to the difficulty of this question that it would require him to widen the scope of the inquiry, to move from the narrower question of the popular prejudices latent and prevailing at a given hour (what Shapiro calls "cultural history")[17] to the broader question of how responsible statesmanship would have to discern and guide such prejudices on important public issues such as the Jew Bill.

Let us come closer to the point at hand. Given at least the modest success of enlightened statesmanship in 1753 in overcoming the derogatory images of Jews admittedly found in Shakespeare's then popular play, wouldn't we have to ask — as Shapiro does not — whether Shakespeare himself might have had enough statesmanlike insight to be able to anticipate and even encourage these same possibilities, however modestly, in his dramatic presentation of Shylock? The moment this question occurs to us, unless we simply decide to rule out certain answers beforehand, we are forced to look again at the manifestly derogatory things said of and by Jews in Shakespeare's play, to see whether they are indeed the play's last word or whether instead they might also call to mind other, more salutary images of the behavior of Jews — and of Christians — embedded as well in the psyches of his viewing and reading audience. But this last question can be answered one way or the other not by insinuation from evidence outside Shakespeare's play, but only by firsthand examination of the play itself.

ༀ II ༀ

Yet point-by-point arguments about the play do not necessarily add up to a satisfactory view of the whole. If we are to be persuaded on the overall issue of whether *The Merchant of Venice* is friendly to Jews, we must confront some general issues as well. Drawing from the foregoing sample of current scholarship about the play what seem to be the most basic obstacles to the view I am proposing, we arrive at the following (mistaken, I believe) premises:

1. that among authors whose characters say more or less nasty things about Jews, one is pretty well as reprehensible as another, their differences being secondary, if not negligible;

2. that a character's apparently anti-Jewish statement can be divorced from its proper dramatic context as a reliable indication of the sentiment of its author — even or especially in the case of Shakespeare;

3. that in the hands of a competent author, an apparently pro-Jewish statement or character is necessarily friendlier to Jews, that is, more salutary and well meaning than an apparently anti-Jewish one;

4. that in public or literary treatments of the relations between Jews and non-Jews, the most important issue is mutual tolerance.[18]

A brief consideration of each of these dubious premises will allow me to indicate how I have dedicated the subsequent chapters of this book to trying to dislodge them.

In the first place, as an alternative to the blanket condemnation of all authors who show some sympathy for characters who hate Jews, I propose instead the maxim that an author's judgment on his character can be seen only with the help of the given dramatic context. This maxim is probably granted on all sides. My differences with the scholars whom I have just cited concern how well they have conformed to it in practice. The case of *The Merchant of Venice* is particularly difficult, probably because everyone agrees that Jewish-Christian relations remain a sensitive theological and political issue. Persecutions and discrimination against Jews, for example, are still matters of living memory, and sooner or later even a critic who is fairly well disposed toward the play is apt to bring up the Holocaust, if only to insist on the innocence of Shakespeare's intent by comparison (as do, for example, Danson [3], Gross [319–23], and Shapiro [84]). In the face of such painful sensitivities, it is perhaps best to begin by conceding that there are anti-Jewish plays, even rather well-written ones, and then go on to examine in what way Shakespeare's may be said to resemble them and in what way not. Critics, moreover, seem agreed that the play that comes closest to *The Merchant of Venice* in its portrayal of a Jew is its immediate forerunner, Christopher Marlowe's *Jew of Malta*. A comparison of Shylock with Marlowe's title character,

Barabas, thus seems in order. So it occasions chapter 2. There I shall suggest their differences by starting from Marlowe's open announcement in the prologue to his play of a hostility to all religion; Shakespeare does no such thing.

My second maxim, which follows closely from the first, is that the very meaning of a character's words (as opposed to the author's final judgment on them) cannot be entirely separated from the dramatic action either. This is especially so for the complicated and, I shall argue, subtle action of *The Merchant of Venice.* In probing the character of Shylock, I must therefore try to give a satisfactory account of the play as a whole, all the while remaining open to the various controversial issues I have begun by raising, in order to see what the dramatic action implies concerning them. In so doing, in chapter 3 I indicate where Shakespeare is at least as capable as Marlowe of considering the question of the virtues — and vices — of revealed religion, Christianity included. The practical teaching of the play, so far as the question of Jewish-Christian relations goes, will be found to reside in Portia's "quality of mercy" speech, in the manner I have already begun to suggest. And yet, as I shall also show by a renewed consideration of Lorenzo's moonlit speech, the play's practical teaching is not entirely separable from its further, theoretical or philosophical teaching.

Next, it remains to consider whether an apparently pro-Jewish statement or character is necessarily more salutary or well meant as far as, say, Jewish-Christian relations are concerned. My third maxim is the denial of this proposition. Hence chapter 4 treats the Jewish character in a most important book by another thoughtful contemporary of Shakespeare. It is Joabin in Francis Bacon's *New Atlantis* (1627). Joabin may be described as an assimilated Jew who is not only wealthy and public spirited but also philosophically sophisticated and politically savvy. He is, moreover, privy to the inner circles of rulers in a modern state governed by high technology and imperialistic aims. (We may recognize in him a sort of combination of Bernard Baruch and Henry Kissinger.) Bacon's book encourages and even forces us to raise the question of the future of Jews of such a stamp and under such a regime. His answer, as it seems to me, is considerably less hopeful — and less friendly to Jews — than Shakespeare's.

Finally, Bacon's question is taken up thematically by Spinoza's *Theologico-Political Treatise* (1670): Spinoza is, if I may say so, the Jewish Bacon. Spinoza's argument for Jewish-Christian tolerance leads him to become the philosophical founder of two institutions that are inseparable from modern religious and political life in general and from modern Jewish-Christian relations in particular. One institution is the so-called higher-critical approach to the reading of the Bible, according to which, for example, the Torah is not the cause of the Jewish people (as traditional piety has taught) but the Jewish people is the cause of the Torah.[19] The other institution is liberal democracy, according to which, in the best case, government would look on the practice of religion as an entirely private matter in the hands of individual citizens, considered as political equals.[20] How Spinoza understands his twin legacy — biblical criticism and liberal democracy — as a solution to what we have since come to call the "Jewish question," the question of how the Jew fits in the non-Jewish world, is worth spelling out in some detail (see chap. 5). In effect, Spinoza's understanding of how mutual tolerance between Christian and Jew might be effected seems to have supplied the unspoken premises for each of the various unsatisfactory interpretations of Shylock that I began by noting. But to say all this, as I do, is to call attention to the fact that Spinoza's solution, which interpreters today tend to take for granted without knowing it, is the product of a deliberate theologico-political argument designed to show the superiority of biblical criticism and liberal democracy to other possible approaches for understanding the place of the Jew in the modern world. I draw the obvious inference that prior to Spinoza there must have existed at least one competing approach, against which Spinoza's own argument strives and against which it could be tested. That such an approach might well be found (quite independently of Spinoza) in *The Merchant of Venice* and that Shakespeare's play should be read with this possibility in mind constitute the last of my maxims.

Differently stated, my final maxim is that Shakespeare's play ought to be read so as not to foreclose on the possibility that his understanding of Shylock's predicament might be, all things considered, superior to Spinoza's. I wish to preserve an openness to what I take to be Shakespeare's own openness to the theologico-political situation of the modern Jew, including his quest for tolerance. Here I am compelled to pit myself against those interpreters who insist a priori that Shakespeare must somewhere down the line have succumbed to the crude and intolerant prejudices of his time. Bluntly stated, I find no evidence to indicate that Shakespeare himself endorses the prejudices articulated by his characters who are unfriendly to Jews and much to indicate that he understands those prejudices fully for what they are, namely, as dubious and damaging opinions, and so encourages his reader to do likewise. If I am correct, it follows that there is a pervasive philosophical element to Shakespeare's "Jewish" play, which has remained by and large unappreciated by current scholars. Not Shakespeare, but scholars themselves seem vulnerable to the charge of having imposed their own dubious prejudices on the events that Shakespeare dramatizes. Inasmuch as Spinoza's argument may be said to underlie their prejudices by supplying the theologico-political suggestions that inform (or, rather, misinform) them here, his *Theologico-Political Treatise* is both the barrier and the bridge for our proper understanding of Shakespeare's Shylock — and, by way of anticipation, of the modern Jew.

2

Shylock and Marlowe's Barabas

*In Machiavelli we find comedies, parodies, and satires but
nothing reminding of tragedy. One half of humanity remains
outside of his thought. There is no tragedy in Machiavelli
because he has no sense of the sacredness of "the common." The
fate of neither Cesare Borgia nor Manilius Capitolinus is
tragic or understood by Machiavelli as tragic; they failed
because they had chance or the times against them. As regards
chance in general, it can be conquered; man is the master.*

— Leo Strauss, *Thoughts on Machiavelli*

I

MARLOWE'S BARABAS, LIKE SHAKESPEARE'S SHYLOCK, is a criminal
in the making. His crime is also prompted by his being a Jew. Marlowe anticipates Shakespeare in making it hard from the outset to
distinguish Barabas's criminality from his Jewishness.[1] There is this
difference, however. Shylock's turning to criminal behavior is, at least
in the eyes of the highest authorities of his city, tantamount to his
stepping outside the bounds of recognized Jewish teaching. This, as
we have already seen, is the view of Venice's duke, and as I shall show
more fully later, it is also the view of Portia in court. Shakespeare

would have us infer that, had Shylock simply followed the religion in which Venice has allowed him to be raised, his lawless action would never have occurred in the first place. In the eyes of Barabas and his fellow denizens of Marlowe's Malta, however, the distinction between Jewishness and criminality is of no comparable importance.

Officially, Marlowe's Malta regards Jews considerably more harshly than does Shakespeare's Venice. According to Malta's governor, Jews "stand accursed in the sight of Heaven" for their infidelity (I.ii.67).[2] According to Barabas himself, the Maltese view (though he finds it dubious) is that "the tribe that I descended of / Were all in general cast away for sin" (I.ii.117–18). Malta thus considers Jews a "scatter'd" and "hated" nation (I.ii.123, 116) and bars them from citizenship as a matter of course. Shakespeare's Venice also bars Jews from citizenship, but Marlowe's Malta is theologically more outspoken about it. True, since Malta's and Venice's citizens are alike professing Christians exclusively, Jews such as Barabas and Shylock would remain resident aliens at either place. They are in the city but not of it, openly tolerated by its laws while denied a share in the authoritative political deliberations by which they are governed. But whereas Venice in the persons of the Duke and Portia publicly emphasizes Jews' routine moral decency, Malta in contrast emphasizes their supposed longstanding odiousness. Malta's one-sided emphasis in turn supplies the theological premise for Barabas's crimes.

It prepares us for the otherwise inexplicable enormity of those crimes.[3] Malta's Jews, their theological odium notwithstanding, are prominent in the city's legitimate business affairs. Barabas himself is the city's wealthiest merchant.[4] He is a famous shipper and trader of Spanish oils and Greek wines and, more lucratively, Indian metals, Moroccan gems, Persian silks, and Oriental spices and pearls (I.i.4–37, 86–90). Still, his profits are only as safe as his shipping routes, and concurrently the eastern Mediterranean, through which his ships must pass, is under the sway of a Turkish naval blockade mounted against Christian Europe and imminently threatening Christian Malta.[5] Marlowe thus places Barabas in pressing political circumstances that at the same time call attention to his inhospitable theological circumstances. For his part, when profits flow easily, Barabas takes them to be the fulfillment of the "blessings promised to the Jews" through their biblical ancestor Abraham (I.i.105–15). When he soon suffers temporary bankruptcy at the hands of Malta's tax-hungry rulers during the Turkish emergency, however, he laments that his misfortunes exceed the biblical Job's — and he plots to recoup his losses and to avenge his adversaries by cunning and unscrupulous means, which Job himself would scarcely have countenanced (cf. I.i.105ff. with ii.184–212). He very nearly succeeds. He conspires, he dissembles, he murders (two suitors, one daughter, two friars, his personal slave, a courtesan, her pander, several carpenters, and a whole nunnery, not to mention a besieging Turkish garrison), and he betrays (his own country of residence as well as its mortal enemy), until he is unexpectedly caught in a trap-door device of his own making and scalded to death in a boiling cauldron. Marlowe goes so far as to have Barabas's morally reprehensible means endorsed by a morally disreputable and atheistic "Machevill" — a disciple of Machiavelli, or perhaps Machiavelli himself — who introduces "the tragedy of a Jew,"[6] as he calls it, in the play's prologue.

The prologue is a dramatic element that Shakespeare's play forgoes. It sets forth the standard by which Marlowe's Jew and the other participants in the "tragedy" are meant to be judged. The standard is that of pure political expediency, of a politics untempered and unhindered by theological or other restraints. Accordingly, Marlowe's Machevill is blatantly antitheological: "I count religion but a childish toy, / And hold there is no sin but ignorance" (Prol. 14–15). He thus repudiates in advance the biblical point of view to which Barabas appeals when comparing his misfortunes to Job's. In announcing the repudiation of biblical religion before his Jewish character even sets foot onstage, Marlowe, unlike Shakespeare, tells his audience ahead of time what to think of that character. Since what he tells them is not entirely complimentary, we may say that he prejudices his audience, or at any rate reinforces certain prejudices that they may already have about Jews.[7] Yet if as a result an anti-Jewish prejudice permeates Marlowe's play, I must immediately add that, so far as the playwright himself is concerned, it is deliberately referred to or explained by the play's explicit Machiavellianism.[8] Meanwhile, as we shall see, the action of the play invites its audience to extend the Machiavellian princi-ples spelled out in the prologue to all three revealed religions. If Marlowe's prologue is any guide, then, his play aims to pry away the religious veneer from human beings as such, in order to display the underlying workings of political life, or of what the characters of the play call "policy,"[9] in all its harshness and seaminess. In the end, Marlowe's Jew is little more than the entering wedge in that prying action.

It follows that the blurring of boundaries between Jewishness and criminality, which in Shakespeare's play proves to be merely ap-parent, is in Marlowe's entirely necessary. Marlowe would have us look beneath the obtrusive theological differences among the three biblical religions so as to establish their fundamental homogeneity. This last cannot be understood entirely in biblical terms, if only be-cause the biblical teaching to which each appeals is thought to be one, whereas the resulting theologies are diverse and conflicting. Once theological considerations are undercut, however, Jew and Christian and Turk all turn out to be unlike the naïve image each gathers for himself from the Bible. Each is instead simply self-seeking. Hence, in the extreme situation to which all three are pushed, none can help becoming criminal. As a case illustration of the Machiavellian lesson of his prologue, Marlowe's play is thus a *reductio ad absurdum* of biblical theology. It even proceeds dramatically by way of a shock-ingly crude parody of the Book of Job.[10] Whereas Job takes morality with the utmost seriousness, Barabas and the others, following the manifesto of Marlowe's Machevill, grow increasingly morally obtuse. As Barabas's crimes mount to the point where they can be effectively countered only by the even greater criminality of his adversaries, Mar-lowe's audience (if his Machevill is correct) will be forced to doubt the firmness of the moral basis on which each claimant presumed to stand when the dramatic action began. That the action that corrupts Marlowe's characters ends up corrupting Marlowe's audience as well is by no means inconsistent with the play's Machiavellianism. It is above all in its strikingly flattering presentation of moral obtuseness that Marlowe's play, unlike Shakespeare's, may be said to be anti-Jewish. Glorifying or encouraging moral obtuseness, even or especially in connection with Jews, is not part of Shakespeare's design, except insofar as it involves correcting that obtuseness.

✌ II ✌

To see more clearly the contrast between Shylock and Barabas, we must examine Marlowe's prologue a bit further. I have already said that part of the difficulty in understanding Shylock has to do with the general principles to which one may be in the habit of appealing, often tacitly, in trying to come to terms with the particulars of Shakespeare's play. At the very least, then, the Machiavellian principles to which Marlowe explicitly appeals ought to invite our considering whether there might be alternative principles, less accommodating to anti-Jewish prejudice and more compatible with Jews' own self-understanding. If so, we might go on to ask whether the latter principles could also have been available to Shakespeare and somehow embodied in his play. Meanwhile, as it happens, Marlowe's Machevill spells out the principles governing his Barabas with unusual boldness and bluntness.

The Machevill's statement of principles is complicated, however, by his not letting us identify Barabas with them completely. This seems to be the point of his describing Barabas's drama as a "tragedy."[11] The description might otherwise be hard to take seriously, for there is a noticeable incongruity between the sober implications of the principles as he would have us apply them to a "tragic" Barabas and the casualness of his own exposition of those principles. The Machevill does not particularly present himself as a connoisseur of tragedy. His actions during the prologue are, if anything, rather comic. Ludicrously, for example, he seems to forget that the purpose of his remarks is to introduce a play. He begins instead, seemingly inadvertently, with a "lecture"[12] about who he is and what he stands for and how he is to be received on his sudden arrival in Britain — and only after twenty-seven lines does he stop short, having recognized the inappropriateness of his lecture, in order to speak directly about the play in the prologue's last half-dozen lines. Marlowe's Machevill makes himself laughable by appearing to act with gross ineptitude.

To be sure, we surmise from the principles he expounds in his abbreviated lecture that his ineptitude may be feigned or duplicitous, since he is evidently a shrewd and unblinking observer of a human baseness that he claims to find everywhere and of the base means often required, according to him, in order to protect oneself against it. So too is his "tragic" Barabas, whose wealth was gotten, as the Machevill says, "not . . . without my means" (Prol. 32). And admittedly Barabas's own overtly comic moments during the drama need not by themselves have been out of place in a larger "tragedy." Nevertheless, when the Machevill finally turns his serious attention (and ours) to Barabas's "tragedy" and asks us to "grace him as he deserves, / And let him not be entertained the worse / Because he favours me" (Prol. 33–35), there is an implied disclaimer. Barabas may not "favour" or resemble the Machevill altogether, or to the Machevill's satisfaction. We are thus prepared for the likelihood that, if "tragedy" is inseparable from a protagonist's serious practical error,[13] Barabas's error is simply that he is not Machiavellian enough.

In any case, the Machevill's comic gestures have a dark shadow.[14] His arrival in Britain is, if not immediately serious, at least potentially so. It allows him to correct what he alleges are two widespread misconceptions about himself: that he is dead and that his odious reputation is deserved. True, he does not appear at first to take either misconception altogether seriously. But his lecture addresses each in turn at some length.

As for the report of his death, he begins his lecture by contradicting what the world may think. His soul, he says, has instead merely flown from Italy across the Alps and eventually to France, home of the late Duke of Guise, whom Marlowe's readers know to be the notorious instigator of Catholic France's recent nationwide massacres of Protestants.[15] Since the Machevill does not exactly say of his visit to France, as he says of his visit to Britain, that he came "To view this land and frolic with his friends" (Prol. 4), he leaves unsaid to what extent he was a mere observer of the Duke's massacres and to what extent he played a serious role in them. But from the fact that the

Duke of Guise was his main reason for remaining in France it is hard not to doubt his moral innocence. Nor, in any case, does he add to what extent the Duke, who was assassinated during the aftermath of the massacres, was the Machevill's friend with whom he frolicked. But from the very mention of the Duke's name and from further shocking examples to come in his lecture, we might not be mistaken in suspecting that, for the Machevill, the theological and political issues over which Frenchmen and others shed blood are just a game, if a sometimes deadly game. The same may be so, from the Machevill's quasi-comic viewpoint, of Barabas's violent and bloody "tragedy" too.

As for the Machevill's odious reputation, his contention that it is not deserved has two parts. In the first place, he argues *ad hominem* against his critics. He does not call them by name. Nor does he take their criticisms personally, since he claims to "weigh not men, and therefore not men's words" (Prol. 8). Nevertheless he implies that the most outspoken among his critics are clerics, and he indicates their hypocrisy. By their deeds, if not by their words, they show that they read and admire Machiavelli's books no less than do his friends. His argument is that even clerics are politically ambitious (they seek to "attain / To Peter's chair," Prol. 11–12)[16] and privately recognize that in order to succeed, they cannot but follow the base political principles supplied by those books, which notwithstanding they publicly vilify from their positions of authority. Even so, the moment such men abandon Machiavellian principles (or "cast me off," as he says in Machiavelli's name), they become "poison'd" or ruined by others who are ambitious like themselves and whom the Machevill in Machiavelli's name calls "my climbing followers" (Prol. 12–13). Marlowe's Machevill by implication vaunts the ongoing validity of his Machiavellian principles, in contrast to the transitoriness and precariousness of those who may be seen to have embodied those principles hitherto.

In the second place, then, he cites three ancient examples as if to illustrate the longstanding truth of those principles.[17] First, Julius Caesar, the destroyer of the Roman republic from within, illustrates the principle that crowns and empires are first acquired not by legitimate right but by might (Prol. 18–20).[18] Second, the harsh Athenian lawgiver Draco illustrates the principle that laws in order to command must be "writ in blood" and backed by a "strong built citadel," that is, enforced by use of arms, over and above what mere "letters" or words can effect (Prol. 20–23). Finally, the Sicilian tyrant Phalaris illustrates the principle that even a political ruler who successfully observes the two aforementioned principles — that might makes right and that arms outweigh words — is still subject to the dangers of others' envy if he becomes lax in his observance of them: Phalaris, the Machevill reports, was tortured to death by envious "great ones" who roasted him in a hollow brass bull, the same means he had used against his adversaries in the consolidation of his tyranny (Prol. 24–26).[19]

Phalaris's error makes us wonder whether the Machevill's two other ancient examples made comparable errors that he does not need or bother to mention. Caesar, as is well known, was assassinated, and Draco's harsh laws were eventually repealed by Solon.[20] The common shortcoming illustrated by the Machevill's examples thus appears to be the impermanence of their otherwise glorious successes because they forgot the principle just associated with Phalaris's misfortune: that the "means" whereby political glory is maintained must be the same as those whereby it is acquired. That none of the Machevill's ancient examples perfectly fits his principles suggests the purpose of his outspokenness here and now. That is, the Machevill, following Machiavelli himself, seems to have raised the question whether one can imitate the political glory of men such as Caesar and Draco and Phalaris without suffering their chief misfortune by forgetting the preconditions for that glory. Here, it seems, might and arms, while necessary, are not sufficient. "Letters" are needed as reminders. Hence the serious purpose of the present "tragedy": it reiterates through Barabas's pitiful failure the hitherto neglected principle that one's political good fortune is maintained only by the same base means as it is acquired.

Barabas's "tragedy" thus proves publicly the ongoing indispensability of Machiavellian books, or makes Machiavelli posthumously enviable, even or especially among his pious vilifiers. Differently stated, the Machevill's playful appearance in Britain belies or dissembles his serious purpose of showing in the face of the vilifying authorities both that Machiavelli (or his transmigrated soul) is still at large and that his odious reputation is undeserved. If the Machevill is correct, then despite what his vilifiers say, he deserves immortal glory for teaching friends and enemies alike the timelessly true principles, or "means," of "policy."

ح III ح

Before turning to look at how Marlowe's "tragic" Jew is designed to fit the aforementioned Machiavellian principles, it may help, in order to sharpen the contrast I intend to point out, to see in a preliminary way where Shakespeare differs. Most obviously, where Marlowe or his Machiavellian mouthpiece is self-glorifying, Shakespeare is self-effacing. By omitting a prologue, for example, Shakespeare bypasses the opportunity to communicate his own philosophical principles directly. Nevertheless *The Merchant of Venice* articulates at least one set of principles that run counter to those of Marlowe's Machevill. It is the Pythagoreanism that Shakespeare entrusts to his philosophical poet, Lorenzo.[21] Within the role that Shakespeare sets for him in the play, Lorenzo might well be expected to have learned those principles in turn from the philosophical writings of Plato or Aristotle — or perhaps from the most philosophical of Christian authorities, Thomas Aquinas, or even *per improbabile* from the most philosophical of Jewish authorities, Moses Maimonides.[22] I mention Lorenzo's (or Shakespeare's) possible literary sources here simply in order to suggest beforehand that, to the extent that Lorenzo is his spokesman, Shakespeare's own philosophical purview, unlike that of Marlowe's Machevill, is not on the face of it hostile to either Judaism or Christianity but may instead prove hospitable to both religions.

I have already quoted from the first of two, adjacent Pythagorean speeches by Lorenzo.[23] Their moonlit setting is Portia's pastoral estate in Belmont, where he finds himself at leisure to woo his recent bride Jessica with the accompaniment of instrumental music to be provided by Portia's servants. Music's audible harmonies, says Lorenzo to Jessica, are like the pure but inaudible harmonies of the mathematically ordered movements of the heavenly spheres. Such harmony, he adds, is in "immortal souls" (V.i.63), by which he could mean either the souls of the spheres as understood by the received doctrine or else the human soul, or both. Lorenzo is forced to expand on the human and practical implications of the Pythagorean doctrine, following Jessica's terse response in the form of a confession that she is "never merry" when she hears sweet music (V.i.69). His gentle rejoinder constitutes a second Pythagorean speech:

> *The reason is, your spirits are attentive.*
> *For do but note a wild and wanton herd,*
> *Or race of youthful and unhandled colts,*
> *Fetching mad bounds, bellowing and neighing loud,*
> *Which is the hot condition of their blood:*
> *If they but hear perchance a trumpet sound,*
> *Or any air of music touch their ears,*
> *You shall perceive them make a mutual stand,*
> *Their savage eyes turn'd to a modest gaze*
> *By the sweet power of music. Therefore the poet*
> *Did feign that Orpheus drew trees, stones, and floods,*
> *Since naught so stockish, hard, and full of rage*
> *But music for the time doth change his nature.*
> *The man that hath no music in himself,*
> *Nor is not mov'd by concord of sweet sounds,*
> *Is fit for treasons, stratagems, and spoils;*
> *The motions of his spirit are dull as night,*
> *And his affections dark as Erebus.*
> *Let no such man be trusted. Mark the music.*   (V.i.70–88)

The philosophical point of Lorenzo's speech is the politically salutary character of "music." Briefly—for I shall extend my remarks in the next chapter, when we look more closely at Lorenzo's role in the play as a whole—the proof he offers is the temporary taming effect of earthly music on wild animals. He describes that effect by alluding to the legendary figure of Orpheus, the musical poet. Orpheus's music is said to be so harmonious as to attract and astonish not just animals and human beings but also trees and stones and floods.[24] As a practical matter, Lorenzo avers that human beings who are unmoved by music are, politically speaking, not to be trusted. Their souls, he warns, are "fit for treasons, stratagems, and spoils." They remain closed to the shared order of things around them, to which "the sweet power of music," according to the philosophical poet, would open them.

A mere glance at Lorenzo's remarks is enough for the moment to indicate the presence in Shakespeare's play of un-Machiavellian principles offered as a guide for political life. We shall need to wait until our fuller exposition of the play before seeing whether those same principles, if properly observed, might have resolved the conflict between Shylock and his Christian adversary peaceably, without the sordid events that do in fact occur during the dramatic action (and which Marlowe's Machevill, were he also present there, might have gloated over). Among the questions we shall have to answer then is why Shakespeare entrusts a philosophical statement of political principles to a character who does not himself appear to act entirely in accord with those principles but whose actions in eloping with Shylock's daughter may even be said to have acerbated the conflict between Shylock and his Christian adversary. My provisional answer is that, by entrusting the practical solution of the conflict to Portia rather than Lorenzo, Shakespeare — like Marlowe — shows in his own way that he is able to separate principles from practice, that is, philosophical theorizing from political prudence. In that respect, one may say for now that Shakespeare's Lorenzo is the un-Machiavellian counterpart to Marlowe's Machevill.

᧖ IV ᧖

The Machevill, for his part, glorifies "policy." He does so, as we have already seen, by depreciating theology. He purchases the one at the expense of the other, and his "tragedy" solicits our approval of the trade-off. By the standards implicit within *The Jew of Malta* itself, however, Marlowe's Machiavellian approach to the theologico-political situation of his Jewish character strikes one as inferior to Shakespeare's. Marlowe's play makes a point of inviting a derogatory comparison with the Book of Job, the biblical text that Jewish and Christian tradition alike identify as closest in spirit to the sort of philosophizing exemplified by Shakespeare's Lorenzo.[25] The resulting difficulty, which Marlowe does not adequately face and which therefore inclines us toward Shakespeare, is that the Book of Job may well understand his protagonist better than he does. Marlowe's Machevill is able to recognize in his protagonist's appeal to the figure of Job only a "tragic" error — an unfortunate lapse from the putatively salutary (but morally dubious) principles of the prologue.

Certainly Barabas's comparison of himself with Job is, from the biblical viewpoint, superficial and misleading. Barabas laments that he suffers worse than Job because he has lost more than Job (II.ii.185–202 with Job 1–3). He thinks exclusively in terms of wealth. He boasts that in his prosperity he could easily have bought out Job and still kept plenty to live on. He overlooks that the biblical Job lost his ten children along with his chattel goods and that Job did not even begin to complain until after losing his health as well. Still, we are not left unprepared for Barabas's theological unorthodoxies. In a lengthy soliloquy just preceding the events leading to his temporary bankruptcy, Barabas speaks of Jews' wealth as the fulfillment pure and simple of the biblical promises made to Abraham and his offspring:

> *Thus trowls our fortune in by land and sea,*
> *And thus are we on every side enrich'd.*
> *These are the blessings promis'd to the Jews,*
> *And herein was old Abram's happiness:*
> *What more may heaven do for earthly man*
> *Than thus to pour out plenty in their laps,*
> *Ripping the bowels of the earth for them,*
> *Making the sea their servant, and the winds*
> *To drive their substance with successful blasts?*   (I.i.105–13)

Barabas reads the Bible selectively, for although "old Abram" may have been wealthy, his retinue and chattel goods were at best a consequence, or perhaps a presupposition, of the "blessings" or "happiness" actually promised him, which concerned the numerousness, reputation, and beneficence of his descendants as well as their eventually possessing the Land of Canaan.[26] Barabas's language here recalls the prophet Isaiah, who speaks of the wealth of nations (including the precious stones and metals in which Barabas deals) which will be transported to the Promised Land from afar by land and sea, except that the imported wealth is not said to flow unrestrictedly but presupposes Israel's justice, that is, its fidelity to the Law.[27] The biblical prophet announces God's promises, moreover, by reporting them in God's name in the first person, and generally speaking, these are paired with God's equally personal threats of national destruction and dispersion for disobedience, whereas Barabas speaks only of the promises made by a somewhat impersonal "heaven" (I.i.109).[28] In short, Barabas idiosyncratically accepts the biblical promise of Jews' prosperity quite apart from the biblical insistence that Jews live up to the demands of justice as embodied in the Law.

Yet to the observation that his theology is idiosyncratic, Barabas might well reply, as he suggests in the subsequent lines of his soliloquy, that to live strictly according to the Law, or at any rate to aim high-mindedly at what he calls "conscience" (I.i.121f.), is of dubious worth nowadays when Jews must struggle not only like all men to survive but also to overcome Christian hatred.[29] The unbridled pursuit of wealth, on the other hand, suggests a solution to the latter difficulty as well as to the former, since wealth is arguably the basis both for one's own happiness and for others' respect: "Who hateth me but for my happiness? / Or who is honour'd now but for his wealth?" (I.i.114–15). It follows from the heaven-sent character of wealth for Barabas that conversion to Christianity is hardly a prudent option for a Jew, since Christianity unlike Judaism lacks proper "fruits" in this world (I.i.118ff.). Those who follow Christian teaching, he argues, are either poor or hypocritical. In Barabas's estimation, Jews, despite being "scatter'd" around the world, have accumulated far more wealth per capita than Christians (I.i.123ff.). He even

lists some of the wealthiest by name and country of residence, including himself. And yet political rule — Barabas thinks of kingship —
seems out of the question for Jews, since one becomes king either by
succession (but Jews are too few in number to be in line to inherit
crowns) or by force (but what is "urg'd by force" is impermanent, so
he has heard [I.i.134f.]). Barabas is therefore content for Christians
to rule, so long as they leave him in peace to mind his business. His
unorthodox theology serves instead to underwrite his habit, which
exile together with the unbridled pursuit of wealth would appear to
dictate in any case, of looking at the larger political events around him
to suit his merely private interests.

Up to the moment of his temporary bankruptcy, it seems, Barabas has succeeded in privately anticipating and adapting to Malta's
public "policy" at every financially important turn. Thus three fellow
Jews seek his prudent counsel concerning the sudden arrival of a
Turkish naval embassy at Malta's council house and a concomitant
summons of Malta's Jews to the senate house. Barabas guesses correctly that the Turks are demanding Malta's payment of tribute owed
for ten years' naval protection, an exorbitant sum beyond Malta's
current resources given her wartime shipping losses. He infers, again
correctly, that the Turks' demand is a ploy to seize Malta as a base for
its naval operations against Europe. He is confident that he can make
shift to prosper under Turkish rule if necessary. Barabas has no public-
spirited loyalties, whether to Christian Malta or to his fellow Jews, to
whom he dissembles his private calculations.[30] Nevertheless his calculations fall short. He fails to consider that Malta will seek a month's
delay from the Turks in order to raise the tribute by dunning Malta's
Jews, hitherto tax exempt, and that afterward Malta will withhold the
tribute and break its alliance with Turkey in favor of a new alliance
with Christian Spain. Arriving with his fellow Jews in the senate
house, he is therefore taken aback — or left without "means," as Marlowe's Machevill might say — by the unprecedented, confiscatory, and
punitive terms suddenly imposed on them: one-half of each Jew's
estate in taxes, immediate conversion to Christianity for any Jew who
demurs, and total expropriation for any Jew who resists the foregoing
provisions. Demurring and resisting by indignantly claiming a per-

sonal exemption from the sudden tax on the grounds that half his substance is "a city's wealth," Barabas quickly incurs expropriation (I.ii.51–89 with 159–63 and II.ii.24–56).

Legally outmaneuvered, he nevertheless continues protesting to Malta's governor with theological objections that allow him (and us) to question the justice of Malta's actions. "Is theft the ground of your religion?" he asks (I.ii.99). In the subsequent disputation that he provokes, the governor and First Knight together rebut each of Barabas's objections concerning justice with theologically sanctioned maxims such as the following: it is better that a private man suffer in order to prevent public ruin than vice versa (I.ii.101ff.); the "curse" of being "poor and scorn'd of all the world" results from Barabas's "inherent sin" as a Jew and is not Malta's fault (I.ii.111ff.); Barabas should be ashamed to try to "justify" himself as an individual, as if the Maltese could forget his Jewish profession of faith (I.ii.123ff.); excessive wealth causes covetousness, a "monstrous sin" (I.ii.128); finally, Barabas has received from Malta "naught but right" (I.ii.156). Angrily resigning himself to forfeiting his wealth, Barabas soon finds the words to dismiss the Christian-Jewish disputation he has just suffered through as moot, once he overhears the First Knight advise the governor on leaving the senate house that Malta renege on paying the Turks the tribute she has just collected and break her alliance with them; it is, says the First Knight, a matter of "simple policy" (I.ii.163). To his three fellow Jews who remain with him, Barabas immediately retorts that the Maltese are in fact motivated by "policy" rather than by the "simplicity" they profess as Christians (I.ii.164ff.).[31] Henceforth Barabas, unlike Job, no longer speaks of his sufferings in terms of their injustice but only in terms of their intensity.

He thus abandons all pretense of deferring to a standard of behavior beyond his own self-interest as he sees it. Focusing above all on his private distress, Barabas implies that it alone is sufficient to warrant, or confirm, his imminent denial of God's particular providence, which Job, in contrast, had never doubted. True, in front of his friends, Barabas calls on God to curse Malta with the "plagues of Egypt," with "Earth's barrenness," and with "all men's hatred," but he addresses God here in impersonal terms as *Primus Motor,* while he himself, kneeling and striking the earth, goes on to banish his adversaries' souls to "everlasting pains, / And extreme tortures of the fiery deep" (I.ii.166–72).[32] When Barabas's three friends unsympathetically counsel patience and admonish him with the example of Job, he replies with his contemptuous comparison of himself with Job, and when they leave, he soliloquizes, not like the biblical Job, that he is innocent of injustice but rather, that in contrast to his simple-minded friends, he is "born to better chance" and so resolves to "search his deepest wits / And cast with cunning for the time to come" (I.ii.219–28). With his daughter Abigail a few moments later, he attributes the circumstances occasioning his suffering not to a just and providential God, as Job does, but to "You partial heavens" and "luckless stars," which "leave me in the ocean thus / To sink or swim," and he then infers, from the transitoriness and precariousness of his life in an uncaring cosmos, that "in extremity / We ought to make bar of no policy" (I.ii.265–79). Barabas's utter vulnerability, as he sees it, leaves him with no "means" but to oppose Malta's extreme "policy" with his own, as befits one who would recover the "city's wealth" just expropriated from him. Abandoning justice in favor of a "policy" that defers to no higher authority, Barabas, the anti-Job,[33] becomes a city unto himself, warring against Maltese and Turks alike.

Barabas's noticeably un-Job-like character permeates his entire "tragedy." It not only attaches to the fringes of his actions — for example, to his radical contempt for his three friends (I.ii.219ff.),[34] to his cursing not once but twice the day he was born (I.ii.195ff.),[35] to his reported sleeplessness (II.i.17ff.)[36] — but colors the very fabric of the play. It lets us in on how Barabas's Machiavellianism flourishes as, and only as, his conscience fades. By merely alluding to, rather than spelling out, the biblical principles by which we are in the habit of judging what makes men such as Barabas morally unconscionable, Marlowe induces us to complete each allusion for ourselves as it occurs. Barabas's moral repulsiveness notwithstanding, we are delighted to cooperate. The satisfaction we hope to gain is not that of, say, antiquarians or literary scholars documenting historical antecedents. Simply in following the dramatic action, we are drawn to the Book of Job and its presentation of moral integrity under duress, in order to begin to understand by way of comparison what makes Barabas's deeds both as unconscionable and as intriguing as they appear to us at first blush. At the same time, we notice how the biblical principles we have begun to retrieve by a modest effort of thought are deliberately disregarded or overruled one by one during Barabas's crimes-in-progress, which we are allowed to witness and which are guided instead by the Machiavellianism of the prologue.[37] As interpreters engrossed in Barabas's actions, then, we cannot help privately trying to reenact the full sweep of his otherwise hidden criminal thoughts and, like him, both wincing and smiling at his inner movement from biblical principles to Machiavellian ones. From being Barabas's spellbound observers, we become his silent coconspirators.[38] Without much more than a rather naïve and trusting attempt on our part to follow a spectacular case history of moral corruption, we soon find ourselves instructed by the perpetrator himself in becoming morally corrupt.

A single illustration may suffice. Barabas's speech to his daughter, which first sets him on his resolute course of action against Malta, contains in its opening line a remarkable allusion to the Book of Job.[39] Barabas, though penniless on paper, has all along kept a secret cache of gold and pearls and precious stones under the floorboards of his daughter's bedroom as insurance. But he now hears from her that the Maltese have already seized his house to use as a nunnery, and he despairs loudly: "My gold, my gold, and all my wealth is gone!" (I.ii.264) Barabas's lament recalls the biblical Job's having excluded just such a misplaced trust in gold from the inventory of his own deeds:

> *If I made golde mine hope, or have said to the wedge of golde, Thou art my confidence,*
> *If I rejoyced because my substance was great, or because mine hand had gotten muche,*
>
> . . . .
>
> (*This also had bene an iniquitie to be condemned: for I had denyed the God above*).   (Job 31:24–25, 28)

Job's introspective self-examination goes on to list several other unjust practices which he has eschewed but which Barabas, on the contrary, will soon embrace:

> *If I rejoyced at his destruction that hated me, or was moued to joye when*
> *euil came vpon him,*
> *Neither have I suffered my mouth to sinne, by wishing a cursse vnto his*
> *soule.*
>
> . . . .
>
> *If I have hid my sinne, as Adam, conceiling mine iniquitie in my bosom,*
> *Thogh I colde have made afraied a great multitude, yet the most*
> *contemptible of the families did feare me: so I kept silence, and went not*
> *out of the door?*   (Job 31:29–30, 33–34)

It is not simply that Marlowe here anticipates the un-Job-like
gloating, cursing, deceiving, and cowering that Barabas's money worship will set in train. It is that the reference to the Book of Job recalls
to us, even if we are only casually aware of its contents, something
about the question of divine providence, of God's support for morality under adverse conditions. Obviously Barabas is no Job; but he is
like Job in suffering undeservedly (at least to begin with) and in
having his complaints ignored or misunderstood by those around
him who are in a position to assuage — and who by their indifference
deepen — his suffering. Having been wealthy, respected, and happily
complacent, both men are suddenly alone in their thoughts and their
pain, and each must search his deeds thoroughly with a view to dis-
covering how to restore the status quo ante. In asking what he might
have done or left undone to warrant his continuing suffering, Barabas
and Job each wonder whether there is some new, not yet considered,
or not yet supplied alternative that lurks just outside his purview. For
Job, the alternative comes to him via a voice from God, which reminds him of what he has up till now considered only hazily: the
narrow limits of his understanding of the vast world around him
which have been imposed by his otherwise admirably complacent
piety, his very habit of uncorrupted justice or unquestioning faith-
fulness to the Law which has made his suffering so morally un-

deserved.[40] Barabas, in contrast, deliberately abandons that piety and its outlook on things, not merely in thought (as Job does, momentarily) but in deed. And as Marlowe lets us watch, both fascinated and horrified with Barbaras's feigned biblical exemplar in mind, he (or his outspoken Machevill) would take us with him.

Consider in this connection, however, Barabas's decisive inference from the alleged uncharitableness of the heavens and the moral indifference of the stars to a need for political ruthlessness. From the biblical viewpoint, Barabas's inference is, to say the least, hasty. The biblical Job, through his suffering, is likewise brought to recognize, among other things, his human incapacity to bend the heavens and stars to his will. God himself reminds him:

> *Canst thou restraint the sweet* influences *of ye Pleiades? or loose the bands of Orion?*
> *Canst thou bring forthe Mazzaroth in ther time? canst thou also guide Arcturus with his sonnes?*
> *Knowest thou the course of heaven, or canst thou set the rule thereof in ye earth?* (Job 38:31–33)

Barabas's inference that justice is useful when the heavens and stars are favorable but negotiable and perhaps dispensable when they are not requires an additional, unbiblical premise, namely that justice is merely a "means" (to use the Machevill's word) for adapting to the heavens and stars, for coping with, or mastering, fate or fortune. But Job would seem to look on justice as a means for adapting not to the heavens and stars but to the will of their divine creator. Here his view differs from Marlowe's fundamentally. For Job, justice is a necessary supplement to his admitted dependence on the heavens and stars and on much else whose workings are beyond him. Suffering and misfortune therefore do not by themselves prompt Job to abandon either justice or the piety that fosters it. Job remains, throughout his heaven-sent misfortunes, God's "servant."[41] Even so, in his extremity, Job is prompted to *consider* abandoning justice, if only by way of being brought to reflect on what human life would be without it. God offers Job a private whirlwind tour of the mysteriously uncaring universe, as if to show him how a human life without justice would be a life that is transitory and precarious, in a world with no proper home for man — unless by his own ruthless and willful making.[42] In Marlowe's considerably narrower terms — which beg rather than confront the far-reaching theological question deliberately posed by the biblical book — it would be the life of Barabas, the "tragedy" promoted one-sidedly by Marlowe's Machevill.

ᔓ V ᔓ

Where, then, has Barabas's Machiavellian "policy" gotten him? By act V, scene ii, just prior to the final episode, which brings his downfall, Barabas has pursued his vengeance against the city to its farthest limits. He climbs a mounting trail of misdeeds. He stealthily recovers his reserve cache by having Abigail feign a wish to convert in order to enter the nunnery that is his former home; he entices the governor's son into a mutually fatal duel over Abigail's affections with her suitor, whom she loves; he poisons the entire nunnery including Abigail, when, heartsick over her father's cruelly disposing of her innocent suitor, she returns to convert in earnest; he murders two friars who have become aware of Barabas's complicity in the fatal duel through Abigail's dying confession; and he poisons his Turkish slave, who has been his chief accomplice, together with the slave's courtesan and her pander, who have been blackmailing Barabas and eventually report him to the authorities. Finally, after pretending suicide, he rises to become governor of Malta under the besieging Turks, to whom he has betrayed his knowledge of subterranean passages through the city's walls. Barabas is now in the position of tyrant over Malta. He therefore faces the classic predicament of a tyrant.[43] He enjoys, as he says, "no small authority" in the city, but having achieved that authority "by wrong," he also suffers the city's hatred and threats of assassination (V.ii.28–38). He wonders in the circumstances whether his success has been worth the effort. Nevertheless, as if mindful of the Machevill's third principle in the prologue or of the fate of the forgetful Phalaris as the Machevill describes it, Barabas resolves to maintain his tyranny "bravely with firm policy" (V.ii.37).[44]

But Barabas's resolution here only hastens his undoing. Having reached the evident limits of what he can accomplish by himself (V.ii.39–47), he offers his friendship to the deposed governor. In return, the governor must help in restoring Barabas's financial fortunes by collecting money from the city's wealthy, and also Malta's political fortunes by implementing a "strategem" designed to assassinate the Turkish commander and detonate the occupying garrison (V.ii.49–111). Barabas soliloquizes that his friendship is intended solely for his own private advantage and is revocable whenever the Turks come back with a better offer. He adds that he has learned to limit his friendships in this way partly from "the life we Jews are us'd to lead" and partly from imitating the Christian examples around him (V.ii.112–25). Yet Barabas's calculations remain seriously incomplete. He fails to anticipate that the ex-governor will deftly subvert Barabas's strategem in order to cause Barabas's own death and the taking of the Turkish commander (who is also the sultan's son) as hostage (V.v.21–94). Perhaps we could feel pity and fear for Barabas's "tragedy" more readily, and so become more edified by his Job-like situation,[45] if we had not instead been instructed beforehand by Marlowe's Machevill on just what we are supposed to think about him all along. It is hard to be moved by casebook examples. Nor, on the other hand, are we as thoughtful onlookers expected simply to cheer at the resumption of political rule by Malta's Christians, for *ex hypothesi* their fates are governed by the same base principles as are those of Marlowe's Jew and the visiting Turks.[46] Meanwhile we cannot help suspecting that the governor and others will be set aside by yet another, more resolute climber.[47] (One candidate might be the First Knight, or whoever dreamed up Malta's emergency tax scheme in the first place — which in hindsight appears to have been perhaps intentionally contrived to provoke Barabas's indignant protest, hence to expropriate him without further struggle.)[48]

Appreciating Marlowe's plot, it seems, is mainly a matter of sharing in the astonishment and delight of whoever finds himself in an opportune position to scheme ruthlessly against an adversary. But again, if his Machevill is correct, all are adversaries and all are doomed to fail. Only the Machevill, postulating their eventual failure in principle, has the last laugh.

Shakespeare's un-Machiavellian difference from Marlowe, on the other hand, has to do with his never losing sight of the moral issue. Among other things, we shall have to see how Shakespeare, or his Portia, faces more fully the practical question of the relations between Christians and Jews, which Marlowe, following Machiavelli, has preferred to downplay into the question of personal glory even at the calculated risk of personal survival.[49] Shakespeare's superiority, I shall suggest, derives from his openness to yet a third human pursuit over and above bare survival and political glory: it is philosophical wisdom.

3

᪣ ᪣

Shylock and Shakespeare's Antonio

*If Shakespeare allowed Shylock to be freely pardoned, he would
be blurring his central theme. If we forgave Shylock, we could
forget him. Because it disappoints our expectations and offends
our sense of justice, Shylock's unreconciled suffering remains
in accord with his author's iconoclastic intention.*

— Robert Grudin, *Mighty Opposites*

᪣ I ᪣

MY SCATTERED OBSERVATIONS SO FAR HAVE LED ME TO DOUBT the
received picture of *The Merchant of Venice* as unfriendly to Jews.
Shylock's willingness to transgress Jewish dietary laws, the Duke's
public appeal for Shylock to live up to Jewish teaching concerning
mercy, Portia's understanding of the Lord's Prayer as a Jewish prayer,
and Lorenzo's nonsectarian philosophizing about the politically salutary effects of music — none of these details fits easily with the current
scholarly supposition that Shakespeare's play is, inadvertently or otherwise, anti-Jewish. It is better, then, to look for an alternative hypothesis, which will account differently for those elements of the play
that tend to put its Jewish (or nominally Jewish) character in an
unfavorable light. I have already touched on what seems to be a much

better hypothesis about the play, by way of the denial of the unsupported assertion that Shakespeare has no thought of correcting Christians' longstanding hostility toward Jews. On the contrary, the evidence of the play requires us to suppose that Shakespeare might mean just that — to correct what he sees as the theologically unwarranted and politically deleterious abuse of Jews as Jews in the name of Christian teaching. This new hypothesis would have the advantage, first and foremost, of allowing us to reckon more fully with the likelihood that, as I have already suggested in chapter 1, Shakespeare by no means considers Shylock a model Jew. Meanwhile, given Venice's morally questionable treatment of Shylock, which I began by noting (his public harassment on the Rialto, the Jew-baiting in court, his legally sanctioned self-incrimination, his forced conversion, etc.), my new hypothesis has the further advantage of remaining open to the possibility that Shakespeare understands, clearly and deeply, the moral and other shortcomings of his Venetians — even or especially those of his title character, the merchant.

The foregoing reflections, and their perhaps shocking implications (for Shakespeare's contemporaries, to say nothing of ourselves), may go a long way toward explaining the peculiarity of the play's title. Its title, *The Merchant of Venice,* is evidently unique in the corpus of his plays. If we divide the corpus's thirty-seven titles into those that identify their protagonists (e.g., *Hamlet Prince of Denmark*) and those that do not (e.g., *Much Ado about Nothing*), *The Merchant* clearly belongs to the former group. Of those, however, most (like *Hamlet*) identify their protagonists by a proper name. Many even add a political description to the proper name (as *Hamlet* is also called *Prince of Denmark, Pericles* is *Prince of Tyre, Othello* is *the Moor of Venice,* and still others are identified as *King . . .*). Only three such titles leave their protagonists anonymous: alongside *The Merchant* stand *Two Gentlemen of Verona* and *The Merry Wives of Windsor.* To judge by its title, then, *The Merchant* is unique in being about one politically identifiable protagonist (not two or more, like *Gentlemen* or *Wives*) who is nevertheless not identified by his or her proper name.

The absence of a proper name in Shakespeare's title is no small matter. In the case of *Othello the Moor of Venice,* for example, the title calls attention beforehand to the fact that its particular protagonist, and no one else in the play, is characterized by the announced description: Othello is the only Moor of Venice, as Hamlet and Pericles are the only princes in their respective polities. But Shakespeare's unnamed merchant could offhand be anyone in Venice. We do not know exactly which Venetian is being described in Shakespeare's title until his play actually gets under way. Even if, as it happens, *The Merchant*'s first scene includes a conversation with a merchant, Antonio by name, and that conversation touches on his business concerns, we cannot yet be sure whether the play is primarily about *that* merchant, unless and until other emergent possibilities are excluded. Shylock himself, who does not appear until the third scene, is also in his own way a merchant, as his conversation with Antonio there is meant to suggest.[1] Shakespeare's title, then, has the peculiarity of distributing the announced description of the play's one protagonist among more than one of its city dwellers, perhaps even among all of them to some extent, whether citizen (like Antonio) or mere resident (like Shylock). This peculiarity, it seems, goes to the heart of the subject of the play. Shakespeare sets his play in a peculiar political light, wherein the general outlines of the subdued moral antagonism between Christians and Jews suddenly become obtrusive and demand renewed attention.

Shakespeare thus follows Marlowe in homogenizing his characters to a remarkable extent, by indicating their common dependence on a given political setting. All are visibly touched or tainted — or, as in Shylock's case, transformed — by the mercantile character of their city. Shakespeare's Venice is a commercial republic. Its merchants, hungry for venture capital, cannot always draw their fill from fellow citizens. Hence they must turn to outsiders — such as Shylock, whose Jewish profession of faith (like that of Marlowe's Barabas) does not fit with Christian Venice's citizenship prerequisites. Venetian citizens, being Catholic Christians, are forbidden by church teaching from borrowing or lending at interest among themselves.[2] Business loans among respectable Venetians are instead either friendly transactions, interest free except perhaps for a penalty clause (presumably strictly monetary, not the life-threatening kind contrived by Shylock), or else joint ventures between entrepreneur and financier, where both alike share the profits as well as the risks of the lender's investment. At the same time, the church's biblically inspired restrictions on interest taking do not necessarily extend to Christians' borrowing from non-Christians. Nor, for that matter, are Jews prevented from lending at interest to Christians. Both Jews and Christians rely, separately, on the authority of scriptural texts such as Deuteronomy 23:19–20, which prohibits charging interest ("usury") only to one's "brother," not to the "stranger":

> *Thou shalt not give to usurie to thy brother: as usurie of money, usurie of meat, usurie of anie thing that is put to usurie.*
> *Unto a stranger thou maiest lend upon usurie but thou shalt not lend upon usurie unto thy brother, that the Lord thy God may blesse thee in all that thou settest thy hand to, in the land whether thou goest to possesse it.*

Jews traditionally interpret *brother* here to mean, in effect, "coreligionist," with whom community solidarity must take precedence over personal profit, and from whom interest taking of any sort is unfair exploitation, damaging to community well-being. So, in practice, do Christians. It follows that Venetian merchants in need of loans beyond what friends or fellow citizens can supply may well find themselves turning to usurious "strangers" in their midst. And strangers like Shylock are content to oblige them.

The peculiar setting that both exposes and colors the deeply rooted conflict between Christian and Jew is thus the burgeoning mercantile life of Venice as a nominally Christian city. There, paradoxically, bonded notes between Christian and Jew, whether interest bearing or not, carry the full sanction of Venetian law. As his trial date approaches, Antonio recognizes as much. He dismisses a sympathetic friend's well-meant but (in Antonio's opinion) empty assurance that the Duke, who presides over the Venetian court, will declare Shylock's penalty clause null and void. Like the Duke, Antonio sees that the city's profitable international trade depends on honoring all lawful contracts with strangers:

> *The Duke cannot deny the course of law:*
> *For the commodity that strangers have*
> *With us in Venice, if it be denied,*
> *Will much impeach the justice of the state,*
> *Since that the trade and profit of the city*
> *Consisteth of all nations.*   (III.iii.26–31)

Shylock too takes his stand on the simple basis that his penalty clause is binding *pro forma* quite apart from its substance. "I'll have my bond," he filibusters, spurning Antonio's pre-trial attempts at an informal, life-saving settlement (III.iii.12–17).[3] To do otherwise would be to allow mitigating circumstances, in which strangers may be at a disadvantage, to interfere with the security of a sealed contract. Such circumstances, Shylock surmises, are extralegal, hence not binding. Shylock insists throughout that he is bound only by the law, no more and no less, and that Venetian law, generally speaking, leaves him free to contract as he wishes.[4]

Shylock's insistence on his "bond" points to the legal and more-than-legal difficulties facing the Duke or anyone else who must confront the practical implications of the cosmopolitanism emblematic of Venetian commerce. The Duke himself is no expert jurist, as his legal bafflement during the trial testifies. He has sent to Padua beforehand for learned advice on whether there may be a loophole to save Antonio, and he goes so far as to plead on Antonio's behalf by urging pity for the latter's reported shipping losses, which evidently prevent his timely repayment of the note, and he even threatens to dismiss Shylock's suit altogether if Shylock fails to show mercy toward Antonio in court (IV.i.3–34, 88–107). Nor need the Duke's predisposition in Antonio's favor be traced to some base private motive (a longstanding business partnership? covert xenophobia?).

On the contrary, the presence of Venice's magnificoes in the courtroom suggests the trial's wider public importance.[5] The Duke is Venice's leading statesman. With Antonio, the Duke shares a bond of civic solidarity denied the stranger. Here, then, is his legitimate motive for favoring Antonio, for he seems expected first and foremost to honor that bond and protect a fellow citizen. Perhaps his sympathies also come from having heard, through mutual friends if not directly, Antonio's own explanation for the Jew's relentless proceedings against him. As Antonio relates it shortly before his trial, it is that his own habit of Christian charitableness is bad for Shylock's business:

> *He seeks my life. His reason well I know:*
> *I oft deliver'd from his forfeitures*
> *Many that have at times made moan to me.*
> *Therefore he hates me.*   (III.iii.21–24)

Other things being equal, to deliver friends and fellow citizens from harsh forfeitures and to denounce those such as Shylock who would profit from them are to act according to the spirit (if not the letter) of Deuteronomy, and so in the spirit of civic well-being. In any case, to decide between Antonio and Shylock here is not simply to decide between Christian and Jew. It is to judge whether priority should be given to public-spirited friendships as opposed to private profits. It is thus to face the dilemma peculiar to a modern commercial city such as Venice: whether the community at large is better served by strengthening the bonds that unite citizens as citizens or instead by reinforcing those bonds that unite citizen and stranger alike simply as freely contracting individuals.[6]

Perplexity over this moral issue permeates the Shakespearean political setting in which the tensions between merchant and moneylender, Christian and Jew, citizen and stranger are allowed to play themselves out. Nor are those tensions ever fully resolved, despite appearances to the contrary. Certainly Shakespeare's Christian citizen (Antonio) wins a devastating victory in court over the Jewish stranger (Shylock), albeit under the vexing circumstances that I noted in chapter 1. Still, victory over that stranger is part of a larger dramatic action, of which the trial scene is only the public reflection. For the moment, it suffices to say that Antonio's victory is made possible by yet another stranger, Portia, the amicus curiae who poses as the emissary of the learned Paduan advocate to whom the Duke had sent for legal advice, but who is also Antonio's disguised private rival in a different kind of suit and takes the opportunity to seal a

decisive victory over him on her own. Likewise Shylock's loss is miti-
gated by the facts that he is never without a certain nobility, as befits
his occasional appeals, however misguided, to his humanity and his
biblical roots,[7] and that the play's larger action teaches how he might
have avoided the extreme baseness that leads to his ultimate downfall.
These larger circumstances require us to look at Shakespeare's Christian merchant and Jewish moneylender more closely.

In considering Shylock's mistreatment, then, we must begin
where Shakespeare begins, by noting how Antonio and Shylock find
themselves in similar dramatic situations. Each is, at the outset of the
play, on the point of suffering the forfeiture of a bond that is neither
contractual nor political but (we may say) personal and familial. It is
in either case a bond of love. In Antonio's case, he is about to risk his
close friendship with his young relative Bassanio, for whom he must
seek an emergency loan in order to finance the latter's wooing of a
young heiress — again, the same Portia who later appears as the disguised stranger who saves Antonio's life and afterward properly dis-
places him in Bassanio's deepest affections.[8] In Shylock's case, on the
other hand, he is about to lose his daughter Jessica through elopement to the poet Lorenzo — who alone among his fellow citizens tries
to articulate a salutary teaching that addresses citizen and stranger
alike and which, if properly heeded, would conceivably correct the
vices that have brought Antonio and Shylock into open conflict in the
first place. The two love triangles are, as we shall see, intricately connected and mutually illuminating. But first we must look at each
separately.

꒦ **II** ꒦

Even before he knows that he will be entering into negotiations
with Shylock over a portentous loan, Antonio has a complaint. He is
sad. Worse, he appears not to know the cause of his sadness, though
he would like to, since it is recent (see I.i.73–76) and hence traceable.
It remains, he says, something "I am to learn" (I.i.5). Meanwhile his

lack of success at self-knowledge has become wearisome both to himself and to his companions Salerio and Solanio, to whom he first confesses his sadness. Antonio's sadness is doubly frustrating to him because it inhibits the self-knowledge he would seek, while it occasions his very seeking. No wonder his sadness, having philosophical as well as practical import, makes of him, as he says, a "want-wit" who has "much ado to know myself" (I.i.6–7). If Antonio speaks the truth about himself, as he swears he does ("In sooth" [I.i.1]), then in saying that he lacks self-knowledge, he anticipates the confusion that his sad words and deeds soon bring upon himself and others around him.[9] The subsequent action of the play may be said to end with some resolution to Antonio's unhappy confusion, but only after much ado, including the fortunate help of Portia, who, to begin with, stands well outside the circle of Antonio's immediately susceptible acquaintances. Only late in act V, following the fortunate outcome of his ill-conceived joint venture with Bassanio in pursuit of Portia's hand, and in the midst of the newlyweds' very first marital spat, which he has unwittingly occasioned, does Antonio come to recognize himself as "th' unhappy subject of these quarrels," to which his confused and confusing doings throughout the play have somehow led (V.i.238). Seen in this light, Shakespeare's comedy is less about a Christian merchant's involvement with a Jewish moneylender than about his unfortunate ignorance about himself and the damage it nearly causes him and his companions in the city.

Of all his companions, his closest friend and "most noble kinsman" (I.i.57), Bassanio, appears to know him best—though evidently not well enough to know whether he himself may be the hidden cause of Antonio's sadness.[10] This possibility is broached during the play's opening scene. There Salerio and Solanio, in conversation with Antonio, are said to be mistaken and even impertinent in attributing the cause of his sadness either to his business worries or to his being in love. Nevertheless there may be some truth to what they say.

As for his business worries, Antonio immediately expresses confidence to them that his current shipping ventures are sufficiently diversified and his other investments long term. When Solanio then infers that he must instead be in love, Antonio indignantly refuses the suggestion outright ("Fie, fie!" [I.i.46]). But in the light of what follows, Antonio's objections seem a bit hasty. Consider that Antonio will shortly be telling Bassanio that his shipping ventures have left him without liquid cash or secure collateral, hence with a low credit rating on the Rialto,[11] so that he must be prepared to face the dispiriting prospect of dealing for Bassanio's sake with a usurer like Shylock. Likewise these same circumstances will soon lead to his being unable to repay Shylock on time.

Nor does Antonio's protest that he is not in love prove entirely convincing, especially to Solanio, who does not limit his notion of love to women or to sexual intimacy. Later on, when Salerio recounts to him Antonio's dockside farewell to Bassanio at the latter's setting sail for Portia's country estate at Belmont, he connects the visible sadness of the one with the departure of the other:

> *And even there, his eye being big with tears,*
> *Turning his face, he put his hand behind him,*
> *And with affection wondrous sensible*
> *He wrung Bassanio's hand; and so they parted.* (II.viii.46–49)

Solanio then remarks, "I think he only loves the world for him" (III.viii.50). Certainly Antonio in the play's first scene professes a willingness to do anything on Bassanio's behalf, so long as it stands, as Bassanio himself does, "Within the eye of honour" (I.i.137).

Having already heard from Bassanio before the play begins that he has sworn a "secret pilgrimage" to a certain "lady," Antonio honorably awaits the promised details. These include Bassanio's purported need for yet another loan from him — the latest in a continuing series — in order, he says, to marry her and so free himself from what he describes to Antonio as his "chief care": "to come off fairly from the great debts / Wherein my time, something too prodigal, / Hath left me gag'd" (I.i.127–30). Bassanio's "prodigal" spending habits have long exceeded his means and depleted his estate. Now they prompt his turning once more to Antonio's financial as well as emotional largess:

> *To you, Antonio,*
> *I owe the most, in money and in love;*
> *And from your love I have a warranty*
> *To unburden all my plots and purposes*
> *How to get clear of all the debts I owe.* (I.i.130–34)

Since Antonio in his charitableness has been the chief enabler of Bassanio's prodigality, and as there is little evidence for other shared interests between them beyond their unspecified family kinship, Antonio's recent sadness may well be both caused and obscured by the newly arisen worry that Bassanio's announced pilgrimage in quest of marriage and financial solvency will soon clear him of his outstanding "debts" not only of "money" but also of "love." That is, Antonio would seem to be upset by the sudden possibility that his love as well as his money — his charity in both senses of the term — will soon become dispensable for Bassanio.

Antonio's worry that Bassanio will no longer need his charity would account for his giving, in the opening scene, two different versions of his financial picture. The prosperous version he gives Salerio and Solanio and the desperate one he gives Bassanio cannot both be true. To whom does Antonio then misrepresent? Perhaps it is not necessary to decide between the two obvious possibilities, for both point in the same direction. If, on the one hand, Antonio misrepresents his financial picture to Salerio and Solanio, his motive may be to protect his reputation as a "royal merchant" (III.ii.237; IV.i.29). Consider that Salerio and Solanio are not as close to Antonio as Bassanio is; their friendship with him seems based on admiration rather than on intimate acquaintance.[12] Indeed, Salerio and Solanio may well be among those whom Antonio has rescued from defaulting on usurious loans, so that to conceal from them his own financial straits would be to remove his crusade from any suspicion that it might be causing his financial ruin. Given that Antonio's companions are less pious or more frivolous than Antonio, such suspicion, whether well founded or not, might open him to ridicule rather than respect.[13] It follows that Antonio's public crusade has the disturbing private implication that he prefers to treat his friends as charity cases. This implication, as we have already seen, has characterized his friendship with Bassanio as well.

If Antonio misrepresents his financial picture to Bassanio, on the other hand, perhaps it is only his misguided move to offset the likelihood of Bassanio's imminent independence.[14] Consider in this regard that Antonio's ready consent to enable Bassanio to acquire yet another loan has the immediate effect of increasing rather than decreasing Bassanio's reliance on his charity. Wittingly or not, Antonio even goes to extremes on this occasion. He puts, as he says, "My purse, my person, my extremest means" (I.i.138) at Bassanio's disposal. Meanwhile he leaves "knowledge" of what is to be done with the loan entirely to Bassanio (I.i.157–60). Possibly Antonio is in the habit of remaining indifferent to how Bassanio spends his borrowed money on the grounds that Bassanio's free spending is a kind of flattering worldly imitation of his own charitableness. However that may be, Antonio's extreme commitment to "means" and indifference to ends leaves room for further wondering: Is the loan really salutary for Bassanio?[15]

It is possible to argue that Bassanio's loan is an altogether needless encumbrance. Assuming that he can already afford to make the twenty-mile overland trip to Belmont on his own (see III.iv.81–84), we are forced to ask why he must arrive as he does by hired ship and with lavish trappings.[16] Portia, the heiress in question, already knows of his poverty, given that he has told her openly at their first meeting (see III.ii.250–58).[17] Even so, she regards him, albeit privately, as "the best deserving a fair lady" (I.ii.109f.). Indeed, after a steady stream of insufferable suitors, she may well be wondering what is keeping him so long from returning for her hand. Nevertheless when Bassanio finally arrives, he does so with a costly retinue and bearing "Gifts of rich value" (II.ix.91). Are Bassanio's expenses here not frivolous? Does he not simply continue, thanks to Antonio's charity, to act the part of a prodigal?

And yet Bassanio's need for the loan is more than the tail end of an ongoing spending spree. Consider further that his one and only meeting with Portia has been during a visit to her late father, where Bassanio had traveled as "a scholar and a soldier" in the company of another Italian nobleman (I.ii.104ff.). There, as he tells Antonio by way of leading up to the subject of the loan, he discovered not only her wealth, her beauty, and her "wondrous virtues," said to befit or exceed those of her ancient Roman namesake ("Cato's daughter, Brutus' Portia"), but also the intense rivalry for her among "Renowned suitors" whom "the four winds blow in from every coast" (I.ii.65–69). When at that time he imparted his love to her, he immediately confessed, as he himself reminds her later on, that "all the wealth I had / Ran in my veins" (III.ii.251–53)—presumably lest she draw false inferences about his financial condition from his being well born. Yet the only acknowledgment Portia then offered in return was, as Bassanio recalls to Antonio, occasional "fair speechless messages" from her eyes (I.i.163–64). Bassanio, as we shall soon see, is not one to be satisfied with mere appearances. How then could he be certain whether his frank confession of poverty might not prevent Portia from reciprocating his love fully? Would not such uncertainty account for his delay until at least after the death of her father before undertaking the "secret pilgrimage" he had promised to her? At any rate, it might account for his wishing to appear as if he had become wealthy in the meantime. Conceivably his wealthy appearance might increase his chances with her, so long as Portia were to infer from it his liberality or high-minded indifference to wealth. If so, it would be a sign to her that Bassanio was interested not particularly in her fortune but only in her.

Still, Bassanio's flashy arrival in Belmont is intended not simply as a fortune hunter's ostentatious display but as a lover's way, however dubious, to the heart of his beloved. Fortunately, that way is never given a chance to work—or rather, to fail, since Portia has meanwhile not been favorably impressed with any of Bassanio's rivals despite their wealth. From that point of view, the salutariness of the loan in question is limited largely to the fact that it finally brings Bassanio back to Belmont. On his arrival, however, he becomes aware that he must pass what amounts to a character test as a requirement for claiming Portia's hand. It is in fact the sole requirement. According to the terms of her father's will, Portia may not choose a husband freely (I.ii.21–31, 98–100). She is instead bound by a contest. Serious suitors must determine which among three sealed caskets — made of gold, silver, or lead, respectively — contains Portia's picture. Each suitor must swear in advance to keep his choice secret, and in the likelihood of failure to leave Belmont immediately and not seek marriage ever afterward. Suitors are to be led, or rather misled, by the respective inscriptions on each casket. The correct casket, as Portia's lady-in-waiting reminds her during a moment of despondency about ever winning a proper suitor after a seemingly endless series of losers, "will no doubt never be chosen by any rightly, but one who you shall rightly love" (I.ii.29–31).

We are prepared for Bassanio's correct choice as Portia's rightful beloved by watching two previous suitors choose mistakenly. One suitor is taken with the gold casket's inscription "Who chooseth me shall gain what many men desire," the other with the silver one's "Who chooseth me shall get as much as he deserves" (II.vii.1–77, ix.1–78).[18] Both men are deceived by the apparent meaning of the inscriptions into judging Portia's worth by some inadequate measure — what the many desire, or what someone else deserves. Bassanio, having implicitly discovered with the contest the futility of his scheme to put on a wealthy facade for Portia's sake, will not himself be misled by the deceptiveness of appearances, as his extensive deliberations just prior to choosing show (III.ii.73–107). Portia, to be sure, supplies him with subtle and encouraging hints to guide his actual choosing, as though she were playfully harboring doubts about his success. For example, she commissions musical accompaniment in the form of a song whose couplets or hemistiches rhyme with "lead" (III.ii.63–72).[19] Yet her other remarks suggest that she expects Bassanio to choose correctly quite apart from such hints (III.ii.4–6, 40–41). How does she know? Here it is plausible to speculate that Portia's father, an "ever virtuous" and "holy" man (I.ii.26), has devised the contest precisely with Bassanio in mind.

Consider how the contest accomplishes what Bassanio's loan might have been meant to accomplish but in principle never could. By separating the quest for Portia's hand from the question of wealth, the contest affords Bassanio the chance both to discover the truth behind her apparent gesture of love (her "fair speechless messages") and to display the truth behind his own (his "Gifts of rich value," etc.). Discovery of the former truth becomes possible on the premise that no one would choose the correct, or lead, casket except one whom Portia "shall rightly love," that is, by virtue of her father's wisdom as matchmaker. Discovery of the latter truth is made possible insofar as the contest is an improvement over wealth as a means for any suitor's showing his love for Portia. Recall that in order to compete against his rivals, Bassanio in obtaining the loan seems to have supposed that he must signify to Portia that he loves her not simply for her wealth or other worldly advantages (e.g., that she is desirable to the many or that he is somehow deserving of her) but for herself. It follows that Bassanio intends his display of borrowed wealth to indicate that, having become sufficiently wealthy on his own, he no longer needs her wealth but now needs only her. Of course, Bassanio here forgets his own prodigality, his longstanding habit of excessive spending, which Antonio's charitable funding and example may well have encouraged in him. To Portia or anyone else recalling Bassanio's previous poverty, his newfound wealth might instead raise questions about its source and so lead to the fuller truth, which he would for the moment prefer to conceal, namely to his prodigality in risking not only his own but also another's wealth simply in order to relieve Portia's putative worries about his poverty — a risk compatible equally with love for her and love for her fortune, and which therefore remains inconclusive for his present purpose.

But the contest simplifies matters. The lead casket reads "Who chooseth me must give and hazard all he hath." Of the three caskets, its inscription alone both demands everything of the one who chooses it and promises nothing in return — except Portia herself. It therefore appeals to Bassanio precisely because of its unpromising, even hazardous character (III.ii.104–7). It lets Bassanio display just that willingness to risk all for her and for her alone which he has wanted to make plain from the beginning, while concealing for the moment his prodigal tendencies, which questions about his newfound wealth might otherwise have disclosed inopportunely. It gives Bassanio the benefit of the doubt. In addition, it anticipates the necessary means by which his prodigality might be corrected, namely the elimination of his need for Antonio's charity following his marriage to Portia. Even so, immediately after having chosen correctly and winning Portia's hand, Bassanio must confess to her the fuller truth of his indebtedness and worse, as Salerio arrives from Venice with a letter from Antonio announcing that all Antonio's ships have miscarried and that the bond authorizing Shylock's pound of flesh is now overdue (III.ii.216–304). The truth that Bassanio has wished to disclose to Portia, his willingness to give and hazard all he has for her, has suddenly been shown to be only a half-truth, and Bassanio must now abandon his bride before their wedding night in order to comply once more with the — last? — wish of his best friend, whose charity has been the prop and possible model for Bassanio's own unfortunate prodigality.

Antonio's shadow now hangs over the newlyweds' marriage, as it has over their courtship. There it will hover till the play's final scene. As his charitable contribution to Bassanio's prodigality has delayed the consummation of their courtship, though ultimately it furthers it, so too it will delay the consummation of their marriage bond. Everything, as it were, awaits Antonio's fate. Were Antonio to die as a result of his last act of charity, it is difficult to see how Bassanio could fail to hold his marriage to Portia responsible. Were Antonio's charitable influence over Bassanio to continue as before, however, it is difficult to see how Portia could remain tolerant of it. Of the newlyweds we may therefore say that their marriage, though legally binding, nevertheless remains incomplete. So far it is only a contract, a set of mutual promises yet to be fulfilled — and perhaps impossible of fulfillment in the present circumstances. In this respect, the marriage bond is typical of every other contractual bond in the play, including Antonio's with Shylock. Something must be done beyond mere formal ratification and legal enforcement in order to fulfill the mutual promises that the contract specifies. Shakespeare's comedy here intimates the limits of all such bonds by posing the further question of how each might be performed to suit the best interests of everyone concerned. Yet if there is one successful example of such a performance in the play, it is Portia's execution of her father's will, which has been so wisely designed as to require of her only the modest encouragement of her intended. In order to settle the larger difficulties surrounding both her marriage bond and Antonio's bond with Shylock, then, Portia must prove by her own wisdom to be heiress to her father's virtue as well as to his wealth.

ᳵ III ᳵ

Portia turns to the law, to Venetian law, because Shylock has already done so in order to enforce his contractual bond with Antonio. Shylock seems to be the one person in Shakespeare's Venice who is most zealous about the law: it alone, quite apart from any friendships with the Venetians, so he thinks, is the ultimate guarantor of his civil liberties.[20] By contrast, Antonio's extreme opposition to Shylock's usuries, which is not shared by anyone else in the play, is neither enjoined nor forbidden by Venetian law, which leaves the issue open in the manner I have already indicated.[21] Antonio's anti-usuriousness, being all of a piece with his Christian charitableness, amounts to private proselytizing and is to that extent theologically rather than legally motivated. Yet for reasons I noted in chapter 1, Shylock's peculiar zeal for the law cannot simply be traced to his being a Jew who understands himself by and large in terms of traditional Jewish law. If that were so, then Venice's repudiation of Shylock might easily be thought to be tantamount to its Christian repudiation of Jewish law, and the trial scene simply another version of the millennial antagonism between Christian and Jew, New Law and Old, with the unfortunate Jew as the loser.[22] But I have already cast doubt on that gross oversimplification by pointing out that Shylock, who has proposed his nefarious penalty clause as a "merry sport" under pretense of seeking Antonio's friendship (I.iii.140), consents to dine at Bassanio's in order to celebrate the signing of their bond—even though he has earlier protested to Bassanio that to do so would be to contravene Jewish dietary restrictions.[23] Shylock here exempts himself from Jewish law. Far from being a paragon representative of it, he is knowingly inconsistent with regard to it, if only in order to "feed fat the ancient grudge" he bears Antonio (I.iii.40) by personally helping to consume the fruits of Bassanio's spendthrift habits and so perhaps increasing the likelihood of Antonio's defaulting on the loan.

Shakespeare thus indicates Shylock's ambivalence vis-à-vis Jewish law. Shylock stands, as it were, somewhere between Jewish law and Venetian law. His demands of others are marked by a moral strictness that resembles that of Jewish law. Yet his demands concerning himself share in the permissiveness that accompanies Venice's openness to commerce. Unfortunately, the two will not hold together in Shylock, and he soon breaks. Long before the trial scene, we glimpse the tension, both in his justification of his business practices and in his behavior at home. Indeed, Shylock's home life seems little more than an extension of his business, and vice versa — a circumstance that may be only partly excused by his being a widower, with an only daughter who must be left in charge of servant and household. Shakespeare's Shylock is less an example of a law-abiding Jew than of what Plato's Socrates would call an oligarchic or moneymaking man.[24] Having departed from the ways of his forebears, to whom honor was more important than wealth, he turns his natural abilities instead, so far as possible, to the opportunities that mercantile Venice affords him for satisfying his private moneymaking desires.

During his preliminary negotiations with Antonio over the loan, for example, Shylock justifies his practice of interest taking by way of a rather loose and self-serving reading of a biblical text. He does not appeal to any of the relevant legal passages of the Hebrew Bible.[25] He cites instead the example of the patriarch Jacob and his sheep-breeding activities while in his uncle Laban's employment (I.iii.66–92).[26] Laban had agreed that Jacob's wages would include all "streak'd and pied" lambs, the natural offspring of mixed black and white sheep parentage (I.iii.74f.). Jacob, however, found a clever way to increase their numbers, and his profits, by planting certain peeled branches in front of the ewes during conception as a fertility device. Jacob's cleverness is the model for Shylock's "thrift" (I.iii.45, 85). How Jacob's own thrift decides the issue of usury in particular, though, Shylock does not say. When Antonio objects that the success of Jacob's venture was hardly in Jacob's hands but was "sway'd and fashion'd / By the hand of heaven" (I.iii.84–86), and moreover doubts whether the incident was meant to justify usury inasmuch as gold and silver, being "barren," are not the same as ewes and rams, Shylock merely replies, "I cannot tell; I make it breed as fast" (I.iii.91). Evidently Shylock admires his ancestor Jacob chiefly for his high rate of productivity. He remains comparatively indifferent to the strictly theological considerations that are Antonio's main concern. Shylock seems to take the Bible rather as a sourcebook for the creative businessman. From Shylock's worldly point of view, to obstruct the dealings of the marketplace as Antonio does — by lending gratis to interest-paying borrowers threatened with arrears and so spoiling Shylock's profits and also by insulting Shylock's religion and abusing him bodily as if he were a "stranger cur" (I.iii.113) — is not just morally intolerable but economically naïve.[27] Even so, Shylock's appeal to the Bible may also be either uninformed or hypocritical, for whereas outwardly he professes to have borne Antonio's interference and invective patiently, on the professed principle that "suff'rance is the badge of all our tribe" (I.iii.105), privately he inveighs angrily against Antonio's profit-damaging crusade as "low simplicity" and swears by "my tribe" never to forgive him (I.iii.46f.).

Where Venetian law is silent or powerless to stop Antonio from hurting his business, then, Shylock will seek his own redress. Nor does he bother to claim legal or even biblical precedent here. He only follows, as he says in his "I am a Jew" speech, "Christian example":

> *If a*
> *Jew wrong a Christian, what is his humility? Revenge.*
> *If a Christian wrong a Jew, what should his sufferance*
> *be by Christian example? Why, revenge. The villainy*
> *you teach me I will execute, and it shall go hard but I*
> *will better the instruction.* (III.i.59–64)

Shylock's spirited plea, which he makes public once Antonio's bond appears forfeited after reports on the Rialto of his extensive shipping losses, infers a right to vengeance from the premise that any Christian would do the same. Shylock argues that Jews and Christians are alike in a low but undeniable respect: having eyes, hands, organs, dimensions, senses, affections, passions, and so forth, their behavior is equally subject to the overriding needs and susceptibilities of the human body. Conditioned alike, they may therefore be expected to act alike. Should not the same desire for vengeance which overcomes a Christian who has been wronged by a Jew, therefore, overcome a Jew wronged by a Christian? Shylock here speaks of what Jews and Christians do rather than of what they ought to do.[28] What they share, he implies, is not the high moral demands of the Hebrew Bible but the base animal appetites of the human body. Reacting in kind perhaps to Antonio's treatment of him as if he were subhuman, Shylock is led to understand both himself and others around him in terms of their common animal characteristics — and subsequently, both in the eyes of Antonio's Venetian friends and in his own, to act accordingly.[29]

Like Socrates' oligarchic man, who is also guided by his baser nature, Shylock thereby confuses what is necessary for maintaining himself and his household, namely wealth, with what is sufficient. Indeed, he attempts to rule his household with the same parsimoniousness of money and love that characterizes his business dealings. His only conversations with his daughter, Jessica, it seems, are about money and property (II.v.3–54; cf. III.ii.282–86). In saying goodbye to her on his way to dine at Bassanio's, for example, he mainly warns her to watch the house for some unsettling ill, which he has anticipated from his having dreamed of money bags the night before. In particular, Jessica is forbidden to look outside and must close the house's "ears" or upper casements (II.v.33) in order to stop the sounds of masqueraders with their loud music who are reportedly in the street that evening. To forbid the music is to deny Jessica any share in the socializing activities of Venice's youth. Not surprisingly, Jessica finds her home life stifling. "Our house is hell" (II.iii.2), she remarks to their youthful servant, her sole source of domestic amusement — who, however, succeeds in leaving Shylock's harsh employment that day for the more adequate food and clothing at Bassanio's.[30] Jessica is "asham'd" to be her father's daughter, and will shed his "manners" by betraying him and eloping that same evening with Lorenzo, who has arranged to use Bassanio's dinner party and the street festivities as a cover for the elopement.[31] As she leaves, she despoils her father of considerable cash and jewels, and Shylock afterward is unable to separate the loss of her from the loss of his savings (III.ii.95ff. with II.viii.12–26). Lorenzo praises Jessica's virtues — she is "wise" and "fair" and "true" (II.vi.51–57) — and perhaps we are meant to infer that she derives these from her mother or even from Jewish law itself, rather than from Shylock; nevertheless her final scene with Lorenzo, in act V, indicates a defect that she shares with her father and which Lorenzo will try to correct.

It is her unmusicality. This shortcoming occasions Lorenzo's two Pythagorean speeches about music, to which I have already called attention.[32] Lorenzo and Jessica as wandering honeymooners have by chance met up with Salerio and joined him on his way to deliver Antonio's letter to Bassanio in Belmont. As Bassanio and Gratiano hurry back with Salerio to attend Antonio's trial in Venice, Portia quietly leaves Lorenzo in charge of her estate, for she and Nerissa soon depart also — ostensibly (so she tells Lorenzo) to spend the rest of their wedding day and night at a nearby monastic retreat, but actually to determine the trial's outcome in lawyer's disguise. The honeymooners stay outdoors all that night to welcome Portia and Bassanio back on their separate, predawn returns, and Lorenzo meanwhile calls for instrumental music from Portia's servants. He expounds to Jessica the kinship between earthly music and the harmonies of the mathematically ordered heavens. According to the philosophical tradition on which he implicitly relies, the motions of the heavenly bodies occur in concentric orbits, each body moving unceasingly in a perfect circle, at a speed and with coordinates differing from its neighbors yet in harmony with them. Hence the cosmos is orderly and its combined movements may be said to generate sounds that are in principle audible to human souls, except that the bodies in which all souls are confined obstruct or blur those sounds. Music, at any rate, has a cosmic significance, for it alerts human souls to their proper place in the larger order of things. Here Jessica interrupts Lorenzo's philosophizing with her personal complaint: "I am never merry when I hear sweet music" (V.i.69).

In his second Pythagorean speech, Lorenzo then suggests the cause of her melancholy. It is that her "spirits are attentive" (V.i.70). That is, he connects Jessica's persisting sadness with her being overly spirited, or headstrong. Her high-spiritedness, he implies, blocks the potentially moderating effect of music on her soul. Speaking with therapeutic as well as philosophic intent, Lorenzo urges Jessica to note the soothing powers of a chance trumpet sound or any other "air of music" on a "wild and wanton herd, / Or any race of youthful and unhandled colts," whose crazy leaping, bellowing, and loud neighing are attributable to "the hot condition of their blood": the music civilizes those animals for the time being, by causing them to "make a mutual stand" and turning their "savage eyes" to a "modest gaze" (V.i.71–79). Hence the feats ascribed poetically to Orpheus, of moving even trees and stones and floods by means of his music. There is nothing, Lorenzo argues, whose "nature" is so "stockish, hard, and full of rage" as to resist music's erstwhile taming force (V.i.80–82).

Curiously, however, the ending of Lorenzo's speech is not quite consistent with what has preceded. He concludes with a practical warning against trusting anybody "that hath no music in himself," that is, who remains unmoved by music's putatively salutary harmonies (V.i.83f.). Such men are "fit for treasons, stratagems, and spoils" (V.i.85). Lorenzo finds their spirits and emotions impenetrable and unfathomable — "dull as night" and "dark as Erebus" are his words (V.i.86–87). It is not immediately clear whether Lorenzo realizes that he is contradicting himself by admitting that there are indeed human beings who, unlike Orpheus's animals, and so on, cannot be swayed by musical sounds. In Lorenzo's defense, it may be that he is simply focusing on the practical meaning of his words, namely that Jessica not join the ranks of those loners who are prone to "treasons, stratagems, and spoils," and the like — but if so, he forgets that his plea comes too late. Jessica's entire elopement with Lorenzo is the play's most obvious incident of "treasons, stratagems, and spoils," for it is hardly separable from the betraying, outwitting, and despoiling of her own father. A more plausible explanation of Lorenzo's self-contradiction, then, is that despite his Pythagorean philosophizing, or perhaps because of it, he does not quite understand Jessica, nor *a fortiori* himself. But in order to confirm this explanation and see its larger implications, we shall have to retrace the steps by which Shakespeare has led Lorenzo to make his last-act speeches, or rather (as we shall see), to withhold them till the last act.

As Lorenzo and Jessica moon-gaze outdoors at the beginning of act V, the night's silence reminds them of the nocturnal settings of four well-known love affairs, each of which ended unhappily: Troilus and Cressida, Pyramus and Thisbe, Dido and Aeneas, Jason and Medea.[33] Bantering, they add their own names to the list, until they are interrupted by messengers reporting their hosts' homeward progress. But Lorenzo meanwhile fails to reassure Jessica that they do not belong on the list after all. He resumes his attempt at reassurance only by calling for music and then philosophizing about it in the poetically stirring but philosophically unconvincing way we have just seen. Then again, this is not our first glimpse of Lorenzo's evidently halting ability to persuade. Only with some difficulty, for example, has he, as Portia's interim trustee, been able to give orders for dinner to the clownish Launcelot, formerly Shylock's household drudge now serving Bassanio in Belmont (III.v.44–56). Launcelot wittily misinterprets Lorenzo's every order as a pun and undermines Lorenzo's domestic authority with ease. Afterward Lorenzo confides to Jessica what amounts to his frustration at having to deal repeatedly with such fools (III.v.59–62).

From these considerations and others, one is inclined to think that Lorenzo's brief and unsought trusteeship in Belmont has been his one and only position of authority over human beings anywhere. Again, he is quite shy and apologetic for showing up in Belmont in the first place, having been talked into it, he says, by Salerio (III.ii.224–28). Similarly, although the lovers' despoiling of Shylock and their subsequent wild spending can only have been Jessica's idea — for Lorenzo, in confessing to his friends that he loves Jessica, does not make much of her father's wealth[34] — nevertheless Lorenzo does not bother trying to talk her out of it. Earlier, to be sure, he had successfully talked his friends into helping with the elopement masquerade, but only at the last minute and as part of the holiday pranks (I.i.70–71; II.iv.21–27, vi.21–24). Most instructive for all these instances seems to be Lorenzo's acknowledgment in the play's very first scene that he is not very talkative, especially as his close companion Gratiano does not let him get a word in edgewise (I.i.106–9). We may therefore say that Lorenzo's actions throughout the play point to his being someone who, for all his thoughtfulness and congeniality, mostly philosophizes privately. Having fallen in love with a woman of excessive spiritedness, whose upbringing under Shylock has made her rebellious and sad, he himself suffers from the contrary vice, a lack of spiritedness. Only at long last, then, is he driven to make his Pythagorean speeches about music, and then, too, not out of a habit of public-spirited concern for the well-being of his fellow citizens but primarily as a last-ditch effort to cheer up his unhappy bride before their honeymoon is over.[35]

Lorenzo's very last words in the play point to Portia rather than himself as the one who has somehow been able to resolve the outstanding difficulties that all the Venetians including himself have gotten themselves into. He expresses his heartfelt, almost religious gratitude to Portia and Nerissa for handing him the Venetian court's "special deed of gift" (V.i.292) making him officially Shylock's heir: "Fair ladies, you drop manna in the way / Of starved people" (V.i.294f.). Portia has announced the deed as providing "some good comforts" for Lorenzo (V.i.289). Her broad suggestion (since the "comforts" are plural) is that it saves Lorenzo's marriage not only from insolvency but from possible collapse as well (cf. IV.i.373f.). Portia's graciousness toward him and the other Venetians thus confirms his earlier praise of her "noble and . . . true conceit [or understanding] / Of godlike amity" (III.iv.2f.). The question therefore remains why Shakespeare has entrusted Lorenzo and not Portia with the philosophic manifesto that, other things being equal, might well have prevented or solved everyone's difficulties — though by now we know it did not. The answer, it seems, is twofold. On the one hand, Lorenzo's speeches alert us to the play's irreducibly philosophical dimension. On the other hand, they let us in retrospect avoid the mistake made by, say, Marlowe's Machevill, of somehow reducing the dramatic action to an abstract formula. Since these two themes prove necessary for an adequate appreciation of the confrontation between Shylock and Antonio, I elaborate them further.

ᣔ IV ᣔ

Let me do so by reviewing Lorenzo's position in the play as a whole. He is in possession of a philosophical teaching that, as he understands it, implies that the conflict between merchant and moneylender that has brought Venice to the point of crisis is in principle avoidable. His remedy is "music." He takes music to be a proven pacifier, for all subhumans at least and, therefore, for humans as well. If Lorenzo is right, music would be the play's most pressing political desideratum, just insofar as the dramatic conflict descends or threatens to descend into subhuman savagery. Yet this is exactly what happens: Shylock, that self-described complex of animal drives and desires, comes to see and treat Antonio as little more than "carrion flesh" (IV.i.41), while Antonio, who has all along been abusing Shylock as if he were a dog, soon describes himself in turn as a "tainted wether [or castrated ram] of the flock, / Meetest for death" (IV.i.114f.). It follows that the more those two are disposed to behaving as beasts, the more they ought to be susceptible to the humanizing influences of Lorenzo's music, which would turn "Their savage eyes . . . to a modest gaze" (V.i.78).[36] Although we do not become aware of it till after the play's savagery or near-savagery has taken its toll, Lorenzo's philosophizing suggests in retrospect that the animosity between Antonio and Shylock, other things being equal, need never have gotten out of hand. Differently stated, the prominence given in the last act to Lorenzo's philosophical optimism may account for why Shakespeare's play, unlike Marlowe's, is nowhere called a "tragedy."[37]

And yet, as we have seen by way of criticism, Lorenzo has kept his philosophizing mostly to himself. It is perhaps no slur on his views to observe that he has difficulty persuading his own wife. More telling as regards his specific claim about the salutariness of music, is that Jessica and Shylock are not the only ones who are unmusical. Antonio is indifferent to music too, as his standoffishness toward Lorenzo's fife-and-drum masquerade indicates (II.vi.62f.). Hence, despite what Lorenzo says, any purely spontaneous or private reconciliation between Shylock and Antonio would remain unlikely, even if the musical summons toward it were to occur. All in all, these circumstances indicate the central difficulty in Lorenzo's philosophizing. In looking to understand the savage behavior of human beings exclusively by reference to the animals that they then resemble, Lorenzo has neglected to consider human beings in their own terms. He has been content to view what they are poetically, in terms of what they are merely like. He therefore blurs the differences between the human and the subhuman, as is evident in his incomprehension of the place of "treasons, stratagems, and spoils" in unmusical human beings such as Jessica, Shylock, and Antonio. In failing as a result to understand a figure of speech — that human beings act like animals — for what it is, Lorenzo the poet likewise misunderstands himself. Fortunately, his suggestive but incomplete philosophizing is not the play's last word.

Immediately following Lorenzo's second Pythagorean speech, Portia nears home on the last leg of her return from Venice with Nerissa. She recognizes a light that they had begun to notice only a short distance away as a candle shining brightly from her own hall. The two women muse about how the moonlight had been outshining the candle, making it unnoticeable even though, when viewed in isolation, the candle may be seen to radiate quite far — like "a good deed in a naughty world" (V.i.91). Then, hearing the distant music of her household servants, Portia observes how much sweeter it sounds than in its usual daytime setting. Nerissa ascribes the improvement to the night's silence. Portia meanwhile begins to speculate on the principle uniting the two separate circumstances, seeing the candle and hearing the music:

> *Nothing is good, I see, without respect.*
> . . . .
> *The crow doth sing as sweetly as the lark*
> *When neither is attended; and I think*
> *The nightingale, if it should sing by day*
> *When every goose is cackling, would be thought*
> *No better a musician than the wren.*
> *How many things by season season'd are*
> *To their right praise and true perfection!* (V.i.99, 102–8)

To the reader, Portia's speech supplies the needed correction to Lorenzo's. Music or light unnoticed, she implies, is music or light that fails to benefit, but the noticing is always in a particular "respect" or "season" or setting (cf. IV.i.194f.), and the benefits themselves emerge, humanly speaking, only within that setting. Lorenzo's indifference to such settings renders him incapable of distinguishing properly between larks and crows or between nightingales and geese, that is, between relatively musical and relatively unmusical beings, along with their human counterparts. No wonder he is shy—being unable to address his fellow citizens fully for what they are or persuade them of what he understands might benefit them. His philosophizing is too abstract, too unpolitical, both in its failure to pay attention to human things in the terms in which they are first found in the give-and-take of human life in particular cities such as Venice, and in its failure to attract fellow citizens to pursue an understanding of things which would enhance their lives together there. Only Portia, as we have already begun to see, unfailingly directs her understanding to the particulars of human life around her and to the principles governing them, and without in any way compromising that understanding, succeeds in benefiting both herself and the others with whom she must deal.

Still, I do not wish to leave the mistaken impression that Lorenzo the philosopher is entirely without influence among his fellow Venetians. One such beneficiary is easily found. It is Gratiano, his boorish and overly talkative companion who, so Lorenzo claims, "never lets [him] speak" (I.i.107). But we have already seen Lorenzo's influence at work, albeit in a manner unexpected by him, in Gratiano's crude Pythagorean outburst against Shylock in court. Gratiano, confused and outraged at what he regards as Shylock's "wolvish, bloody, starv'd, and ravenous" designs against Antonio, attempts to "hold opinion with Pythagoras" by attributing those designs literally to the presence in Shylock of the transmigrated soul of a wolf executed for manslaughter while Shylock was gestating in his mother's womb (IV.i.128–38). At the same time, he cannot quite bring himself to hold to that opinion, for to do so would be to let go, so he thinks, of

his Christian "faith." Because in the circumstances, Gratiano's frag-
mentary notions about Pythagorean philosophy in contrast to Christian faith can have come only from Lorenzo,[38] we cannot conclude
our review of him without raising the further question of whether or
not Lorenzo's general lack of persuasiveness vis-à-vis his fellow citizens is simply of his own making.

Gratiano must have presented a formidable challenge during
Lorenzo's attempts to initiate and sustain a philosophical conversation, for he seems unwilling to pause or listen long enough to concentrate. When trying to dissuade Antonio from his sudden "melancholy," for example, Gratiano wonders out loud why anyone "whose
blood is warm within" should "Sit like his grandsire cut in alabaster,"
and he professes a contempt for "peevish" men who put on a solemn
show of "wisdom, gravity, [and] profound conceit" to mask their
underlying foolishness (I.i.79–102). Gratiano, in no way disclaiming
his own foolishness, prefers to "play the fool" honestly, outspokenly,
as his friend Bassanio subsequently confirms:

> *Gratiano speaks an infinite deal of nothing, more than*
> *any man in all Venice. His reasons are as two grains of*
> *wheat hid in two bushels of chaff. You shall seek all day*
> *ere you find them; and when you have them, they are*
> *not worth the search.*   (I.i.114–18)

Later on, Bassanio, who is normally unfailingly courteous and generous to a fault, for once upbraids his easygoing friend—for being
"too wild, too rude, and bold of voice" to be indulged in his sudden
request to accompany Bassanio to Belmont for the purpose of wooing
Portia's lady-in-waiting, Nerissa (II.ii.164–75). Gratiano must first
promise "To allay . . . [his] skipping spirit," as Bassanio calls it, "with
some cold drops of modesty." Gratiano's extravagant way of promising to behave himself reveals the larger difficulty that Lorenzo or anybody else would face in moralizing to his fellow Venetians.

Acceding, if only temporarily, to Bassanio's wishes, Gratiano
swears he will observe a sober decorum that would please even his
pious grandmother:

If I do not put on a sober habit,
Talk with respect, and swear but now and then,
Wear prayer books in my pocket, look demurely,
Nay more, while grace is saying hood mine eyes
Thus with my hat, and sigh, and say amen,
Use all the observance of civility
Like one well studied in a sad ostent
To please his grandam, never trust me more.   (II.ii.177–84)

To Gratiano, the "observance of civility" includes such Christian "os-tent[s]" as the sober habits, prayer books, grace at meals, and amen-saying of his grandparents' time. He thus recognizes Christian moral-ity, or at any rate the Christian beliefs and practices of two generations back, as the bond of polite society. But if so, what holds polite society together would seem to be opposed to the wildness and frivolity of Gratiano's more commercial and cosmopolitan generation, of which he himself is only the most extreme example. Moreover, as Gratiano himself suggests in his outburst in court, Christian beliefs and prac-tices as Gratiano understands them would also seem opposed to a philosophical teaching such as Lorenzo's, which might well be useful to help guide Venetians through the newly arisen conflicts and crises for which the old ways have left them unprepared. It follows that anyone who would appeal to some such philosophical teaching in order to strengthen the bonds of civility in cosmopolitan Venice, without thereby eroding whatever salutary political influence remains of a Christianity on the wane, must do so with considerable circum-spection — that is, either privately, as Lorenzo has evidently tried to do without much success, or else in a prudent public disguise, as Portia herself does in court.

ॐ **V** ॐ

Consider in this regard that the disguised Portia's unsuccessful exhortation of Shylock to exercise mercy toward Antonio may be thought to fail of its immediate practical purpose precisely because of its Christian overtones. Yet the fault here, if there is one, is not Portia's but rather Shylock's for misapprehending her meaning. Portia's "quality of mercy" speech is indeed the dramatic corrective to Shylock's pretrial attempt to justify his morally dubious pursuit of vengeance against Antonio by way of an appeal to "Christian example" (III.i.62). In substance, however, it is not specifically Christian but addresses Christian and Jew alike in a highly statesmanlike manner. At the same time, being inherently nonsectarian, it is both open to and dependent on the philosophical premise implicit in Lorenzo's speech, that the hoped-for reconciliation between Christian and Jew does not lack cosmic support.

In order to see the nonsectarian and statesmanlike character of Portia's argument, it is first necessary to recall its immediate dramatic context. Echoing the Duke's own appeal for mercy from Shylock at the beginning of the trial, Portia herself begins by confirming in open court that Shylock's suit, though "Of a strange nature," is legally unassailable in its own terms and that Antonio in consequence "stand[s] within his danger" (IV.i.175–79). When she quickly infers, enthymematically, that "the Jew [must then] be merciful," Shylock at once interjects, "On what compulsion must I?" (IV.i.180–81) Her exhortation is her reply:

> *The quality of mercy is not strain'd;*
> *It droppeth as the gentle rain from heaven*
> *Upon the place beneath. It is twice blest —*
> *It blesseth him that gives, and him that takes.*
> *'Tis mightiest in the mightiest. It becomes*
> *The throned monarch better than his crown.*
> *His sceptre shows the force of temporal power,*
> *The attribute to awe and majesty,*
> *Wherein doth sit the dread and fear of kings;*
> *But mercy is above this sceptred sway;*
> *It is enthroned in the hearts of kings,*
> *It is an attribute to God himself;*
> *And earthly power doth then show likest God's*

> *When mercy seasons justice. Therefore, Jew,*
> *Though justice be thy plea, consider this —*
> *That, in the course of justice, none of us*
> *Should see salvation. We do pray for mercy,*
> *And that same prayer doth teach us all to render*
> *The deeds of mercy. I have spoke thus much*
> *To mitigate the justice of thy plea;*
> *Which if thou follow, this strict court of Venice*
> *Must needs give sentence 'gainst the merchant there.* (IV.i.182–203)

To be sure, Portia's words here are in harmony with Christian teaching. For example, she describes mercy as "an attribute to God himself" and as something "We do pray for" over and above strict justice in order to gain "salvation." But her argument, strictly speaking, is no more Christian than it is Jewish. Like Shylock's pretrial argument, it is neutral with regard to the differences between the two faiths. Unlike Shylock, however, Portia appeals to the highest aspirations common to Christians and Jews. Nor does she maintain, as do Bassanio and Gratiano, among others, that Venetian law ought to be bent or overlooked in favor of Christian mercy (IV.i.212–20, 128–42). On the contrary, she insists that the two are inherently separate: unless the exercise of mercy remained "above" the "sceptred sway" or "temporal power" of the law, it would be neither possible nor necessary for mercy to "season" or "mitigate" the justice enforced by the law. Portia appears rather to take her cue from the Duke's implicit bow in the direction of Judaism, which I cited earlier. Remarking that "the world" expects "a gentle answer" from the "Jew," inasmuch as Antonio's reported losses would "pluck commiseration" even

> *From brassy bosoms and rough hearts of flint,*
> *From stubborn Turks and Tartars, never train'd*
> *To offices of tender courtesy* (IV.i.31–33)

the Duke could not help suggesting that, Shylock aside, the world expects Jews, unlike Turks or Tartars, to be properly habituated to acts of compassion and humanity over and above the sternness of their law-governed circumstances.

Nor, any more than the Duke, does Portia proceed in a simply adversarial manner against Shylock. Instead she gives him every possible opportunity to extricate himself from the harsh legal predicament in which she, alone at this point, knows he will otherwise find himself. Her opening remarks — that Shylock's suit is "Of a strange [*sic*] nature" and that Antonio "stand[s] within his danger" — would indicate to anyone alert to the Venetian law in question (as the Duke and the others are not) that the final charge against him is almost inevitable, namely, that he is a stranger who deliberately endangers the life of a Venetian citizen. His only hope of escaping the charge is to display just that "mercy and remorse" of which the Duke has already spoken (IV.i.20) and which Portia's speech is designed, among other things, to elicit from him. Indeed, her withholding any warning at the outset that Shylock's right to a pound of Antonio's flesh entitles him neither to any of its blood[39] nor to anything more or less than exactly one pound is hardly a disservice: to have disclosed that information publicly before her exhortation to mercy has had a chance to work its possibly soothing or taming effects on its Christian hearers might well have prevented the Duke — possibly swayed by the savage passions of Gratiano and others — from exercising mercy toward Shylock at all.[40] In short, the "salvation" of which Portia speaks is legal and political, not just theological. Her opportune silence concerning the full legal implications of Shylock's bond, far from constituting entrapment *tout court* or from being mere casuistic cleverness on her part, is rather just such an act of mercy as she herself describes. Prudently viewing the scope and limits of Shylock's bond from "above" the "sceptred sway" of the law, she discloses the high ground on which Christian and Jew might meet amicably to resolve their legal differences, their theological differences notwithstanding. She thereby offers Shylock a gracious exit from the legal constraints of his bond, as well as from the logical constraints of his justification for lawful revenge. She gives Shylock, both as Venetian resident and as Jew, a chance to repent. As in the case of her own father's will, so too here, her more-than-legal wisdom allows her to view the legalities by which they are severally bound as a means for encouraging the worthy and foiling the unworthy.

۶ **VI** ۶

Portia gives Antonio in turn the opportunity to render mercy toward Shylock, now recognized to be legally culpable. If she has calculated that Antonio may have ulterior motives, she does not show it. Still, statesmanlike prudence would dictate that Portia not publicly restrain Antonio, for Venice continues to honor Christian morality as the bond of society even in the breach of it, and Antonio is the city's exemplary Christian. Her subsequent actions, however, show that she knows full well that she is placing Shylock's fate in the hands of a man whose extreme charitableness (for this is the chief fruit of Antonio's religious practice) has had a morally corrupting effect on others in the city — notably in encouraging Bassanio's prodigality. Portia will move to correct Antonio's excesses only after the fact, by calling attention to their unacceptable practical consequences.

Antonio's rendering of mercy to Shylock is meanwhile neither unconstrained nor unconstraining. It is filled with provisos. In the name of mercy, Antonio stipulates a series of contractlike conditions, each one a quid pro quo (IV.i.378–88). Whereas Portia has argued for the separation of acts of quid pro quo, or justice, from acts of mercy, Antonio merges the two. He thus leaves open the question of whether his rendering of mercy, or more generally his charitable deeds, may be unjust.

Antonio proposes to bind Shylock, in effect, to a fourfold contract. He does so at Portia's prompting in response to Shylock's lament that he would rather die, now that half his wealth belongs to Antonio, even though the Duke has already pardoned Shylock's life and has offered to reduce the city's claim on its half of Shylock's estate to a fine in return for contrition (IV.i.366–76). Shylock prefers death, on the grounds that to be deprived of his wealth is to be deprived of the means necessary for supporting himself and his household. Yet Shylock has all along been confusing means and ends, or what is necessary for living well with what is sufficient. Shylock's claim that he is being deprived of his means of livelihood, moreover, holds only so long as he continues to make his living as a moneylender. Antonio's proposals therefore aim to benefit Shylock by charitably depriving him of that livelihood — though they also figure in Antonio's estimation to benefit himself.

Antonio signifies in the first place that he would be content if the court were to forgive Shylock even the fine that the Duke has offered to substitute for Venice's legally authorized claim on half of Shylock's estate. He thus urges the court, at no cost to himself, to extend his mercy even further than it already has. At the same time he links that proposal to a second one. He stipulates that, instead of owning his half of Shylock's estate outright, he be allowed the "use" of it so long as Shylock remains alive. Antonio does not specify to what use he plans to put Shylock's wealth, whether to reinvest in the wake of his reported shipping disasters or to continue his charitable crusade against other usurers, although the latter remains likely, especially given the surprise announcement, later in the play, that three of Antonio's six argosies have arrived in port safely and profitably after all (V.i.273–79, with III.i.86–88). Be that as it may, the harshness of Antonio's second proposal counterbalances the leniency of the first so far as Shylock is concerned, since the money he will have saved by being forgiven the Duke's fine is now offset by his having to grant Antonio what amounts to a lifelong interest-free loan. Antonio mitigates — or perhaps intensifies — the harshness of this proposal by adding as a codicil that after Shylock's death the principal sum will revert to the "gentleman / That lately stole his daughter" (IV.i.382f.) — to his otherwise alienated son-in-law, Lorenzo. However admirable Antonio's generosity here, we cannot help noticing that, like his protégé Bassanio, Antonio is generous with what would ordinarily not be his to give. Perhaps, then, he makes his third proposal — that Shylock immediately become a Christian — in order to dignify the preceding one, for as a Christian, Shylock will no longer be permitted to charge interest to any fellow Christian and will no longer have a reason to disinherit his daughter for marrying a non-Jew.

It is possible to imagine that Shylock's conversion might be sufficient by itself to bring about everything that Antonio has proposed so far, including his escaping the penalties he has incurred as a stranger in Venice and his freely endowing Antonio's charitable campaign, but Antonio himself excludes this possibility by speaking of Shylock's conversion as necessary in connection with the "favour" constituted by his interest-free use of Shylock's wealth — the "favour" in these circumstances being granted by Shylock, not Antonio (IV.i.384f.).[41] Antonio's wording here implies a tacit recognition that he himself remains the chief financial beneficiary of his mercy toward Shylock. Still, that Antonio's motives are not simply mercenary is confirmed by his fourth proposal. It is that Shylock revise his will in court in order to "record a gift / . . . of all he dies possess'd" to his daughter and son-in-law (IV.i.386ff.). Antonio's charitable concerns extend not just to the use of Shylock's money but also to the welfare of Shylock's family. Even so, we are left to wonder whether this last proposal does not restore, *mutatis mutandis,* the dangers of Antonio's meddling in the private lives of others with which the play began, now that Jessica and Lorenzo will become indebted to him, just as Bassanio has been, in matters of money as well as of love (see I.i.130–34).

Portia can do nothing directly to save Shylock or his heirs from the possibly harmful effects of Antonio's subsequent interference in their family affairs. But she can protect her own marriage and so take steps to moderate Antonio indirectly. Has she not already seen for herself how Antonio has interrupted Bassanio's marital duties by taking him away from Belmont on their wedding night? Has she not also found occasion to reprimand Bassanio for asking her, in disguise, to twist Venetian law in Antonio's favor? Does she not even hear Bassanio say in court that he would sacrifice his wife, who is "as dear to me as life itself," together with "all the world," for Antonio's sake (IV.i.281ff.)? How then could Portia fail to see that Antonio, if left unchecked, remains even more of a danger to life in Venice and environs than Shylock could ever be? Shylock's excesses, as Portia's actions have already proved, can be contained by a more prudent reading and writing of contracts or, failing that, by a greater attention to the civil protections inherent in Venetian law. But Antonio, like Bassanio, has just now shown a willingness to wrest the law to his own private purposes, and he seems to have succeeded where Bassanio has failed. Like mercy itself, Antonio would place himself "above" the law (see IV.i.191). Hence, unlike Shylock, he would not be constrained by law. Portia can only appeal to Antonio's charitable impulses toward Bassanio in order to induce him to restrain those impulses.

The process of self-correction which Portia imposes on Antonio begins in the aftermath of the trial. The Duke prevails upon Antonio to "gratify this gentleman," meaning Portia, to whom in the Duke's mind Antonio is now "much bound" (IV.i.404f.). When Bassanio spontaneously offers Portia three thousand ducats, the principal sum previously owed Shylock, on his and Antonio's behalf, and when Antonio immediately adds that he and Bassanio "stand indebted, over and above, / In love and service to you evermore" (IV.i.411f.), Portia demurs, stating that she is "well paid" by being "well satisfied" at having delivered Antonio from Shylock's danger (IV.i.413–16). And yet her exact words, "in delivering you," are implicitly addressed as well to Bassanio, whom she has now all but delivered from Antonio's having interrupted the consummation of their marriage. Bassanio nevertheless presses her to take some remembrance of Antonio and himself as a "tribute" (IV.i.420f.), and she consents by asking first for Bassanio's gloves and then for his wedding ring. By her latter gesture, she tests whether Bassanio will continue his old habit, which Antonio has encouraged, of being generous with what is not entirely his to give. Bassanio properly hesitates, presumably recalling his betrothal promise of yesterday wherein he had gone even further than Portia on receiving her ring. Portia had then merely warned that parting from the ring would "presage the ruin" of his love, whereas Bassanio had boldly equated its departure with the departure of his very life (III.ii.171–74, 183–85). Now Portia is therefore unsparing. She accuses him of being "liberal" or free in his offers, that is to say, of not being bound by his word (III.ii.436; cf. II.ii.172; V.i.226). In two subsequent lines, which the disguised Portia means as mocking disapproval but which would equally serve as a compliment of Bassanio were they somehow to point to the concluding action of the play, she offers a critique, at once damning and praising, of Bassanio's hesitating to part with the ring: "You taught me first to beg, and now methinks / You teach me how a beggar should be answered" (IV.i.437–38).

How one should answer a beggar, or generally speaking, someone who asks favors, whether the favor be a loan or deliverance from a loan, Portia indeed indicates in the play's final episode. Bassanio's "teaching," at least in the version that Portia ultimately approves of, is that one's answer must be consistent with the fostering and maintenance of marriage and the family. It is the very teaching that Bassanio's mentor, Antonio, meanwhile continues to ignore, as he persuades Bassanio to send his ring after the departed Portia, although or because to do so is to "Let his [the disguised Portia's] deservings, and my [Antonio's] love withal, / Be valued 'gainst your wife's commandëment" (IV.ii.448–49). No wonder that next morning, after their separate returns to Belmont, Portia exercises her prerogative to "exclaim" on Bassanio for giving up the ring and to threaten her own marital unfaithfulness, until Antonio, recognizing himself to have been the cause of their momentary domestic unhappiness, offers to guarantee Bassanio's keeping faith with his marriage promises henceforth (V.i.184–255, with III.ii.169–74). As Antonio's once lent his body to guarantee Bassanio's loan, so he will now risk his soul as collateral to guarantee Bassanio's valuing his "wife's commandëment" above his own. Antonio thereby promises to limit his excessive meddling, and Bassanio his excessive generosity. Thus Portia corrects the excesses of Antonio's charitableness by correcting his erstwhile disciple.

ꙅ VII ꙅ

Let us now return to the questions with which we began, about whether Shakespeare's Venice treats Shylock fairly. My four original questions concerned Antonio's unrestrained harassment, Gratiano's unreprimanded Jew-baiting, Portia's legal entrapment, and Antonio's

court-authorized sentencing of Shylock. The aim of my analysis so far
has been to help the reader discover Shakespeare's own answers here.
I have tried to avoid the unhelpful alternative, all too prevalent in
current scholarship (as the examples in chap. 1 suggested), of attributing motives to the playwright which patient attention to the
evidence of the play might render doubtful. I have appealed instead to
the principle that, before one can claim to know whether one's own
offhand opinions in these matters are superior to Shakespeare's, one
must first come to know, as clearly as possible, Shakespeare's opinions
in the terms in which he has set them forth, that is, in his play.

Consequently, we have been led to doubt what seem to be two
unspoken premises of much of current scholarship concerning the
play's understanding of Christians and Jews. As I see it, Shakespeare's
Shylock is no simple (or stereotypical) Jew. Nor is his Venice simply a
Christian city. Both Shylock and Venice are altered by the city's newly
prominent, far-reaching commercial life. Modern commerce opens
the city to strangers such as Shylock, and vice versa, it opens Jews such
as Shylock to Venetian ways. Built into Shakespeare's play, then, is the
examination of what becomes of the old habits and expectations that
have up till now made Venice Venice and Jews Jews. His comedy lets
us contemplate the various dynamic possibilities, while favoring us
with the most salutary among them.

As regards the first question, then, about Antonio's public harassment of Shylock, which has evidently started the personal enmity
between the two, Shakespeare's answer seems to be that we are not
meant in the end to condone it but to see it for what it is. Consider
that, so far as his crusade on the Rialto is concerned, Antonio literally
acts alone. True, not one of his fellow Venetian merchants intervenes
to stop the harassment. But not one imitates the gentler and more
endearing side of Antonio's behavior either — by offering later on to
pay his defaulted note, as Portia does through Bassanio, for example,
or at least to lend him Shylock's principal interest free. So far as we
can tell, the other Venetians remain admirers or consumers rather
than producers of charitable works. Hence my description of Shakespeare's Venice as Christian mostly in name. Commerce has offset
Christian morality in Venetians' private lives. Thus, when Salerio first

tries unsuccessfully to trace Antonio's sadness to his business worries, he does so among other things by imagining himself at worship in Antonio's place:

> *Should I go to church*
> *And see the holy edifice of stone*
> *And not bethink me straight of dangerous rocks,*
> *Which, touching but my gentle vessel's side,*
> *Would scatter all her spices on the stream,*
> *Enrobe the roaring waters with my silks,*
> *And, in a word, but even now worth this,*
> *And now worth nothing? Shall I have the thought*
> *To think on this, and shall I lack the thought*
> *That such a thing bechanc'd would make me sad?*   (I.i.29–38)

What a pious churchgoer would view as a "holy edifice" serves to remind Salerio (if he went to church) rather of "dangerous rocks" threatening Antonio's ships and luxurious cargo.[42] Profit-and-loss calculations have replaced pious contemplation.[43]

We are left to wonder how far Antonio's fellow citizens may be said to share his Christian zeal except that they stand to benefit from it financially. We begin to suspect that, in Antonio's own eyes, his anti-usurious crusade against Shylock may represent a last-ditch effort in an otherwise losing cause, to restore Christianity as the social bond among the now too worldly Venetians. But if so, it would follow that, were there no Shylocks in lieu of respectable Venetians to satisfy the local market for cash loans at interest, Antonio's savage resentment and the resulting crusade might have been directed instead against his fellow citizens.

Nor, as regards my second question, does the playwright expect us to condone Gratiano's savagery in court. We have already seen how Lorenzo's philosophizing is meant to suggest that there is a viable alternative to such savagery. Lorenzo, to be sure, is not sufficiently political to supply the "music," or the words, which would tame his fellow citizens during their savage moments. But Portia, in her statesmanlike way, is. Although Lorenzo's intended lesson backfires in

Gratiano's case, since Gratiano ends up interpreting Pythagorean re-incarnation in a most savage way, Shakespeare's play cannot be said to give savagery, whether religiously motivated or not, the last word. Neither is his last word particularly Christian. Rather, the very need for Lorenzo's philosophizing or (better) Portia's statesmanship may be seen to arise from the weakness of Christian morality — of which Antonio's religious backlash on the Rialto is a symptom. Consider how little moral guidance Antonio actually provides his fellow Venetians, who, as we see them, are mostly idlers. Gratiano himself is drawn to Pythagoreanism precisely during that moment when he realizes that his Christian faith, as he is given to understand it, is inadequate to account for men such as Shylock. Without the quiet companionship of Lorenzo, whose moral decency seems informed by philosophy rather than by religion, Gratiano's personal life might have come to resemble that of Shylock's former servant Launcelot, who casually if playfully deceives his blind father, undermines household decorum, and impregnates a Moorish woman out of wedlock (II.ii.32–95, v.7–9; III.v.26f., 33–38). Like Gratiano and Lorenzo, Launcelot too is unable to find satisfactory answers from Christian teaching for his most serious theological questions: whether or not to run away from his harsh master, Shylock, and whether or not Jessica's marrying a Christian will be sufficient to save her (II.iii.1–29; III.v.1–23). Lorenzo turns unsatisfactorily to Pythagoras, and Gratiano returns briefly to the religion of his grandparents, but Launcelot is left to face his theological crises with little more guidance than his own private convenience or taste.

The answer to my third question, about Portia's apparent entrapment of Shylock in court, has already been spelled out in some detail. What may appear as legal entrapment to the uninformed in the Venetian courtroom is, to more discerning eyes, nothing less than Portia's delicate public-spirited attempt to extricate Shylock from his grim predicament as an alien who deliberately endangers a Venetian citizen's life. It is an extrication that would be possible only with Shylock's simultaneous — nay, spontaneous — moral reform, from being a pursuer of vengeance to becoming a dispenser of mercy. Again, to untutored eyes, it looks as if Portia would prefer Shylock to be a good Christian, or to act like one despite his being a Jew, but that is not how she (any more than the Duke, at least publicly) sees things. Her being introduced to the court as "a young doctor of Rome" (IV.i.153) perfectly captures the complexity of her situation: she is not only someone who has purportedly received an education in Rome — both at its modern university and, as I shall suggest in a moment, from its ancient heroes and heroines — but also one who may have something to teach Rome, that is to say, the Church. In exhorting Shylock to mercy, she appeals not simply to what is parochially Christian, much less to the de facto morality of contemporary Italy,[44] but to an originally Jewish prayer that Christians now share and which reminds its votaries to pursue mercy over and above strict justice.[45] Portia thus indicates that her understanding of things is far from being merely sectarian. It is philosophical. In her opening conversation with Nerissa, for example, the two women speak of the burdensomeness of bodily life in "this great world" and of happiness as being "seated in the mean" (I.ii.1f., 6f.) — themes of Platonic and Aristotelian political philosophy, respectively.[46]

Belmont itself is conducive to philosophical study: it is quiet and orderly and has an unobstructed view of the heavens, the appropriate backdrop for Lorenzo's Pythagorean speeches. But Belmont ("beautiful mountain") is not just an ivory tower, for if Portia is like her Roman namesake in having been educated by her "ever virtuous" and "holy" father in Platonic political philosophy,[47] hers is an education as well in the ways of political society, as her facility in court and elsewhere testifies.[48] Portia's daring descent from Belmont to Antonio's trial in Venice resembles nothing so much as the descent of the Platonic philosopher into the cave (to use Plato's image of the relation between philosophy and political society). As the philosopher's descent is not quite freely chosen but compelled or necessitated in the interest of the justice of the city, so too is that of Shakespeare's Portia, whose actions accord well with the description of her ancient forebear in Shakespeare's literary source: "being addicted to philosophy, a great lover of her husband, and full of understanding courage."[49]

Finally, the answer to my culminating question is that Shakespeare does not wish us to condone Antonio's court-allowed private sentencing of Shylock either, much less Shylock's harsh conversion. But the play's critique of its title character is necessarily indirect. It takes the form not of a global assault on Antonio's piety but of a local skirmish over its practical consequences. Antonio's piety may be summed up, as I have shown, as a charitableness that is barely distinguishable from meddlesomeness. Portia criticizes that piety by insisting on the right of the family and by inducing Antonio to swear to respect that right, at least in the case of her own family. Further she cannot go. To the extent that Christianity remains the — admittedly slackened — bond of society, Shakespeare or his Portia would not in good conscience see it thrown off altogether without an adequate replacement. Meanwhile, Christianity remains the chief ennobler of Venetians' personal lives, as is evident from the lips of almost all of them: even the pagan-philosophical Lorenzo considers Jessica's conversion preferable to her remaining a Jew (III.v.28–35). Shakespeare's conclusion here seems to be that in the circumstances it is better to strengthen Christian piety, especially by reminding pious Christians of their political responsibility to encourage proper marriages and families, so that it can continue to grace souls through the storms and stresses of a more commercial and cosmopolitan age.

Still, Portia's statesmanlike endorsement of a theologically tolerant Christianity, together with Shylock's eloquent plea for the political equality of Christians and Jews although or because neither are saints, would suggest that Shakespeare himself may have seen even farther down the road toward Christian-Jewish tolerance than his Shylock. At any rate, he seems to have not only anticipated but also wondered about the arguments for the political disestablishment of Christianity which we tend to take for granted nowadays and which find their first fullblown expression in the "Jewish" writings of Francis Bacon and Benedict Spinoza. The next two chapters investigate this possibility. Both Bacon and Spinoza start with the critique of Christian charitableness already found in Shakespeare's "Jewish" play and go from there to argue that the political disestablishment of religion is both desirable and possible. It is possible, they argue, since although the impulse to charitableness tends to be above reproach in nominally Christian societies, it can nevertheless be redirected under quasi-

Christian auspices to new and improved goals. And it is desirable, since the new goals — the technical mastery of nature (Bacon) and the expansion of political freedom (Spinoza) — would make religious persecution both theologically implausible and politically unlikely. But as we shall see, arguments like Bacon's and Spinoza's, which take tolerance to be the highest standard for judging revealed religion, are not without difficulties of their own, difficulties that are perhaps best appreciated by keeping Shakespeare's play in mind.

4

Shylock and Bacon's Joabin

*It is often claimed that civil religion is superior to prophetic
religion in that it does not bring crusades in the wake. . . . The
Anglican doctrine of religious unity has stood the British in good
stead. It helped to furnish a patriotism which aroused a free
world in the days of the Battle of Britain, and it helped also to
provide that religious toleration for which the British people are
famous. These considerations are, however, considerations of
prudence, not of faith, and certainly one may question whether
practical wisdom is the first consideration of a religion.*

— Howard B. White, *Peace among the Willows*

I

WITHIN THE LIMITS OF MY SET PURPOSE, I am led to Francis Bacon's
Joabin as a kind of foil to Shakespeare's Shylock. My aim so far has
been to suggest a plausible alternative to the complacent insinuation
these days that Shakespeare is somehow anti-Jewish. I cannot help
finding the insinuation — for that is what it is — dubious. If my appreciation of the evidence of *The Merchant of Venice* is correct, it means
that Shakespeare sees his Shylock as a Jew who has drifted away from
the sensible ethical teachings of his religion and his Portia as a states-

manlike philosopher who would correct Venice's Christians for giving Shylock some provocation to do so. Portia's (or Shakespeare's) practical solution to Shylock's predicament is to remind Jews and Christians alike of the need for mutual respect and tolerance, which is implicit in the prayers for mercy common to both religions. The larger message of Shakespeare's play is thus political moderation as grounded in, or bolstered by, religious repentance.

Dissatisfaction with the play's outcome, then, has rather to do with the unfortunate consequence that neither Shylock nor Antonio willingly takes up Portia's sage advice, at least not so far as we can tell. By the end of the play, we have every reason to believe that Shylock as a forced convert is a broken man, as his exit line in court suggests, and we lack any warrant for supposing that Antonio will ever stop meddling in others' family business, even though Portia may have laid down the law to him privately as far as interference in her own family is concerned. Antonio's spontaneous public acknowledgment of his share of the blame for the whole Shylock affair, together with a solemn promise to mend his ways vis-à-vis the rest of Venice, would have been nice but would be too much to expect. At the same time, Portia's public humiliation of him, as I have already said, might have been ill advised in the light of his unofficial role as moral exemplar in a nominally Christian (but religiously corrupt and potentially volatile) city, where Christianity still underwrites public morality and where there is little else in sight to take its place. The question of a public reform that would prevent sectarian conflicts from becoming public crises by removing Christianity entirely from the common bond of society — a possibility of which there is some glimmer in Shylock's "I am a Jew" speech — must meanwhile be downplayed in the interest of safeguarding the city's tenuous moral life, or else left on the far horizon. With the posthumous publication of *New Atlantis* some thirty years after Shakespeare's play,[1] however, that horizon comes to be occupied by Bacon's fictitious Jewish character, Joabin, and eventually by his real-life Jewish disciple Spinoza.

And yet to look at Jews and Christians by and large from the vantage point of that horizon, as Bacon encourages us to do, is to catch a glimpse of them which is perhaps exhilarating and instructive, but at the same time rather shadowy and remote. To speak less meta-phorically: Bacon (like Spinoza after him) proposes a society where Jews and Christians can meet on an equal political footing. At the moment Bacon writes, his proposed society exists only on paper. Nevertheless he means to suggest to his serious readers how it might come to be, for all practical purposes, in a foreseeable future. In such a society, Christianity would lose much if not all of its privileged position as chief custodian of public morality. Bacon's candidate to replace it is, or includes, scientific technology.[2] For reasons we shall see when we examine *New Atlantis* more directly, the radical extent to which Bacon plans to rid society of the authority of biblical religion is not so clear at first reading. Much of the unclarity arises because he writes for nominally Christian readers, whom he must persuade to embrace his revolutionary proposal under quasi-Christian auspices. He must show a broad consensus between Christian goals and his own, so as to suggest that a way of life ordered around high technology not only brings about what pious Christians would wish for anyway but has other advantages besides. The sorts of readers Bacon has in mind here are moved less by the technical details that would presumably make his proposed transformation possible than by a vivid narrative description of that transformation, replete with Christian and other appealing imagery. Even so, the actual description of Christians, Jews, and others in *New Atlantis* is rather thin. His human beings of the future are more like manikins, whom readers themselves must help clothe by means of recycled materials to be gathered and pieced together from old allusions that Bacon's narrative strews in passing. Because *New Atlantis* points the way to a merely projected — hence strictly unknown — future, Bacon cannot quite populate it with full-blooded characters drawn from the wide range of concrete observations that we find, say, in Shakespeare's play. We shall have to consider as we go along whether the philosophical and moral fabric of Bacon's narrative is correspondingly shrunk-to-fit as well.

The overall point in this chapter is that a comparison between the Baconian and the Shakespearian solutions to what may be called Shylock's problem — the predicament of the Jew who, whether innocently or not, invites Christian persecution — seems required in order for us to see the full merits and drawbacks of either. Shakespeare's solution, to repeat, amounts to having his Portia sermonize from her bully pulpit in order to exhort Christians and Jews alike to political moderation. Yet meanwhile she is also required to scheme quietly (notably against Antonio) in order to nip stubborn and unwarranted Christian meddlesomeness in the bud. The obvious difficulty with Shakespeare's solution, then, is that it depends in great measure on the extraordinary virtues and opportunities of someone like Portia. Fortune or providence has not always appeared in the form of wise and timely intervention in order to spare Jews and others from persecution at the hands of Christian tormentors. Furthermore, even if such persecutions are (certainly by Portia's standards) a Christian sin, what guarantee is there outside Shakespeare's play that sinners will pay much mind to admonitory voices such as hers? Bacon's solution therefore recommends itself at first glance for its improved efficiency over Shakespeare's. Politely but firmly, Bacon would revoke Christians' license to meddle altogether.

Still, Bacon's difficulty is like that of Shakespeare's Portia in that he cannot remove Christian meddlesomeness without some Christian cooperation, as I have already indicated by pointing out the manner in which he had to approach the writing of his revolutionary book. The difficulty is compounded, in Bacon's case as in Portia's, because meddlesomeness is not so easily separated from Christian charitableness in the first place, that is, from Christianity's teaching of love, to which Portia, for one, would have her listeners return. If, however, Bacon cannot be sure of purging his Christian readers of unwelcome meddlesomeness, he can, under the literary conditions I have begun to describe, redirect it to the ends mandated by his new dispensation. He can recommend scientific technology as the consummate charitable enterprise. And he can hope that his society of the future will become so enthralled with the practical benefits of scientific technology as to tolerate or overlook a modicum or more of meddling in practical life, as traditionally understood, so long as it comes from scientists or enthusiasts of science in the spirit of scientific progress. Nevertheless the question will remain whether a certain meddlesomeness that is both morally and philosophically objectionable continues to taint the Baconian solution. This question comes into clearer focus the moment we recall the moral and philosophical dimensions of the Shakespearian solution that Bacon would have us leave behind.

As for *The Merchant of Venice*'s philosophical dimension, we remember that we were alerted to it by the Pythagorean speeches of Lorenzo, especially their appeal to the music of Orpheus. We may therefore anticipate the contrast with *New Atlantis* by looking briefly at Bacon's own direct treatment of the Orpheus figure in his *Of the Wisdom of the Ancients*.[3] It is his thematic summary and (Baconian) explanation of some thirty-three Greek myths. In his chapter on "Orpheus, or Philosophy," Bacon identifies Orpheus with philosophy personified. He does not limit himself there to describing Orpheus's ability to move animals, trees, and stones with his music, as Lorenzo does. He includes it instead as part of a larger account of Orpheus's musical exploits. In so doing, Bacon indicates, even before giving his own explanation, how we are to understand the philosophical activity of his Orpheus. Prior to exercising his remarkable ability on animals, Orpheus had used his music to charm the rulers of the underworld in order to retrieve from them his prematurely deceased wife, whom he dearly loved. He was then allowed to lead her out, yet only on condition that she follow after him and that he not look behind until they both reached daylight. But at the last moment, "in the impatience of love and care," he looked behind anyway, and when his wife at once fell back into the underworld forever, he himself grew resentful and shunned women and made his way to "solitary places" (3:647 [720f.]). There his sweet music "drew every kind of beast to him, so that shedding their nature, they stood around him in the manner of a theater, not remembering [their] angers or ferocity, not driven suddenly by the stimuli and furies of lust, not caring any more to satisfy gluttony or to stare at prey, having become benign and tame among themselves and offering their ears only to the chorus of the lyre" (ibid. [721]). So great was "the force and power of the music," Bacon adds, that Orpheus moved woods and stones to assemble around him too — until Thracian women worshipping Bacchus drowned out Orpheus's lyre with the "hoarse and monstrous" sounds of their horn. Beasts and woods and stones immediately returned to normal, since "the bond of that order and society" — that is, their hearing of Orpheus's music — was now dissolved, and the women in their fury tore Orpheus to pieces and scattered his limbs through the fields (ibid.).

Bacon's chapter goes on to argue that the two separate uses to which Orpheus put his music correspond to the two parts of philosophy. The music by which Orpheus charmed the underworld is said to correspond to natural philosophy, whose "noblest" task is "the very restoration and renewal [*instauratio*] of corruptible things, and (as a lesser degree of this) the preservation of bodies in their state and the retarding of dissolution and decay" (3:648 [721]). On the other hand, the music by which Orpheus moved the wild beasts, and afterward the woods and stones, is said to correspond to "moral and civil" philosophy, which comes about initially as a result of natural philosophy's lack of success in its efforts to renew and restore natural bodies, that is, to counteract their natural tendency to decay. It aims instead to "make crowds of peoples join together into one and accept the yoke of laws and submit to imperiums and forget [their] untamed emotions while they listen to and obey precepts and discipline — from which soon afterward buildings are constructed, towns are founded, and fields and gardens are planted with trees, so that stones and woods are not irrelevantly said to be called together and shifted" (ibid. [722]). The connection between the two parts of philosophy, according to Bacon, is the quest for immortality. Whereas natural philosophy seeks but fails to restore dead bodies to life, as Orpheus sought but failed to restore his dead wife, moral and civil philosophy seeks a substitute immortality, namely merit and fame, by persuading humans to found cities.

Shakespeare may be seen to recognize a similar distinction, by indicating the difference between Lorenzo's politically inept philosophizing about nature and Portia's philosophizing in the service of statesmanship. But the contrast between Shakespeare and Bacon here is evident in how *The Merchant of Venice* differs from *Of the Wisdom of the Ancients* in describing music's transforming effect on "nature." Whereas Shakespeare's Lorenzo connects the transformation of the wild beasts with the harmonious movements of the heavens according to the Pythagorean cosmology, Bacon grounds it simply in Orpheus's art. The contrast has to do with whether or how there is cosmic support for Orpheus's music, that is, for human philosophizing. The question becomes unavoidable for Bacon's readers, as for Shakespeare's, since both men's books point to the need for a philosophical clarity that is not simply arbitrary in order to guide practical life. For Shakespeare's Lorenzo, philosophical clarity is in principle possible (though Lorenzo fails to find it to his satisfaction or ours) insofar as the intelligible order is accessible to us through music, which calls our attention to that order and so induces us for the moment to put aside so far as possible the practical distractions that normally bar our awareness of it. Shakespeare's Portia does not disagree here, except that she corrects Lorenzo implicitly by insisting that we know the intelligible order to which the music points only as it is reflected in the particulars close at hand to us.[4]

For Bacon, however, the ultimate grounds for philosophical clarity are not so easily indicated. If *Of the Wisdom of the Ancients* provides any indication, Bacon does not separate knowledge of the intelligible order from art, that is, from the attempt to control nature by intervening in the inherent tendency of natural bodies to pass away. To understand nature for him is akin not to noticing its orderliness as imitated in the music of Orpheus's lyre but to the "due and exquisite tuning" of the lyre itself (3:648 [721]). In other words, our understanding of nature according to Bacon is measured by our ability to adjust nature mechanically as if it were our instrument. Yet if so, then the intelligible order that Bacon would have us seek cannot be said to be simply inherent in things. It must somehow be imposed on them. If Bacon is correct, it seems, we cannot know things without first meddling in them.[5] That is, we cannot know things as they are in themselves but only as we make (or "tune") — or perhaps mar (or inadvertently "untune") — them. Yet although we may for practical purposes be able to tell the difference between making and marring here, we cannot strictly know, according to Baconian principles, what it is that ultimately lets us tell.

This darkness at the root of Bacon's scientific project suggests a similar darkness, or at any rate an unclarity, at the heart of his practical solution to what I have called Shylock's problem, the problem of

Christian meddlesomeness, since Bacon's solution stands or falls with a claim to the moral salutariness of scientific technology. The practical need for scientific technology to lubricate and fuel the workings of Bacon's religiously cosmopolitan society is evident at any number of places in *New Atlantis*. It makes a marked impression on readers even during the narrative's frequent rhetorical gaps, or silences, where readers themselves must supply connections that are left for the moment unspecified. Bacon helps us along by having his narrative point, at virtually every step, to an otherwise insurmountable neediness in human beings, which would invite technology's ongoing and authoritative presence. As technology or technology-related activities come to relieve each pressing human need the moment it emerges, we as readers are relieved vicariously. The range and depth of human needs are meanwhile seen to expand and intensify with the very progress of the narrative. Eventually, in the narrative's culminating episode, technology's spectacular role in meeting the full panoply of human needs comes to be described, quite matter-of-factly, as "the enlarging of the bounds of Human Empire, to the effecting of all things possible" (71 [¶ 20]). Baconian technology, we learn, aims in its massive relief efforts at nothing less than world domination pure and simple.

In its narrative context, however, Bacon's description induces us for the moment to overlook the possibly world-shaking moral difficulties implicit here. Given the mixture of concern and relief over human beings' fundamental neediness and its imminent satisfaction which the narrative has been inducing in us all along, Bacon instead both provokes our gratitude for the smooth efficiency with which technology's ultimate aim promises to be accomplished (for Bacon's spokesmen as presented in the narrative are highly efficient and practical men) and postpones our bewilderment over the moral consequences of accomplishing or even trying it. Instead the narrative goes so far as to raise our hopes for the unhindered success of Bacon's project, by limiting its description of human life to just those needs that would admit of direct satisfaction with, and only with, technological means. Life in *New Atlantis,* in other words, is dominated by the — technically satisfiable — needs of the body. As I shall indicate, it is a life that, in its private motivation at least, coincides remarkably with the self-understanding of Shakespeare's Shylock in his "I am a Jew" speech. Pursuing this remarkable coincidence lets us see in Bacon's narrative much that is philosophically dark and morally disturbing, which we might otherwise be inclined to overlook. The analysis of *New Atlantis* which follows is therefore guided by the suggestion, or rather the suspicion, that Bacon's Joabin is Shylock's politically emancipated, philosophically sophisticated (yet morally dubious) cousin.

Admittedly, at first comparison, Joabin does not seem to have much in common with Shakespeare's Shylock beyond their Jewish origins. He seems to have found a way to accommodate himself quietly and comfortably to his political surroundings whereas Shylock has, generally speaking, failed. Bacon draws Joabin to our attention for his being, along with his fellow Jews, a loyal and respected citizen of a prosperous and well-governed South Sea island kingdom called Bensalem, hitherto uncharted on European maps. Joabin even acts as a semiofficial spokesman on behalf of Bensalem's peaceful and luxurious way of life. In private conversation with a thoughtful European visitor who is the book's narrator, Joabin is asked to explain a state-funded household ceremony called the "Feast of the Family," which the visitor has recently heard described and which celebrates the rewards of fatherhood in Bensalem. Afterward he arranges for an interview between the visitor and a Bensalemite official of the highest rank, with whom he has a privileged contact. He is, that is to say, both well informed and well connected in Bensalem. Joabin himself owes much to the regime under which he lives. Bensalem's citizens, cosmopolitan in their ethnic origins, include Jews, Persians, and Indians among others, as well as native islanders (49 [¶ 10]). Although the island is said to have been converted to Christianity since the mid-first century A.D., its civil religion emphasizes charitable works rather than dogma, and its rituals both public and private remain highly syncretistic, and the modified Judaism that Joabin openly professes is no barrier to his active participation in Bensalem's public life. Indeed, Joabin's terse but informative conversation with the narrator is marked by a monetary show of patriotic indignation in support of the Bensalemite law he has been asked to explain. Joabin's apparent indignation serves to belie the generally calm impression we may have derived from the narrative's other conversations. In retrospect, it casts a shadow over the other conversations, as well as over Joabin's own, and therefore strikes us as being comparable in its way to Shylock's anger in connection with Venetian law. It alters any complacency we might have about the regime he represents. All in all, it makes us wonder whether the peace and prosperity that Joabin's Bensalem displays to its visitor are the whole story.

ᠵ᠊ II ᠵ᠊

From a strictly literary viewpoint, *New Atlantis* resembles a narrated Platonic dialogue, though without any disconcerting Socratic cross-examinations. Except for Bacon's nameless, placid narrator, who tends to smooth over the story's potentially worrisome rough spots, its plot reads like a science fiction adventure, concerning sudden peril at the hands of an unpredictable and overpowering nature, followed by gradual redemption in the hands of efficient yet compassionate strangers. Bacon's narrator presents himself as a senior officer of a European explorer ship that almost founders during a storm en route to China from Peru around 1612,[6] but which soon receives unexpected hospitality, if at first cautiously, from the newly sighted island. Bensalemites' wealth and leisure are seen to owe much to an elaborate government-sponsored research institution, whose high technology facilitates the island's covert worldwide intelligence gathering, and *vice versa* whose worldwide intelligence gathering facilitates its technology-intensive production of military, industrial, and consumer goods. It is difficult to know whether, in the end, the fruits of Bensalem's scientific enlightenment are for the sake of her domestic and global politics, or the other way around. The narrator does not exactly say. As we shall see, a correspondingly ambiguous silence pervades the situation of Bacon's Jew as well.

Be that as it may, within a scant week or so following their near shipwreck, Bacon's European sailors recuperate from their ordeal (with the aid of Bensalem's advanced medical and nutritional technology), acclimatize to Bensalem's customs, and even incline toward immigration. Bacon's reader is allowed to follow the narrator's hurried introduction to life in Bensalem through a series of spokesmen, who appear hierarchically arranged: (1) a coast guard officer, who prevents the crippled ship from landing but promises emergency relief and supplies; (2) a senior customs and immigration officer, a "person . . . of place," as he is called, who together with his attendants stipulates the conditions under which the sailors will be permitted to land after all; (3) the governor or administrator of Strangers' House, Bensalem's official visitors' hostel, who recounts to some ten interested sailors the circumstances of the island's conversion to Christianity and its longstanding foreign policy of deliberate isolation; (4) Joabin, who, alone among the spokesmen, appears to be freely sought out or chanced upon by the narrator personally, as befits his ostensibly private station in Bensalem; and finally, (5) one of the so-called Fathers or scientist-priests of Salomon's House, Bensalem's remarkable research institution, also called the College of the Six Days' Works. Although Joabin consents to answer the narrator's questions about marital life which have been raised by the report the narrator has heard from two of his shipmates concerning Bensalem's fatherhood celebration, he does not — despite his indignant outburst, or perhaps because of it — quite answer them fully. Joabin's less than complete account of courtship and marriage is framed, on the one hand, by the narrator's description of him as a Jew and, on the other hand, by the political message that removes him from further conversation with the narrator — except for his brief return next morning to announce the rare arrival in town one week hence of the Father of Salomon's House; his then unobtrusively accompanying the narrator to view the civic parade welcoming the Father; and lastly his informing the narrator three days later that the Father has granted a group audience to the sailors and an exclusive interview to one sailor chosen by his fellows, who turns out to be the narrator himself. In order to understand the prominent yet ambivalent place of Bacon's exemplary Jew, then, it is necessary to consider what he says and does in terms of the narrative as a whole.

But is Bacon's narrative whole? It appears to be a literary frag-
ment. The book ends, somewhat abruptly, with the Father's recruit-
ing the narrator to publish the extensive description of Salomon's
House to which he has just listened. Bacon's literary executor advises
the reader that the author originally intended to add a lengthy "frame
of Laws, or of the best state or mould of a commonwealth," but
preferred to conclude his life's work by compiling a "natural history"
instead (36 ["To the Reader"]). Still, inferences about the book's
evident incompleteness depend on some assessment of its content,
and here Bacon gives us warrant to second-guess his executor.[7] A
lengthy paragraph or more of the speech by the governor of Strangers' House, the book's central spokesman, is devoted to correcting an
account of ancient Atlantis found in Plato's *Critias,* of which Bacon's
readers are explicitly reminded and which resembles *New Atlantis* in
its apparent incompleteness (53ff. [¶ 14]). If Bacon took from Plato
the theme that gave his own book its title, then perhaps he took much
else too, including his de facto literary format. In any case, the book's
appearance of incompleteness may also be seen to suit the rhetorical
incompleteness of its several speakers, and of Joabin in particular.

ᝍ III ᝍ

The narrator's introductory description of Joabin suggests the
benign or salutary effect of Bensalem's official policy of toleration
toward Jews without, however, disclosing the full grounds of that
policy. The policy depends in part on what differentiates Jews in
Bensalem, of whom there are some few ancestral lines, from Jews
elsewhere. Jews elsewhere are said to "hate the name of Christ, and
have a secret inbred rancour against the people amongst whom they
live" (65 [¶ 17]). Bensalemite Jews, on the other hand, combine
extreme patriotism with high praise of Christianity's founder. Joabin
himself "ever acknowledges" that Christ is Virgin born, superhuman,
and ruler over the "Seraphims" or six-winged angels guarding the divine throne. He and his fellow Jews go so far as to call Christ by such

laudatory terms as the "Milken Way" and the "Eliah of the Messiah," terms that indicate among themselves and their Christian neighbors that Christ is a way to heaven and a herald of the biblically promised redemption to come. At the same time, Joabin consciously assimilates his country's ancient lineage and divine mission to those of his religion. Bensalem's founding father is said to be Nahor, Abraham's younger brother;[8] Bensalem's current laws are derived from a "secret cabala" or unwritten teaching of Moses himself; and when the Messiah eventually comes and sits on his throne of judgment in Jerusalem, "the King of Bensalem should sit at his feet, whereas other kings should keep their distance." Joabin's articulate if eclectic merging of patriotism and religion seems not accidentally connected with the narrator's further description of him as wise, learned, statesmanlike, and thoroughly familiar with Bensalem's laws and customs. We are therefore led to wonder in what way Joabin's wisdom undergirds or interweaves his rapprochement between Bensalem and Judaism. Does he speak simply as a private citizen whose scholarly appreciation for his ethnic roots, or what the narrator calls "these Jewish dreams," is strictly antiquarian? Or does he speak rather as a statesman, mediating between ongoing Bensalemite and Jewish interests — and if so, which, if either, does he favor? Bacon's text withholds any immediate answer.

Its passing reference to Jews' alleged hatred of non-Jews, however, invites our sidelong glance at Shakespeare's Shylock. The obvious comparison is that both Shylock and Joabin take a step away from Jewish orthodoxy in order to embrace non-Jewish habits. There the similarity would seem to end, though the more we think about it the less we can be sure. Shylock abandoned the dietary laws precisely for the sake of what Bacon's narrator has rightly, in this case, identified as a "secret . . . rancour" against the Christian Antonio. At the same time, we cannot help noticing that Shakespeare omits the slanderous innuendo that Bacon's narrator allows. No one in Shakespeare's Venice ever makes the suggestion that hatred of non-Jews is in any way "inbred" in Jews or their religion.[9] Shakespeare refuses to countenance any such suggestion, if we are to take the words of his

Duke and his Portia at face value, since both equate Jewish law with moral decency. Even the volatile Gratiano in his momentary flirtation with Pythagoreanism ascribes what appears to him as Shylock's innate currishness to the prenatal transmigration of a wolfish soul into Shylock's mother's womb, rather than to Shylock's religion. And we have already looked at some length into Shakespeare's delicate but decisive disposal of Antonio and his anti-Jewish crusade in the interest of Venice's moral stability.

My point is that Shakespeare's remarkable attentiveness to the moral implications of the situation of his Jew is comparatively absent from Bacon's text. Consider how Joabin's deliberate departures from the ways of his forebears might have warranted some further comment on the part of the narrator. Joabin is seen to innovate not only privately, by ignoring or suppressing the purported habit of hating non-Jews, but also publicly. He bends over backward to publicize his religion's quasi-agreement with Christianity's claim to Jesus' divinity and with Bensalem's political arrangements. More than that we are not told, but it is hard to resist the impression that Joabin's chief motive is political convenience combined with a personal indifference to the claim to sacredness of his own religious tradition. This impression would be strengthened if it turned out that the immediate source for the narrator's passing indictment of Jews elsewhere is Joabin himself, as the text surely permits on second reading. Meanwhile further perplexities arise which Bacon's narrative either ignores or postpones. Does Joabin's publicly voiced theology lead him to modify his private religious practice as well, by abandoning the dietary laws, for example? If so, then we might best describe him as what is nowadays called a Reform Jew. If not, then perhaps his entire theology is simply for non-Jewish consumption, and he and his fellow Jews remain orthodox in secret, like Marranos. The point is that Bacon's narrator, unlike Shakespeare, does not let us linger over the moral implications of such questions. He hurries us on instead to broader considerations about Bensalem's religious and political legacy. If, then, answers are to be found to the immediate moral questions that his narrative provokes in us, they will have to be inferred from what is to come.

♁ IV ♁

On the second day after their three days' quarantine in Strangers' House, ten of the more refined and interested sailors forgo sightseeing to converse with the governor and hear his answer to their question of how Bensalem became Christianized despite its remoteness from the rest of Christendom (47–49 [¶ 6–10]). The sailors' question is evidently prompted by the Christian regalia and formalities of their rescuers, including the customs and immigration officer's preliminary wish to be assured of the sailors' Christian peaceableness, as well as by the governor's statement that he is also by vocation a Christian priest. The governor informs the sailors that the coming of Christianity was prepared, in effect, by a scientifically certified miracle. Twenty years after Christ's ascension, citizens of Bensalem's east-coast port of Renfusa (whose name is Greek for "sheep-natured") saw offshore, one calm and cloudy night, a pillar of light rising toward heaven and topped by a bright cross of light. Viewers on shore sent out boats, which were mysteriously prevented from approaching more closely than sixty yards from the pillar but stood around it, as in a theater. Aboard one boat was one of the "wise men" from Salomon's House. With appropriate prayerful gestures, he suddenly proclaimed before God — and on the basis of his God-given ability to distinguish divine miracles from works of nature, works of art, and "impostures and illusions of all sorts" — that the pillar was a "true Miracle," whose meaning he therefore prayed to God to reveal. As the scientist's boat alone was then allowed to approach the pillar more closely, the pillar dissolved spectacularly, leaving a small ark containing the entire Old and New Testaments in a single volume, including certain as yet unpublished New Testament apocryphal books, and also a letter from the missionary St. Bartholomew assuring "salvation and peace and goodwill" for the people to whom God would ordain the ark. The book and letter were read and accepted by each Bensalemite in his own language (Hebrew, Persian, Indian, etc.).

On reflection, it may well be that the narrator finds that such an appeal to the authority of a natural scientist to validate a supernatural sign is incongruous. Yet none of the sailors interrupts with pointed questions. Nor is the governor allowed to expand his remarks in order to suggest pertinent answers, for after a brief pause as if to allow all present to bask in the miracle story's afterglow, he is called away by a messenger. But then again, the governor, unlike Joabin or the ancient scientist, is never characterized as "wise." Among the questions left unraised and unanswered by the governor's remarks, then, is whether a "wise" account by either Joabin or the scientist would differ significantly from his own merely pious account. The issue here is not primarily epistemological — how to tell miracles from natural or artificial works or "impostures and illusions." It is theological and political. Let us assume that Bensalem's "wise" scientists are technically competent. The question remains whether their official competence extends to the point of being able to decide knowledgeably, that is to say scientifically, concerning the theological and political merits of Christianity itself. The issue may even have a sinister side, since the reader later learns that among the astounding facilities of Salomon's House are laboratories for deliberately implementing artificial light displays, as well as what are called "deceits of the senses." These last include not only "all manner of feats of juggling" and "false apparitions" but also, recalling the governor's own words in connection with the miracle, "impostures and illusions."[10] At any rate, given that Salomon's House predates Christianity in Bensalem, we are left in the dark about whether its endorsement was simply for the sake of scientific enlightenment — either in the innocent sense that the miracle may after all be "true" at face value or in the underhanded sense that, especially if the miracle in question turns out to be among the "impostures and illusions" reproducible at will by Salomon's House, Bensalem's scientifically approved Christianity was chosen chiefly on the grounds of its compatibility or congeniality with Bensalem's science. Or do both science and Christianity necessarily subserve some further public interest — in common, say, with men like Joabin?

The suspicions that Bacon's narrative cannot help raising concerning the possible use or manipulation of religion for ulterior purposes are soon allowed to fade into a consideration of Bensalem's public policy, for on the third day after their quarantine in Strangers' House, the sailors' conversation with the governor resumes by turning to matters of statesmanship (49–60 [§ 11–15]). The sailors hear the governor's answer to their question of how Bensalem, though unknown to the rest of the world, is yet so knowledgeable about the world. The governor describes a time three thousand years earlier, antedating the historical records of present-day Europe, when Bensalem was a great sea-trading power alongside Phoenecia (including Tyre and Carthage), Egypt, Palestine, China, and especially Atlantis (which the governor identifies with America, both North and South). Bensalem's subsequent isolation followed the legendary attempt by Atlantis to conquer the rest of the world, a legend that modern Europe has learned chiefly through Plato, yet which Bacon's governor corrects in several ways, presumably on the basis of Bensalem's own historical records. First, as the governor indicates, Atlantis was not a single island but comprised all of America, including Mexico (then called Tyrambel) and Peru (then called Coya). Second, to Plato's merely "poetical and fabulous" account of how the Atlantian forces attacked Europe, Asia, and Africa through the Mediterranean and were utterly destroyed by the Athenians and their allies, the governor adds that only Tyrambel attacked the Mediterranean, while Coya attacked Bensalem but surrendered before firing a shot, because of Bensalem's superior strength and the military and naval maneuvering of her "wise" king Altabin, who afterward allowed the Atlantians to return home peaceably in an extraordinary act of clemency. Third, however, "Divine Revenge" soon destroyed the civilization of Atlantis anyway, not by an earthquake, as Plato claims, but only by a localized flood, which left survivors whose descendants populate an uncultivated America to this day (1612). Henceforth, the loss of America as a trading power and the general decline of navigation elsewhere left Bensalem isolated. In the wake of these circumstances, Bensalem's greatest lawgiver, King Solamona, around 288 B.C. redirected Bensalem's long-term foreign policy toward the goal of self-sufficiency and to that end set laws prohibiting contact with foreigners, except for (1) relief for travelers in distress, (2) wooing of prospective immigrants from among such travelers by offering favorable jobs and generous subsidies, and (3) covert intelligence-gathering expeditions abroad by a team of scientists from Salomon's House — an institution which Solamona also established.

It is not clear from the governor's revision of the Atlantis myth how much he has read of Plato's *Critias* firsthand.[11] That is, to what extent has he considered the fuller theological and political implications of that myth as Plato lets us glimpse them? The governor may know of Plato only in the way that he knows of Bensalem's conversion to Christianity, namely secondhand at best, through Bensalem's official archives or (more likely) approved textbooks. Either way, he simply assumes that a knowledge of history, albeit of Bensalemite history, is superior to the knowledge that might be gained by studying Plato's "poetical and fabulous" account in its own terms. He thus elevates (Bensalemite) history over (Platonic) poetry. Yet he does not exactly say why. One cannot maintain in the governor's defense that his history by itself refutes the Platonic account. Leaving aside the epistemological difficulty of establishing with certainty the particulars of the remote past, we note that if Plato's account is indeed a poetic fable — a deliberately invented myth — then strictly speaking, it cannot be refuted by a simple appeal to recorded history, by whose standards it is not necessarily bound. It can only be replaced by that history.[12] We are therefore left to examine in somewhat fuller detail the implications of the governor's replacement of Plato's myth with the particulars supplied by Bensalem's authorized records, in the hopes of elaborating the one clue we have learned from the governor so far concerning the distinctiveness of Bensalem's public policy as it affects Jews such as Joabin. It is the support and deference that Bensalem pays to the scientific technology of Salomon's House.

The Platonic discussion, in contrast, is guided by a thoroughgoing critique of science or art (*technē*) in matters of public policy. Briefly, the conversation about Atlantis in Plato's *Critias* continues a previous day's conversation in Plato's *Timaeus,* which in turn follows a conversation the day before as found in Plato's *Republic.*[13] In the *Republic,* Socrates narrates a conversation he once had with Plato's two brothers and others about the perfectly just city. The perfectly just city, Socrates had argued, is politically realizable only if justice is an art that supervises all the other arts in the city, including the art of war, such that each citizen practices only the one art best suited to him or her (*Republic* 370b–376c). The ruling artisan must therefore be a philosopher, who understands the scope and limits of all the other arts and so, paradoxically, minds everyone else's business while minding his own. Establishing such an art politically, however, cannot as such be a matter of art. It is a matter of chance or good fortune (473c–d). The coming into supreme political power of a philosopher, though theoretically possible, is as unlikely for all practical purposes as is the converting of an actual ruler to the way of life of the philosopher, for the philosopher's first priority is wisdom rather than political honor or even bodily pleasure, which are more comprehensible and credible to nonphilosophers (549c–550c, 580c–583b). Nor is it clear how other artisans would withstand the meddlings of the philosopher's art, since its interference with the proven arts would undoubtedly seem counterproductive to them. And even if *per improbabile* an actual philosopher were to rule, his ruling art could not guarantee that his successors would be philosophers either (543a–548d). Chances are thus that the perfectly just regime either would never see the light of day or else would collapse within a generation or two. As a practical political proposal, then, Socrates' argument is a failure. Nevertheless it shows the necessary limits of any attempt to superimpose justice on the city and its everyday arts. For anyone who, like Socrates, seeks as much justice as is humanly possible for the city, the argument indicates that there is a corresponding need to be moderate in his or her practical expectations, or that political life must somehow include moderation over and above art (490c–d, 500b–d). For Plato, the putative art of justice is hardly the solution to the ongoing problems of political life, but it indicates the permanently problematic character of political life, and hence the need for moderation as well.

Still, in Plato's terms, one need not despair entirely of the possible realization of the perfectly just city if it could be shown that such a city was at one time actual. According to Critias in the *Timaeus,* the Athens that had defeated Atlantis some nine thousand years earlier (he says) was just such a city.[14] Critias recalls having heard when young a festive recitation about Athens's great and virtuous victory over Atlantis from his grandfather, who had relied on Critias's great-grandfather's account of a report that the "wise" Solon had heard from an Egyptian priest. Critias's own account of Atlantis thus depends not so much on written records as on oral tradition. It is therefore only as reliable as that tradition. But, to say nothing of other things, Plato indicates by way of the dramatic action of the dialogue that Critias's memory is defective, if only by having his Critias spend full time, including a sleepless night, since the previous day's conversation in order to recollect each detail sufficiently (*Timaeus* 26a–c). The resulting account, moreover, is emphatically harmonistic (26d). Critias wishes to harmonize the perfectly just city of the *Republic,* which according to Socrates he considers a mere "myth" (26e), with his own ancestral Athens.[15] He even asks the natural philosopher Timaeus to introduce the account of Athens and Atlantis with an account of the genesis of the universe up to the point of the founding of those two cities, which Timaeus does at length. But Timaeus (like Critias) ignores Socrates' own prior insistence that the account of ancestral Athens and Atlantis be true, for Timaeus's cosmogony is admittedly only a likely story (29d, 30b). And Critias himself forgets the built-in tension that the *Republic* had shown between the requirement that the perfectly just city be governed by a single art that rules over all the others and the requirement that it be moderate. Critias thus suppresses the problem of the place of the arts in the just city and, with it, the problem of moderation. No wonder, in the *Critias,* he is incapable of accounting for the decline of ancestral Athens from the peak of its virtue following its victory over Atlantis, except by an appeal to the judgment of the gods, for the dialogue ends with Zeus about to recommend to a council of the gods that both Atlantis and Athens, along with Athens's European, Asian, and African allies, be destroyed because of their "unjust acquisitiveness and power" (*Critias* 121a–c).

Bacon's governor reports the details of Plato's Atlantis myth accurately enough as far as he goes (though he limits himself to the three points I mentioned earlier). Even so, his report imitates that of Plato's Critias in seeking to harmonize two potentially incompatible elements.[16] As Critias sought to harmonize the "myth" of the perfectly just city with his own Athens, so the governor seeks to harmonize the corrected "history" of Atlantis with his own Bensalem. The resulting "history" includes not only Altabin's magnanimous victory over Atlantis and the subsequent flood that destroyed Atlantian together with European, Asian, and African civilization, but also Solamona's longstanding policy of self-sufficiency as necessitated or made possible by the flood, as well as Bensalem's eventual conversion to Christianity under the auspices of the scientific technology first patronized by Solamona. Bacon's governor thus follows Plato's Critias in ignoring or smoothing over the tension noted by Plato between history or political life and the arts. To be sure, unlike Critias, the governor thinks of the arts, so far as we can tell, in terms of the scientific technology of Salomon's House. He seems to take for granted that the replacement or improvement of the arts by means of a scientific technology that would master nature as a whole would somehow make Plato's elaborate warning against immoderateness no longer necessary.[17] Given the governor's silence on this issue, we can only infer the implications from the narrative structure of *New Atlantis* itself.

Consider that, unlike Plato's *Critias,* Bacon's *New Atlantis* is not preceded by the *Republic* and *Timaeus,* which would supply the standards for recognizing the tension between politics and the arts; rather, if Bacon's literary executor be trusted here, *New Atlantis* is succeeded by the unfinished natural history. The *Critias,* as I have said, ends suddenly with Zeus about to announce to an assembly of the gods his plan to destroy not only the defeated Atlantis but also the victorious Athens and her allies, for their "unjust acquisitiveness and power." *New Atlantis,* on the contrary, ends with the speech by the Father of Salomon's House, which mentions neither divine justice nor human beings' "unjust acquisitiveness and power" but instead promises human beings a kind of salvation from destruction, a salvation evidently based on replacement of the gods in favor of scientific mastery of nature. We are left to infer that, as Plato's Atlantis together with all the civilized world was once said to be subject to the destructive power of the gods, so Bacon's Atlantis (America) together with all the civilized world, for which global navigation has recently resumed, is now said to be subject to the salvific power of Bensalem's scientific technology. It follows that Bensalem's "history" leaves her in a position, if not already poised, to restore her long-lost global commerce, while possibly introducing a new, post-Solamonic policy of global hegemony. Such a modification of policy might well require or compel Bensalem to imitate the "unjust acquisitiveness and power" of ancient Atlantis and its quondam contemporaries.

From what the governor has said or implied so far, then, it is clear enough that if the name "New Atlantis" in Bacon's title refers to Bensalem as heir to the old Atlantis, perhaps Bensalem differs from Atlantis not at all in its political aim — world domination — but only in its means — peaceable commercial and technological development so far as possible rather than violent military conquest. At this point, Bensalem's need for cosmopolitan and sophisticated men like Joabin — say, as diplomats or international entrepreneurs — becomes more apparent. But what do men like Joabin derive from Bensalem in turn?

ॐ **V** ॐ

As usual, Bacon's narrator does not say enough to allow us a direct answer. But we can make a few cumulative observations on entering the crucial section of the narrative, the description of private life in Bensalem, where Joabin's voice is raised, or rather hushed, in a show of indignation (64–69 [¶ 17]). Afterward, on probing his indignation a bit to see just what might have provoked it, we can turn to consider its Shylockian character while looking at the narrative's final section, the meeting with the Father of Salomon's House, where the drama has been heading all along.

Bacon's narrator has been introducing us gradually to life in Bensalem from the standpoint of the sailors themselves. Our perplexities over Bensalem's beneficence or worrisomeness have, so to speak, been theirs, and vice versa. We may nevertheless infer something about the island's basic practical priorities from what I have called the hierarchical arrangement of its spokesmen. Through them the narrative has taken us from the most immediate urgencies to broader concerns.

Meanwhile the narrative never lets us lose our original sense of urgency. The first urgencies were the immediate security and health of the sailors and, correspondingly, of the Bensalemites, who as the sailors' vessel limped into port, stood silently on shore with night sticks in hand before sending out the coast guard officer's boat with its formal refusal of landing. Subsequently, the momentarily delayed landing and interim quarantine led the narrator himself to warn his crew that the urgencies were hardly over yet. According to him, their hosts were probably taking constant note of the sailors "manners and conditions" in order to decide whether to help them further or to get rid of them (43f. [¶ 3]). Even the governor's subsequent deep-background lectures about Bensalem's civil religion and public policy were of a piece with the salient urgencies, beyond his merely addressing the visitors' pressing need to know. Both the island's adopted Christianity and its deliberate isolationism were responses to ancient emergencies — the "miracle" at Renfusa, or whatever occasioned it (say, the need in the light of Bensalem's religious cosmopolitanism for a politically unifying civil religion that would at the same time be receptive to the activities of Salomon's House), and the attack of the old Atlantians with its global aftermath — and religion and policy have so far remained unchanged ever since. Obviously, the island's resulting self-sufficiency would not have been possible in the long run without the establishment of Salomon's House, then as now the final cause (that is, the originating source as well as the ultimate purpose) of the island's extraordinary bounties and powers, as we are eventually brought to see more directly during the narrator's culminating interview with the Father of Salomon's House. The neediness of the islanders and their visitors alike, hence their common dependence on Salomon's House, is never quite forgotten throughout the narrative, for everything seems said or done under its watchful "eye" and messengers are more than once dispatched to interrupt spokesmen at some higher command.[18]

No one narrated incident by itself, of course, can decide whether we or the sailors (or, for that matter, the Bensalemites) ought to be grateful for rather than fearful of the awesome power of Salomon's House to monitor security, health, religion, and public policy. But the accumulation of incidents such as I have described them cannot help magnifying our suspicions along with our appreciation — unless, that is, the benevolent promises of Bensalem's spokesmen lull us into a kind of forgetfulness, as they did most of the crew early on. And yet both these responses seem not only permitted but required by the narrative, as if mutually complementary. If so, it follows that it is a mark of the narrative's political intent of introducing us to both sides of Bensalem's way of life, the beneficent and the sinister, that it allows us to be lulled if we are so inclined, or alternatively to be suspicious as we are so induced. And it is a mark of its philosophical intent that it lets us see both alternatives with remarkable (though in the end insufficient) clarity.

As for private life in Bensalem, then, the material prosperity of men like Joabin is evident in the celebration to which the two shipmates are invited toward the end of their first week on the island (60–64 [¶ 16]). The so-called Feast of the Family marks a father's becoming a Tirsan, or patriarch, with thirty living descendants over the age of three. (The term, of Persian derivation, suggests "fearful,"[19] but whether it means "God-fearing," "submissive," or just plain "wary" is not immediately clear.) Two days before the feast, all family members are assembled, together with three friends of the Tirsan's choosing and the local governor or civil administrator. With the latter's help, the Tirsan resolves any family discords, relieves any pressing financial needs, reproves any wayward offspring, advises concerning marriages or careers or the like, and designates his chief heir. During the feast, the Tirsan sits on a dais under a homemade canopy fashioned of Bensalem's all-season ivy (a winter-resilient species presumably developed by Salomon's House [cf. 74 (¶ 30)]) and bound or braided by silver and by multicolored silks. The ivy's leaves and sprigs afterward serve as souvenirs for the guests. Strangely, the family matriarch, if there is one, sits aloft behind an elaborate partition and concealed from others' view. Equally strange perhaps is the Tirsan's intermittently absenting himself for private devotions. Publicly, the Tirsan receives a royal scroll and title and a royal gift of a cluster of grapes wrought of gold and delicately enameled with sun or moon signs on each grape according to the preponderance of male or female descendants, the number of grapes being equal to the total number of descendants. After a formal dinner that concludes with an inventively composed hymn praising Adam and Noah as progenitors of mankind and Abraham as "Father of the Faithful," and with a prayer giving thanks for the birth of "our Saviour,"[20] the Tirsan blesses each descendant individually. The feast thus celebrates abundance, both material and familial. It is Bensalem's attempt to reconcile the requirements of family life with the conditions of general luxury made possible by Salomon's House. Indeed, luxury and family seem both its preconditions and its reward. But are these conditions simply compatible in Bensalem?

Something like this question must have been bothering the narrator for some time prior to his conversation with Joabin. Like his fellow sailors, the narrator has been pondering immigration to Bensalem at least since hearing about its favorable jobs and generous subsidies for newcomers (57, 60 [¶ 15]). Maybe for that reason, he now confesses to Joabin that he was "much affected" by his shipmates' report of the Tirsan celebration. He adds that he had never heard of a solemnity so guided or directed by nature. By *nature,* as his further remarks suggest, the narrator means sexual desire and the propagation of children, matters to which the Bensalemites seem to him to be giving the greatest priority. He asks Joabin three connected questions: What are Bensalem's marriage laws and customs? Are Bensalemite marriages happy? Are they lifelong? The narrator thus wonders about the practical rewards and restrictions of married life as such. Possibly he has noticed that the Tirsan celebration would appear to reward the proliferation of offspring even apart from marriage. For example, in saying as they do that "the king is debtor to no man, but for propagation of his subjects," Bensalemites suggest that their king may be indifferent to whether marriages are long or happy or even lawful so long as they produce children (62f. [¶ 16]). More "natural" than marriage and family, it seems, are sexual desire and the need to procreate, as suggested, respectively, by the ivy, classically associated with Dionysus, the Greek god of desire, and by the grape, a biblical symbol of fecundity as well.[21] Above all, there is the visible absence of the mother of the family—if there be one, the shipmates had said (perhaps there are more than one, in which case Bacon seems to be suggesting that none need even be invited) —whereas there is little sexual discrimination otherwise. The celebration's deference to "nature" would thus suggest, so far as the narrator is concerned, that Bensalemites do not consider marriage or the family the natural setting for the satisfaction of sexual desire. But if that is the case, then the narrator must be wondering whether the state-supervised party and pension are anything more than an ingenious attempt at channeling whatever political benefits may accrue from Bensalem's potentially rampant sexual promiscuity, namely a proliferation of children to solve the king's admitted underpopulation problem, while at the same time fending off the threat that promiscuity poses to family life and the political order by offering longterm financial incentives.

With these possibly unsettling implications of the narrator's questions in mind, Joabin launches into a morally indignant diatribe in praise of Bensalem's chastity, as against the promiscuity he finds prevalent in Europe (66–68 [¶ 17]). Bensalem, by contrast, is "the virgin of the world." Joabin resolutely defends Bensalem's virtue by attacking, to begin with, Europe's worldly tolerance of prostitution. Europeans, he charges, excuse prostitution as a necessary evil to protect the institution of marriage. They say it prevents adultery with married women, preserves virginity among eligible maidens, preempts "unnatural lusts," and so forth.[22] But Bensalemites find such excuses lame and sophistical. Europe's "preposterous wisdom" they contemptuously call *"Lot's offer,* who to save his guests from abusing, offered his daughters."[23] Joabin's biblical allusion, however, suggests that his main target is not prostitution, or in general heterosexual promiscuity, but homosexuality, its Lot-inspired trade-off, for he immediately protests in so many words that to condone harlotry in place of sodomy does not eliminate so much as intensify the passions that give rise to the latter, whereas Bensalem, on the contrary, has succeeded in abolishing all touches of "masculine love" in favor of the world's most faithful and inviolate masculine friendships, and Bensalemites even repeat pious mottos daily equating chastity among men with reverence for oneself.

Here Joabin's pause provokes the narrator's own biblical allusion, in lieu of his embarrassed silence. He recalls what the widow of Sarepta said to the prophet Elijah, that he had come "to bring memory to our sins," although the narrator then suppresses the rest of the biblical citation, which continues with the frightened or frightening thought that the sins in question, those of the widow's son, might well have deserved punishment by death.[24] We seem invited to view Joabin's polemic (wise, learned, statesmanlike, and informed, as the narrator would have it) as deliberately designed to elicit from the narrator a tacit admission of the population-stifling evils of homosexuality and to warn him and his shipmates away from those evils as the price of Bensalemite citizenship — or indeed, given our own larger suspicions, of their ever leaving Bensalem alive.[25] In any case, Joabin's savage attack on European sexual mores serves to focus the narrator's subsequent attention on how well Bensalem's marriage laws and customs in fact facilitate its own modification of "Lot's offer," namely its restraining nonproductive homosexuality by liberalizing or emancipating child-producing heterosexuality.

Do Bensalem's marriage laws and customs, then, harness raw sexual appetites in the direction of long and happy marriages, as the narrator had wondered? Only very loosely, we must say, despite Joabin's moralizing gloss. In any event, it is a question that Joabin avoids answering directly. The laws, he reports, prohibit polygamy, stipulate acquaintanceship of at least one month before marriage, and restrict inheritance rights for children of couples who marry without parental consent. Surely the narrator easily surmises that the first law nevertheless permits serial remarriages, the second allows too short a time for couples to reckon the likelihood of a lifetime of happiness together, and the third imposes too long a one. Together, the three provisions seem paltry — too trivial, too little, and too late — unless they are somehow supplemented by the guidance of wise customs. Are they? Here Joabin's all-too-brief comments are most revealing, but also most guarded, concerning Bensalem's giving loose rein to sexual promiscuity. Joabin, who has evidently read Thomas More's

Utopia (and perhaps Plato's *Laws*), revises More's recommendation that prospective betrotheds be allowed to see each other naked (in the company of suitably approved chaperons) to warn of unpleasant bodily defects.[26] Bensalemite couples, says Joabin, would "think it a scorn to give a refusal after so familiar knowledge." Joabin emphatically approves of Bensalem's "more civil" way of conducting premarital body inspections. Near each town is a pair of pools, he says, called Adam and Eve's pools, where a friend of either fiancé is allowed to see his or her intended bathe naked. Bensalemites accordingly replace married or respectable chaperons, the proxies of family authority, with unattached voyeurs, whose loyalty belongs primarily to the adolescents themselves (and so is easily changeable, despite protestations of friendship, when other attractions come into full view).[27] In other words, Bensalem's marriage customs diminish family authority and stability while augmenting adolescent freedom. Despite Joabin's show of indignation, then, the narrator seems entitled to infer that Bensalem's marriages are not necessarily happy or long, or if happy, need not be long and if long, may not be happy.

Joabin's spirited if hypocritical endorsement of Bensalemite marriages anyway seems connected with his understanding of just what it is that Bensalem's premarital couples in their nakedness would be ashamed to refuse each other. Arguably in the circumstances I have outlined, Joabin does not mean marriage. He means sexual intercourse. Assuming that Joabin's "wise" expectations gravitate that low, they may extend as well to the groom's best man when inspecting the bride and to the bride's maid (or matron) of honor when inspecting the groom as Peeping Toms at Adam and Eve's pools. Joabin's unblinking worldliness in such matters, combined with his resolute loyalty to his sovereign, would resemble that of his namesake Joab, the biblical King David's nephew, military commander, and political troubleshooter. Joab, for one, implicitly understood the dangers that resulted when someone like the immoderate David looked on the distant nakedness of a beautiful woman. David's subsequent liaison with Uriah's wife Bathsheba, and her becoming pregnant by him, led to his covertly ordering Uriah's death—and to Joab's politic compliance, at the probable cost of other innocent deaths as well.[28] David was eventually called to account by the prophet Nathan, though Joab seems to have escaped direct prophetic censure. Given the distinct likelihood that Bensalem's religion, unlike David's, is entirely under the supervision of the civil authorities, Joabin's own freedom (along with his supervisors') from any moral censure of his thoughts or actions in such matters seems, for all practical purposes, assured also.[29]

In any case, it follows that the dangers of sexual license in Bensalem are not just private but political, and perhaps this insight allows the narrator to round out his understanding of the Tirsan feast as seen through Joabin's eyes. Three apparent incongruities remain: the meaning of the term *Tirsan,* the reason for his intermittent absence, and the invisibility of his wife. If the foregoing interpretation of Joabin is correct, the apparent incongruities may have a common source in the private desires that the feast is designed to arouse, to channel, and, ultimately, to reward. The invisibility of the Tirsan's wife (or alternatively, the shunning of his concubines) would eliminate from the scene at least one clear and present reminder of past sexual promiscuities or frustrations and so prevent possible soap-opera confrontations that would spoil the outward reverence of the occasion. The Tirsan's intermittent absence in addition lets him offer private prayers and thanks to God for continued protection against David-like competitors for the things he privately desires. Finally, the Tirsan, like Joabin himself, would seem at least as "wary" as he is "submissive" or "God-fearing," for he finds himself in a state in which, governed openly by his private desires, he must secretly worry about meeting a Uriah-like fate, the violent and permanent termination of his private satisfactions at the hands of some equally fearful rival. In the almost Bensalemite language of Bacon's younger friend Thomas Hobbes, the Tirsan's fearful private state is the "state of nature," the state of mind and of being in which each man sees himself in the end simply as a private individual in mortal competition with every other individual.[30]

Joabin's poker-faced hypocrisies in moralizing about the attractions of private life in Bensalem would seem unconscionable unless offset by more compelling reasons befitting the narrator's description of him as wise, learned, and statesmanlike. After all, perhaps Bensalem's need to maintain or augment its population, especially given the likelihood of its imminent re-entry into world commerce and its possible world hegemony, is greater than would appear at first glance, and therefore Joabin has a patriotic duty to present an embarrassingly vulgar subject in its most alluring, not lurid, light; perhaps Bensalem needs the narrator and his shipmates even more than the shipmates need Bensalem. But this consideration in turn raises the moral question of just how far Joabin is justified in going along in that direction, and to what end. Are his tight-lipped efforts to attract outsiders to Bensalem as "the virgin of the world," ripe for gazing upon and embracing, to be praised for the ultimately salutary results that they seem to promise? Or are they no more than elaborately veiled efforts to sustain Bensalem's (and Joabin's own) wealth- and power-seeking propensities?

꒓ VI ꒓

In the end, what draws us to notice the kinship between Joabin and Shylock is that Bacon's narrator routinely neglects such pressing moral questions, whereas Shakespeare (to judge by what we have seen so far) does not. Bacon's *New Atlantis* concludes as the Father of Salomon's House outlines to the narrator privately the aim, facilities, staff, and official rituals of "our foundation," as he calls it, and immediately afterward gives the narrator leave to publish that information "for the good of other nations" (71–83 [¶ 19–59]). Perhaps Bacon's narrator is too overwhelmed by the ceremonial presence of the Father and the astonishing content of his message to ask our questions himself. Still the questions remain, for scientific and practical elements here seem inextricably, and for all we may know unfathomably, mixed.

The stated aim of Salomon's House is not only the (technical) "knowledge of Causes, and secret motions of things," but also the (quasi-political) "enlarging of the bounds of Human Empire, to the effecting of all things possible" (71 [¶ 20]). Its facilities sustain projects related to military as well as consumer uses: experimental laboratories for producing and preserving bodies and bodily life (human as well as nonhuman) and for construction materials and fertilizers; underwater farming; mineral wells; weather control devices and air conditioners; medicinal baths; farms for developing year-round hybrids; experimental zoos, aquariums, insect farms, kitchens, and medical dispensaries; factories for producing rare fabrics, heat generators, lenses, and precious stones; audio laboratories; perfume houses; mobile weapons production, including nuclear bombs, airships, and submarines; mathematical instruments; and finally, the aforementioned laboratory for "deceits of the senses." The scientist-priests swear themselves to secrecy, even from the state when necessary, and publish only after mutual consultation, although this may well include consideration of such mundane practicalities as their collective dependence on state support and funding. And the facilities house museum galleries for venerating scientific innovations and inventors, though whether their larger innovative purposes are broadly humanitarian, as typified by the advanced medical and consumer technology, or more narrowly imperialistic, as typified by the sophisticated military and dirty-tricks capabilities, is not yet clear. That is, the question remains whether the public role of Salomon's House is best emblemized by Bensalem's compassionate rescue and rehabilitation of the sailors, or perhaps instead by its deliberately causing a storm that might bring badly needed immigrants — and a potential publicist — to its hidden shores.

I have already suggested in passing that Bensalem's two faces, the beneficent and the sinister, need not be mutually exclusive. Each may well require the other, Janus-like, in Bensalem's special circumstances. Consider that, taken by themselves, security, health, luxury, religious tolerance, and (now) the revival of international commerce with its strategic implications would seem to be praiseworthy goals of public policy. The difficulty is that, assuming Bacon's narrative to be complete, these are Bensalem's *only* public goals. What is missing from the Baconian discussion is indicated, as I have already shown, by the Platonic sources of whose implications Bacon's governor seems oblivious, or alternatively by the biblical allusions to which Bacon's Joabin gives short shrift—namely, justice and moderation. Whereas the Platonic and biblical texts to which Bacon's narrator alludes in passing are clear in their disapproval of, for example, licentiousness in both public policy and private behavior, Bensalem's spokesmen are not. At the same time, Bensalem's policy goals are to be guaranteed by Salomon's House. *Guaranteed* is hardly too strong a word here. It means not only that the stipulated policy goals are to be given top priority but also that any obstacles or hindrances to their realization are to be eliminated so far as possible, unstintingly and relentlessly wherever necessary by means of the full arsenal of technology available to Salomon's House. It follows that, while Bensalem might tolerate, say, other religions in private competition with its official Christianity, it cannot tolerate the teaching or practice of justice and moderation as found in Plato and the Bible if—or lest—these get in the way of the publicly stipulated goals. But this is to say that only security, health, luxury, religious tolerance, and foreign commerce will receive unconditional moral approval in Bensalem and so be subject to protection and enforcement by Salomon's House, whereas justice and moderation (at least by Platonic or biblical standards) will not. Nevertheless the reader will recall with some perplexity that Bacon's Joabin, in warning the narrator indignantly against the danger of engaging in homosexuality in Bensalem, could not help appealing to at least a façade of justice and moderation. Since Bacon's narrative does not make it easy for us to sort out the grounds for Joabin's (or Bensalem's) moralizing for the sake of ends that by traditional standards are possibly immoral, but certainly insufficiently moral, we must consider taking our bearings once more by way of Shakespeare's Shylock.

Shylock shares with Bacon's Joabin a far-reaching indignation. Both men are upset over not receiving their due. In Shylock's case, to judge by his "I am a Jew" and other speeches, what upsets him is the denial of his putative right to compete for business on the Rialto equally with Christians and free of religious harassment from them. In Joabin's case, it is the uncertainty over whether the sailors as new immigrants will acknowledge his (or Bensalem's) putative right to expect that Bensalemite men will direct their sexual proclivities to child-producing ends. In both cases, the appeal to what is right goes beyond the mere law of the land. Hence it cannot simply be enforced by that law. Each man's indignation is rather a sign of his temporary helplessness in the face of his larger moral expectations. Shylock, as we have seen, tries to overcome his helplessness by means of a futile lawsuit, while Joabin is able to turn with more success to the use of elaborately veiled threats. But in either case there is a moral appeal that would sanction what for the moment lies outside the purview of the law — the equality of Christians and Jews (Shylock) or the need for private sexuality to cooperate fully in the workings of Bensalem's realpolitik (Joabin).

The question we must ponder here is, What, if anything, makes such appeals moral? In Shakespeare's play the answer is clear enough. Both the Duke, who is the play's highest political authority, and Portia, who is the philosophical authority, identify morality with what we would call biblical morality. Remarkably, as I have shown, in their understanding of the latter, they include Jewish law. Both see justice tempered with mercy — with theologically sanctioned moderation — as the chief teaching of that morality, and both therefore plead with Shylock to live up to it. But Shylock in his anger does not listen. The same anger that first raised his sights to the need for justice beyond what Venetian law alone would seem to provide, namely the equal treatment of Christians and Jews under the law, now blocks Shylock from seeing, as the Duke and Portia do, how that justice might for all practical purposes be realized within the bounds of moral decency, namely by the exercise and inducement of moderation from those who habitually claim to defer to the law. Surely Shylock as a Jew is thought by Shakespeare's Venetians to be capable in principle of seeing this much by himself even without the Duke's and Portia's unheeded reminders in court, assuming that their understanding of Jewish law on that point is correct (and Shakespeare gives us no reason to doubt that it is). Why, then, didn't Shakespeare let Shylock, given his presumptive knowledge of Jewish law's prohibition against vengeance, use his ingenuity in the manner of Portia, say, to embarrass Antonio into repenting of his anti-Jewish crusade, for example, by having Shylock refuse publicly to collect on his penalty clause when Antonio's note became overdue? The answer seems to be that

Shakespeare has had Shylock early on in the play disclose his intent to break with the moral demands of Jewish law in matters of vengeance[31] as well as of eating, while subsequently claiming that his Jewishness — as understood by Venice's Christians, his following the way of life prescribed by Jewish law — nevertheless entitles him both to eat the same food and exact the same vengeance as he supposes Christians do. We are led to conclude that Shakespeare finds Shylock's position morally indefensible not because it is Jewish (for in Shakespeare's eyes it is *not* Jewish) but because it is inconsistent, both in its own terms and vis-à-vis Jewish law.

Let me express the same point from within the horizon of Shylock's impassioned "I am a Jew" speech. Shylock, as I have said earlier, defends the moral legitimacy of his taking revenge against Antonio by arguing that any Christian would do the same. It is an argument for the equality of Christians and Jews that has, so to speak, nothing to do with their being Christians and Jews. Or rather, it is an argument that overlooks any need for there being Christians and Jews in the first place. That is, Shylock's argument ignores the prohibition of revenge by both Christianity and Judaism, at least as Shakespeare's Duke and Portia understand them. Shylock disregards Christian and Jewish moral teaching in the name of what he considers more fundamental, namely a pre-moral or natural equality of Christians and Jews which has to do with their both having live human bodies. What they share equally according to him is the neediness that belongs to beings that have such bodies. Of the sixteen or seventeen common human characteristics that Shylock enumerates in a list culminating in his alleged need for revenge, the first seven ("eyes . . . hands, organs, dimensions, senses, affections, passions") are bodily capacities that are named quite apart from the various ways in which human beings exercise them, whereas the remainder of the list would seem to be bodily actions in response to increasingly complicated circumstances that beings who have the aforementioned capacities must suffer or undergo: feeding, being hurt, becoming diseased, healing, being warmed and cooled in winter and summer, bleeding after being pricked, laughing as a result of tickling, dying from poison, and finally, revenging in return for being wronged. Shylock sees revenge, then, as the most complicated of inevitable responses to circumstances over which human sufferers have little or no control and yet, at the same time, as the morally correct thing to do. But if we are to take Shylock quite literally in his own, self-contradictory terms, the only moral basis for revenge is his observation that Christians despite their being Christians (and Jews despite their being Jews), who are forbidden revenge, practice it anyway, so that their revenge somehow partakes of the nobility of the biblical teaching even though those who exercise it thereby disregard that teaching. Shylock, in short, wishes to claim for himself the aura of a moral teaching whose applicability he flatly denies.

Having been alerted by Shakespeare in this way to the moral implications of Shylock's anger, we are encouraged to notice something similar in Bacon's Joabin. Like Shylock, Joabin too is morally at odds both with himself and with Jewish law. That the consequences of his moral incongruities are not simply trivial may be seen by the following consideration.

Joabin claims Bensalem's moral superiority (or what on the surface is meant to look like Bensalem's moral superiority) to Europe in sexual matters. What he means, however, turns out to be the superiority of Bensalem's remedy for preserving some semblance of traditional family life under adverse circumstances. If Joabin's explanation of the Tirsan celebration is any indication, the adverse circumstances include the thoroughgoing individualism that results from Bensalem's liberation of each citizen's private desires for wealth and sexual fulfillment apart from the family. The comparative weakness of any inducements to moderation in Bensalem is implicit both in the silences of Bensalem's laws and in the readiness of Joabin's anger, in the ways I have already suggested. We cannot therefore avoid suspecting that Joabin's moralizing is little more than a stopgap attempt to close the laws' loopholes in order to bring about the necessary sexual cooperation in Bensalemites by a smooth combination of cajoling and threats. Here we must keep in mind that Joabin's philosophical and practical single-mindedness in defense of Bensalem's policy is, in the light of the alternatives, which he dismisses out of hand, a sign of the one-sidedness of his overall position. Philosophically, Joabin's staunch commitment to Bensalem's individualism would seem to deprive him of the possibly illuminating benefits derived from a fuller consideration of the old-fashioned view that marriage and family — not just raw sexuality — are somehow natural.[32] And practically, it is hard to see how Joabin's ultimate reliance on the technology of Salomon's House in support of his cajoling and threats — by way of publicly funded programs complete with artificial celebrations and financial rewards to bolster weak Bensalemite marriages[33] — provides an adequate replacement for a more traditional education designed to show citizens the attractions of wealth and sexual fulfillment within the setting of decent family life. To put what is at issue in terms of the Jewish teachings that Joabin would thereby have us abandon: it is hard to induce the moderation implied by the Fifth, Seventh, and Tenth Commandments once promiscuity and covetousness have received the endorsement of public policy.[34]

From what I have said, it follows that part of the price Jews must pay for political tolerance by non-Jews, according to Bacon — though not according to Shakespeare — is a Joabin-like (or Shylockian) willingness to forgo biblical morality wherever it comes into competition with the policy goals of a Bensalem: for example, security, health, luxury. For Shakespeare, on the contrary, biblical morality remains the chief and proper bond that links Jews as Jews to others in society. To the extent that biblical morality stands at the core of what it means to be a Jew, then, Shakespeare emerges as much the greater friend to Jews for his reminding Christians and Jews alike of their common moral bond. The contrast between Shakespeare and Bacon here could hardly be clearer. My previous argument has mainly tried to show why each must appear to readers offhand in the guise of his opposite.

Yet perhaps my argument at this point is open to the objection that I have made too much of the too little that Bacon's Joabin has said. It might prove more convincing one way or the other, therefore, if we could be shown a fuller and more sympathetic account on Baconian premises of the shared biblical roots of Jews and Christians in order to see what I have called the Shylockian implications of these premises in a clearer light. For that reason, I turn in the final chapter to Spinoza's Joabin-like recipe for Jewish-Christian tolerance as found in his *Theologico-Political Treatise*.

5

ᖷ ᖷ

Shylock and Spinoza's Theologico-Political Treatise

Take as an example the city of Amsterdam, which, with its considerable growth and to the admiration of all nations, experiences the fruits of this freedom; for in this most flourishing republic and most outstanding city, all human beings of whatever nation and sect live with the greatest harmony, and in order that they might entrust their goods to someone, they care to know only whether he is rich or poor and whether he is wont to act in good faith or by cunning: Otherwise religion or sect does not move them at all, since it is of no avail at all in winning or losing a case before a judge; and no sect is so utterly hateful whose devotees (so long as they harm no one and pay each what is owed and live honestly) are not protected by the public authority and enforcement of the magistrates.

— Spinoza, *Theologico-Political Treatise*

ᖷ I ᖷ

LET US RETRACE THE STEPS THAT HAVE TAKEN US from Shakespeare's Shylock to Spinoza's *Theologico-Political Treatise*.[1] I began by wondering about the moral implications of Shylock's forced conversion, in light of the all-too-frequent allegations nowadays that Shakespeare must have succumbed to the anti-Jewish prejudices of his time. On closer examination, however, the evidence of the play has suggested otherwise. Shakespeare measures his Shylock by the standards of Jewish orthodoxy. More than that, Shakespeare equates Jewish orthodoxy, especially the primacy that, according to his Duke and Portia, it gives to justice and mercy, with the moral decency that is seen to be lacking in Shylock's particular case. Here Shakespeare parts company with Marlowe, whose Jewish protagonist Barabas is little more than an occasion for flaunting the views (which are scarcely warranted by the biblical evidence he parodies) that biblical morality is puerile and superficial and that human beings in general are guided instead by considerations of self-preservation and self-aggrandizement, which induce them to be deliberately unjust and immoderate at will. Bacon in turn does not disagree with Marlowe's fundamental claim here, except to add that for practical purposes a way may nevertheless be found for Jewish-Christian tolerance, if not on the basis of a common reverence for biblical morality, as Shakespeare would have it, at least on the basis of a common openness to scientific technology and a technology-friendly political order. Yet because Bacon's own temporizing with the evident likelihood of injustice and immoderateness in such a political order may well leave us perplexed over what we are to make of biblical morality — hence of Judaism — on Baconian premises, we therefore turn for help to Spinoza's philosophical *Treatise,* which proclaims on its very title page (in a manner reminiscent of Bacon's Joabin) a promise to safeguard both biblical piety and civil peace.[2] The practical implications of Spinoza's argument become clearer than they might otherwise be, the more we recognize its kinship as well with Shylock's "I am a Jew" speech.

To judge by the preface to Spinoza's *Treatise,* its philosophical theme is the proper relation between politics and theology. The prevailing relation according to Spinoza — the one that his intended reader takes for granted as he begins to read the book — is a mismatch. On the one hand, there is disagreement among the various religious sects over the meaning of the biblical teaching to which they all profess to defer. On the other hand, biblical religion is held to be the bond of society. The unfortunate result, as Spinoza forcefully indicates, is that theological instruction easily degenerates into sectarian polemics and political society is in turn destabilized by religious conflicts. Nevertheless Spinoza argues that a smooth fit between biblical religion and political society is not only desirable but possible. Theologically, it is a matter of reminding or persuading the warring sects to look first and foremost to what they have in common, namely the biblical teaching of justice and charity. Since that teaching is (Spinoza argues) independent of all sectarian differences, and so detachable from them, its chief practical fruit may be said to be mutual tolerance, implying the freedom to believe or not to believe in any strictly sectarian teaching so long as one is just and charitable otherwise.[3] At the same time, politically, Spinoza aims to weaken or remove biblical religion as the — hitherto problematic — bond of society, in favor of "commerce."[4] Since commerce, when pursued most efficiently, requires a corresponding cosmopolitanism or openness to novelty for the sake of worldly gain, it follows that government must no longer be thought of as deriving from traditional authorities that would place moral restraints on wealth-getting and so on, but instead as catering to the self-interest of its individual citizens as each sees that interest, that is, to individual freedom, so far as this is compatible with the need for political order. The best form of government, then, will be a liberal democracy, which leaves its citizens free to pursue their private interests and even leaves them free to accept or reject biblical religion, provided that they conform to those minimal standards of public decency that, it so happens, are conveniently supplied by the Bible properly understood according to Spinoza: as pure justice now understood as law-abiding peaceableness, and charitableness now understood as a benevolent live-and-let-live attitude.[5]

The foregoing summary is enough to indicate that Spinoza's overall argument is twofold not only in subject matter — theology and politics — but also in how it approaches that subject matter. As the founding document of both liberal religion (the view that religious belief is essentially a private matter) and liberal democracy (the political regime that is guided above all by the private interests of its citizens, regarded as political equals), the *Theologico-Political Treatise* is revolutionary in its conclusions. Yet by appealing to the theological authority of the biblical text and by going out of its way to bow in addition to the moral authority of the Dutch republic (in which the book was originally written), the *Treatise*'s rhetoric is, superficially at any rate, conservative. The link between its superficial conservatism and its inherent revolutionariness may be found in the *Treatise*'s "philosophical" addressee, whom Spinoza's argument is intended to benefit especially.[6] The addressee is said to be among those who "would philosophize more freely" if they were disabused of the opinion that reason ought to be handmaid to theology. Even so, Spinoza warns that his argument will not please nonphilosophers, who are incorrigibly superstitious and would prove "troublesome" to philosophers. By addressing would-be philosophers in the full view of potentially hostile nonphilosophers, Spinoza is therefore compelled to challenge their theological prejudices in a way that only a philosopher alerted to the need for intellectual self-improvement could fully appreciate. In the detailed wording and arrangement of his argument, he silently shows the logical absurdity of those prejudices, or the absurdity of their logical implications as is evident to those who find themselves encouraged to think them through while reading his words, even as he explicitly shows their "theological" plausibility, or their conformity with the theological expectations of nonphilosophers, who will be more or less satisfied by seeing their prejudices reflected in Spinoza's words without necessarily seeing a further need to examine very far the larger implications of those words. So conceived, Spinoza's purportedly theological (but, from the prerevolutionary viewpoint of nonphilosophers, antitheological) argument is the necessary complement to his political liberalism.

The present chapter focuses on the twin strands of Spinoza's argument—his theological argument for religious tolerance and his political argument for liberal democracy—in order to show how, taken together, they aim in effect to prevent the recurrence of the sort of situation in which Shakespeare's Shylock finds himself. To show that much is to indicate where Spinoza's argument joins (or rather underlies) the thinking of the scholars whom I began by considering in chapter 1. Yet along the way I cannot help pointing out the evident shortcomings of Spinoza's argument as well, in the interest of my primary goal of making Shylock's situation intelligible enough to be able to tell whether Shakespeare's understanding of his character is in principle superior to Spinoza's — that is, to the modern scholars' — or not.

I may anticipate my final conclusion by pointing to the most obvious difficulty embedded in what may be called Spinoza's liberal solution to Shylock's problem. Spinoza would make of Judaism, or for that matter Christianity, a private preference to be protected by government. That way, he would eliminate in principle all religious discrimination on the part of government. Yet this solution can hardly be said by itself to eliminate religious discrimination on the part of private citizens. On the contrary, it follows from the religious and political liberalism that Spinoza establishes that government is bound to protect private discrimination, and in fact to subserve it. Any government that acted otherwise would have to give up the claim to be guided by liberal principles, that is, to be simply subservient to the private preferences of its citizens.[7] Our perplexity here might be overcome somewhat if we could recover for ourselves the alternative understanding of religion and politics which Spinoza would have us abandon, so that we might take note of the chief differences between it and Spinoza's liberalism and examine with requisite care the trade-offs. Those trade-offs are embodied to some extent in the *Theologico-Political Treatise* itself — for example, in Spinoza's polemic against Maimonides as the philosophical defender of Jewish orthodoxy.[8] Behind that polemic lies Spinoza's implicit critique (following Machiavelli,[9] Bacon, et al.) of Platonic and Aristotelian political philosophy,[10] as well as his explicit critique of the Bible. In what follows, I shall touch on Spinoza's anti-Maimonideanism and its supporting critiques largely in passing. It is enough for my present purpose to indicate where Spinoza's overall position is doubtful and the position he opposes is by contrast plausible, as I have tried to do with Bacon. It is then a short step to point out that the position Spinoza opposes is more or less that of Shakespeare's Duke and Portia. As with Bacon's Joabin, I then conclude by speaking of the Shylockian implications, and limitations, of Spinoza's liberalism.

ᘑ II ᘑ

To see in a preliminary way how Spinoza's argument connects more directly with Shylock as we have come to understand him, it is enough to look again at Shylock's theological disputation with Antonio during their negotiations over the terms of Bassanio's loan. The disagreement between them centers on whether or not the Bible permits taking "interest" (to use Antonio's term, I.iii.46, 70–72, 89) — or "advantage" (as Shylock prefers to say, I.iii.64) — of borrowers. Presumably Shylock is as aware as Antonio is of the Bible's obvious legal prohibition of interest taking among "brothers,"[11] though neither mentions it directly. Yet surprisingly, in the light of his insistence on strict legalities throughout the remainder of his dealings with Antonio, Shylock here does not seek to justify his apparently going against that prohibition by adducing some legal exemption. He appeals instead to the "skilful[ness]" and "thrift" of the patriarch Jacob in increasing the numbers of sheep and goats owed him by his uncle Laban, in the manner I mentioned earlier (I.iii.79, 85). Shylock's appeal is to the prelegal authority of the ancestral. Jacob is a founder of Shylock's "sacred nation" (I.iii.43). His being the "third possessor" in line from "our holy Abram" is a circumstance owing not to the biblical law, which in any case is not yet promulgated during Jacob's lifetime, but to the manipulativeness of Jacob's "wise" mother in covertly arranging for him to receive an inheritance-blessing from his blind father by having Jacob masquerade as his older brother for the occasion (I.iii.66–69). So far as Shylock is concerned, the justification for Jacob's taking advantage of Laban, as well as for his mother's taking advantage of his father's blindness for Jacob's sake, is that Jacob thereby found "a way to thrive" (I.iii.84). "Thrift" — or business acumen and success — and "blessing" amount to the same thing for Shylock. His biblical precedent serves to sanctify that equation.

Antonio does not dispute the authority of Shylock's biblical example. He differs only on its meaning and relevance. He counters at once that the success of Jacob's "venture" (using a term that Shylock during Antonio's absence a moment before had applied to the latter's shipping investments, I.iii.18, 86) was hardly the product of those who by themselves could not guarantee the final, divinely ordained outcome. Jacob's success was rather "A thing not in his power to bring to pass, / But sway'd and fashion'd by the hand of heaven" (I.iii.87–88). Antonio's further queries about the passage that Shylock has cited as proof—"Was this inserted to make interest good?" "is your gold and silver ewes and rams?" (I.iii.89–90)—are thus rhetorical, for the expected answer to both is obviously no, though Shylock diffuses his adversary's point, as we have already seen, by quipping that his gold and silver may even so be seen to multiply as fast as Jacob's herds (I.iii.91f.). Antonio's way of reading the Bible, in contrast to Shylock's, depreciates human calculation and inflates divine providence. He finds something inconsistent and morally objectionable about Shylock's "producing holy witness" to justify a base act. "The devil can cite Scripture for his purpose," he warns Bassanio, but he leaves it unclear whether the burden of his remark is simply to formulate a memorable maxim for Bassanio's edification or to insult Shylock's own "evil soul" obliquely (for he is, after all, asking Shylock for money) by compounding references to "a villain with a smiling cheek" and a "goodly apple rotten at the heart" (I.iii.93–96). For Antonio, Bible stories are to be taken not just literally, for the ancestral incidents that they record, but spiritually, for the moral, allegorical, and anagogical meanings that present-day believers may attribute to those incidents.[12] Reading them is accordingly a test or sign of one's faith in a divine ordering of the particulars of human life. Shylock, on the other hand, reads the Bible for its business tips.

What is beyond dispute here is that Antonio and Shylock draw fundamentally different practical inferences from a single biblical text. Insofar as each's inferences are guided above all by the enthusiasm of a believing Christian or by the resoluteness of a loyal Jew—that is, without the element of moderation to which Portia later calls attention in her "quality of mercy" speech—collisions between the two become likely, especially where each must face the other daily within Venice's city limits. So long as Christianity remains the official bond of Venetian society, Antonio's biblical inferences cannot fail to win the official nod of approval among his fellow citizens over Shylock's. We see something of the persistence of that bond in the popular esteem

Antonio receives for his religious opinions which, quite apart from the intrinsic merit of those opinions, seems all the more readily — that is, thoughtlessly — granted in the morally disorienting currents and eddies of Shakespeare's Venice, where (if the buoyant Gratiano is our indicator) traditional piety is ebbing and modern commerce is on the rise. And yet concerning the question of moneylending in particular, Antonio stands alone, as we have also seen. No one else on the Rialto steps forward to pay off his debt to Shylock or to lend him sufficient to do so interest free in the way he has done for others. Shylock himself seems to have been correct in intimating that his own thinking is much closer to the everyday business practices of the Rialto than Antonio's (I.iii.38–40). Practically speaking, Antonio's original harassment of Shylock would have been unthinkable if the opinions of the Rialto — of Shylock (and the modern scholars) rather than Antonio — were the ruling opinions of Venice. This is the point of Spinoza's *Treatise,* so far as the practical question of Jewish-Christian tolerance is concerned. Spinoza's argument culminates, as we shall see, with a paean to the prosperous city of Amsterdam, where the spirit of commerce is said to have triumphed unambiguously over the spirit of religious persecution.

ॐ III ॐ

In examining the theological strand of Spinoza's theologico-political argument for tolerance, we must first look separately at its basis in his distinctive way of reading the Bible. What distinguishes Spinoza here from, say, Shylock or Antonio is his insistence on method. Subsequent readers who take Spinoza's achievement for granted may not find that insistence very noteworthy. But Spinoza devotes an entire chapter of the *Theologico-Political Treatise* (chap. 7) to method as a pressing need in interpreting the Bible. Evidently he thinks his method controversial enough to warrant considerable justification. A method, after all, is a means to an end (in this case, understanding the Bible) and supposes prior reflection on its appropriateness. Method, as Spinoza conceives it, moreover, is necessarily imposed on its subject matter as on something inherently lacking in order. Spinoza's view that the Bible requires a method for its understanding, then, must have been arrived at or decided on in advance of any strictly methodical consideration of its subject matter.

What has led Spinoza to the insistence on method, according to his own account, is not so much the subject matter of the Bible per se as the practical effect of that subject matter on its devotees. While the Bible's devotees hold it to be comprehensive and salutary and binding in general, it is often seen to be obscure in detail. Its details thus invite interpretation. Interpretations lead to disagreements. These in turn foment sectarian divisions and public persecutions and, ultimately, religious wars. In the circumstances the Bible as a public document endangers the public peace. Part of the danger, at least, is the intellectual incompetence of its interpreters, who, blinded by sectarian zeal, overlook the element of moderation comprised in the biblical teaching of charity (*Praef.*8.1–9.25 [E6ff.; S52ff.]). Nor are they helped by their occasional appeal for interpretive guidance to the extrabiblical teachings of the classical political philosophers — to Plato or Aristotle, for example. Theologians influenced by Platonic and Aristotelian teachings are no less apt to disagree among themselves, let alone with the biblical teaching, and in fact may well come to view the Bible as little more than an occasion for passing off their own, biblically unauthorized speculations as authoritative. They therefore stir rather than settle conflicts.[13] Spinoza's method, on the other hand, would remedy the aforesaid abuses by reorganizing the study of the Bible so as to prevent politically charged disagreements from ever happening again. Imitating the method of (Baconian) natural science, Spinoza would have Bible interpreters take their bearings by what presumably no one could disagree with, namely the unadulterated or "authentic history" of the Bible as drawn "from certain data and principles."[14] Despite Spinoza's high-sounding language here, as we shall see, the compelling certainty of those data and principles turns out to be not theological but what might be called statistical, deriving as it does simply from the numerical frequency, or relative predictability, of the occurrence of various commonly repeated notions or expressions within the confines of the biblical text.

Spinoza's method would have Bible interpreters begin by reorganizing the "data" found in the biblical text into three different groupings. The first would include a description of the grammatical and rhetorical peculiarities of the Hebrew language, in which the Bible was originally written, or in the case of the Greek New Testament, on which it was evidently modeled. Subsequently he suggests how such a list might look in part, by way of enumerating the practical difficulties facing anyone in search of a satisfactory grasp of biblical Hebrew: there are words and phrases whose meaning we cannot know easily, since no Hebrew dictionaries, grammar books, or rhetoric manuals survive from ancient times; there are features of Hebrew spelling, syntax, and verbs that allow for confusions or ambiguities; also, the utter absence of vowels and punctuation in the biblical text gives rise to further ambiguities. The immediate practical result of this list is to place the biblical text at a distance, to make what has long been familiar to Spinoza's sectarian reader suddenly unfamiliar, to transform traditional certainties into scholarly uncertainties so that certainty may then be restored on Spinoza's new and untraditional terms. What look like matters of style thus prove to be matters of substance as well. That is, Spinoza's method is not innocent of theological and political implications.

To focus on the peculiarities of biblical Hebrew is to focus on the limitations of what can be learned about—or from—what is written in that language, and hence to weaken our habitual attachment to anything written in that language. A further example, which Spinoza in passing has already called attention to in the opening chapter of the *Theologico-Political Treatise,* must surely be included in the list. "The Jews," he says, "never make mention of intermediary or particular causes, nor care about them, but, for the sake of religion and piety or (as is wont to be said by the vulgar) of devotion, they always have recourse to God" (1.16.33–17.1 [E15; S60]). In other words, pious Jews ignore natural causes, as when they say (to use Spinoza's illustrations) that God has brought them money when they mean that they have made a business profit, or that God has disposed their hearts to-ward something when they mean that they desire it, or that God has said something to them when they mean that they themselves have thought it. To take only this last illustration: it is not difficult to see something of the weakening of the Bible's traditional authority which would result among its devotees if the "theological" expression (that God has said something) were in every instance, or even in a consid-erable number of instances, translated into its "natural" equivalent.

The second group of biblical data to be gathered according to Spinoza's method is the authoritative "tenets"[15] expressed in each of the biblical books. These are to be tabulated by subject matter for easy reference. Among them must be noted any that appear obscure, am-biguous, or mutually contrary — the potential sources of theological conflict. Apparent obscurities, and so on, are to be investigated exclu-sively in terms of the meaning of the given expression within the biblical setting, not in terms of its truth or reasonableness outside that setting. Spinoza explicitly warns against "confus[ing]" the true mean-ing with the truth of things" (7.100.19f. [E101; S143]). Meaning here is reduced to a matter of linguistic usage. Spinoza illustrates this point by citing two "tenets" that the biblical text attributes to Moses, yet which at first glance are obscure and even false: "God is fire" and "God is jealous" (7.100.21–101.25 [E101–103; S143–44]).[16] He notes, among other things, that "God is fire" evidently contradicts Moses' more frequently repeated "tenet" that God has no resem-blance to visible things. One way to begin to resolve that contradic-tion, he admits, would be to speculate that "God is fire" is metaphori-cal. But for the political reasons already indicated, Spinoza would rather not have potentially volatile biblical controversies decided on the basis of mere — disputable — speculation. Appeals to the authority of the text must instead be unanswerable. Therefore he proceeds to show that "God is fire" is metaphorical by way of establishing the equivalence of "fire" with "jealousy," on the strength of their identi-fication at Job 31:12. Practically speaking, Spinoza's procedure would have the usefulness of cultivating the scientifically salutary habit of searching for incontrovertible evidence, while at the same time weed-ing out the politically dangerous habit of indulging in raw speculation on theologically sensitive issues. We may go even further and say that his method as a whole rests on the premise, touched on lightly in the course of his discussion, that human reasoning, when left to speculate on its own, is naturally inseparable from "prejudices," that is, from political passions (7.100.16–19 [E101; S143]). From this circumstance alone, even apart from the particulars of the biblical text, reason would seem to warrant methodological guidance.

Spinoza's third and last step in grouping the biblical data requires compiling a case history of each of the biblical books. It would consist of the recorded details of each author's life, mores, and concerns (7.101.27f. [E103; S144]), including who he was, and why and when and for whom he wrote, as well as in what language. There is in addition a need for each book's subsequent "fortune": "namely, how it was first received and into whose hands it fell, then how many variant readings it had, and by whose counsel it was received among the holy and then how all the books that everyone now admits as being holy coalesced into one body" (7.101.30–34 [E103; S144]). According to Spinoza, the biographical information is necessary in order to know "which opinions are proffered as laws and which as moral teachings [i.e., as practical advice intended for a particular time]" — especially since "we can explain someone's words more easily, the better we know his mind and character" (7.101.35–102.4 [E103; S144f.]). Again, Spinoza takes for granted that what "someone" teaches, even or especially if he is a biblical author, can scarcely be separated from the self-interested passions that motivate most human beings most of the time. This assumption would preclude any serious attempt to understand even the most reasonable of authors strictly by their own lights. Spinoza leaves us here to wonder whether or how the Bible's own way of presenting self-interested human beings might nevertheless be instructive for readers at all times. In any event, the bibliographical information concerning each book's composition and circulation, by calling attention to corruptions, copyists' errors, and other textual alterations, would also have the practical effect of casting doubt on the Bible's ostensive claim to timeless authority over its adherents. The political importance of any theological debate over the meaning of the biblical teaching is thereby diminished as well.

Spinoza's subsequent procedure for inferring the "certain . . . principles" contained in the Bible from the foregoing data is deliberately modeled on what he takes to be the method of natural science. Natural science, he says, begins by studying the "most universal" things, which are "common to the whole of nature" (7.102.22ff. [E104; S145]). These are motion and rest, whose "laws and rules" can be known with the most certainty because they describe how nature is seen to behave "always" and "continually" (ibid.). From there, scientific investigation proceeds "gradually" to what occurs less frequently, while preserving certainty at each stage by considering the less frequent as a variant or concomitant of the more frequent. Thus the laws describing the motion and rest of particular things are derived from those describing the constant motion and rest of things in general. Investigating the Bible for Spinoza is similar. The investigation takes its bearings by "what is most universal and what is the basis and foundation of the whole of Scripture" — in other words, "what . . . is commended by all [*sic*] the prophets as an eternal teaching and [the one] most useful for all mortals" (7.102.26ff. [E104; S145]). Examples of notions that the Bible everywhere teaches include: that a single and omnipotent God exists, that He alone is to be worshiped, that He cares for everyone, and that He esteems above all those who worship Him and love their neighbor as themselves. These are to be distinguished from notions over which various prophets more or less disagree, notions such as what God is and by what plan He sees and provides for all things. In Spinoza's scheme, the former notions, being the most agreed upon, are most certain because most frequent, and so have the most compelling prima facie claim to be considered the Bible's fundamental teaching. The latter, being notions that are less agreed upon, are proportionately less frequent, less certain, and therefore less fundamental. Least fundamental of all are the particular revelations or visions that come to one prophet rather than another and which Spinoza therefore comes to consider peripheral to the teaching of the Bible as a whole and explainable rather in terms of the psychology of the individual prophet.

Now the general difficulty that results from strict adherence to Spinoza's method may begin to be seen as follows. By focusing attention primarily on the "tenets" expressed in the Bible according to subject matter, Spinoza implies that the Bible's own arrangement of those "tenets" is negligible. He atomizes the biblical text. That is, he reduces it to its putatively simplest elements, in order to make possible a certainty or predictability about the Bible that would remain immune to any raging theological controversies based on an appeal to the Bible. At the same time, he tries to render such controversies harmless to public life by establishing the widest possible agreement on the meaning of the biblical text. Scientific certainty about the Bible would thus free Spinoza's reader from the sectarian authority of the Bible. By requiring as the price of that certainty a rearrangement of the "tenets" of the Bible from the Bible's own arrangement, Spinoza would in effect substitute an encyclopedia of biblical "tenets," classified and explained as something historically removed from the reader, for the Bible taken in its own terms. To make of the Bible ancient history in that way is to divest it of the immediate authority that the various sects variously attribute to it—or perhaps discover in it. Yet just this last alternative, namely whether the Bible's authority is merely imputed or somehow deserved, is a question to which the reader of the *Theologico-Political Treatise* eventually becomes alerted but which he cannot answer on the basis of Spinoza's method alone. Spinoza's own answer, though implicit in the preliminary considerations by which he justifies his recourse to method in chapter 7, awaits a fuller discussion outside the consideration of method proper.

৵ IV ৵

Evidently what is at stake in Spinoza's discussion of how to read the Bible is not merely a scholarly issue of concern mostly to antiquarians, any more than is the theological dispute between Shylock and Antonio. Its practical implications have to do with whether or how the reader's way of life—Shylock's Judaism or Antonio's Christianity, for example—receives support from the biblical text, looked on as the highest moral authority. Theological controversy over the

Bible's meaning is thus tantamount to moral controversy, and unresolved differences of opinion to moral chaos leading to civil discord. Spinoza's method, on the other hand, promises to restore civil order. It does so by seeking to reduce the need for theological interpretation of the biblical text altogether. It focuses instead on those elements of the text about whose meaning all readers can more or less agree, while overlooking for the moment any further theological meanings that readers might be inclined to attribute to the text but which would (so far as Spinoza is concerned) prove speculative and so breed controversy. Spinoza's premise here is that any interpretation, no matter how erudite, which takes its bearings largely by theological suggestions supplied by the Bible itself is in principle unable to win agreement among readers of the Bible. The Bible has no notion of "nature." Its authors lack awareness of an impersonal, unchanging, self-subsistent order that would make the incidents they narrate intelligible. The narratives are therefore guided by little more than the self-interested passions, chiefly the hopes and fears, of their authors. It is for this reason that Spinoza must maintain that order or intelligibility cannot in the last analysis be found in the biblical text but must be imposed by method. Even so, unwarranted theological inferences from the Bible, which presume more intelligibility than is available there, remain an inveterate habit. Biblical theology therefore needs to be brought under control as well. Otherwise political life could never be made safe from the crowd-stirring excesses of enthusiastic yet fraudulent eisegetes, that is, of sectarian teachers and preachers of the Bible, who cannot help disagreeing among themselves and so setting their flocks in motion against one another unpeaceably.

Spinoza's first six chapters treat the following theological terms, respectively: "prophecy" or revelation, "prophets," the "calling" or choosing by God of the ancient Hebrews, "divine law," biblical "ceremonies" and "histories," and "miracles." The order of topics is a descent, chapter by chapter, from the highest and most all-inclusive to the more pointed and particular — from revelation and its spokesmen, the prophets, to divine providence and law and the like, as embodied in the Hebrews, to reports of particular miracles. First things are important, and so it is worthwhile tracing the broad implications of

Spinoza's initial remarks on prophecy for the narrower topics that follow. Here is how the first paragraph of chapter 1 reads:

> Prophecy or revelation is the certain knowledge of any matter revealed by God to human beings. A prophet, moreover, is one who interprets what is revealed of God to those who are unable to have certain knowledge of the matters revealed by God and who therefore can only embrace the matters revealed by God by mere faith. For among the Hebrews a prophet is called נביא *nabi,* that is, orator and interpreter, but in Scripture he is always taken for an interpreter of God, as is gathered from Exodus 7:1. There God says to Moses, "Behold, I constitute you the God of Pharaoh, and Aaron your brother shall be your prophet." He would say, as it were, since Aaron acts in the person of the prophet by interpreting what you will speak to Pharaoh, therefore you yourself will be, as it were, the God of Pharaoh, or one who acts in the role of God. (1.15.5–16 [E13; S59])

Spinoza thus begins his argument as a whole with definitions connecting the subject matter of his first two chapters. Although the definitions are plausible enough at face value, their untraditional and antitheological implications unfold as the chapters proceed. Prophecy is said to be a kind of "certain knowledge . . . revealed to human beings." A prophet is therefore someone who interprets what is revealed for those who are not certified knowers but can only take the prophet's word for it. Spinoza offers a single biblical proof text that confirms the definition of prophecy while implying prophecy's inferiority in rank to firsthand knowledge, and so he suggests what he will state openly in chapter 2, namely that prophecy is at bottom the work of the human imagination: if (following Spinoza's interpretation of Exod. 7:1) Moses' acting as Pharaoh's God is to be correlated with Aaron's acting as Moses' prophet, then it makes no difference whether, as in this case, the prophet interprets the secondhand words of another human being rather than the firsthand knowledge of God, since in either case he merely elaborates or embellishes a derivative report to suit the uninformed mentality of his audience. Likewise it follows that the "calling"[17] of the Hebrews, as spelled out in chapter 3 of the *Treatise,* has nothing to do with any putatively superior or distinctive knowledge of God supplied by a prophet, but, on the contrary, the term proves to be merely an imaginative way of exhorting the Hebrews to obey their political laws, in a manner befitting what Spinoza calls their "childish" mentality (3.45.24 [E44; S89]). As for Spinoza's discussion of "divine law" in chapter 4, it is prepared by the immediate sequel to the first paragraph of chapter 1, where Spinoza infers from the definition of prophecy that it does not differ at all from knowledge acquired by natural means, except that it is vulgarly imagined to be rare and of supernatural ("alien") origin (1.15.21ff. [E14; S59]): Spinoza, on the contrary, will identify divine law with the laws of physics, which he holds to be knowable with certainty, and only homonymously or derivatively with the law of Moses. The "ceremonies" and "histories" discussed in chapter 5 are also construed with reference to Moses' law, but only as political devices for strengthening the Hebrews' devotion to it. Finally, "miracles" are said to be exceptions to the laws of nature, but since such exceptions are impossible in reality, they must therefore be understood from a simply human viewpoint, as figments of the human imagination.

To the extent that Spinoza's deliberate revision of traditional theology is made for the sake of his peacekeeping efforts among rival theologians, as I have suggested, it is based not on any sectarian tendencies but on an appeal to nature. More exactly, Spinoza argues by analogy with what can be known with certainty about nature, just as he does in chapter 7 when devising a method for interpreting the biblical text proper. Certainty in both instances means predictability, or incontrovertible expectation.

Just as in interpreting the biblical text what is least controvertible is that it consists of various "opinions," so in interpreting the content of those "opinions," or the revelations themselves as announced by the prophets, what is least controvertible, he argues, is that they are all products of the prophets' highly developed imagination. His argument is that experience shows an inverse ratio between the power of understanding and the power of imagining in human minds, such that "those who are most powerful in imagination are least apt at purely understanding things, and on the contrary those who are more powerful in understanding and cultivate it most have a power of imagining [which is] more tempered and more under control, and they hold it in rein, as it were, lest it be confused with understanding" (2.29.25–29 [E27; S73]). Accordingly, the biblical narratives, too, speak of men of outstanding wisdom or prudence, such as Solomon and others, who nevertheless lack any "prophetic gift," whereas even Abraham's untutored handmaid Hagar is endowed with that gift. It is worth noting that Spinoza's argument here takes its bearings by the extreme alternatives — either understanding or imagination, either wisdom or prophecy — and so seems to neglect the more pertinent and intriguing possibilities of prophets or other human beings (such as himself?) who might have both understanding and imagination; Spinoza evidently assumes that the extreme cases are least controversial and looks at the others simply as variants or composites of these.

Be that as it may, the prophet's imagination is only a necessary, not a sufficient condition of prophecy. The prophets themselves admit their own uncertainty about what is revealed to them by requesting from God a sign that what they are supposed to prophesy is certain to happen. The signs may be seen to vary in turn according to what each prophet finds persuasive, in other words according to his temperament as well as to the opinions with which he has been imbued. Finally, inasmuch as certainty is not to be found in the content of the revelation as such, it can be attributed to it only on the grounds that God never deceives the pious. Hence Spinoza infers a third condition of prophecy, over and above the prophet's imagination and the requisite sign: that the prophet have "a spirit inclined only to the equitable and the good" (2.31.30f. [E29; S75]). The certainty that is found in biblical prophecy is thus no more than a "moral certainty," a credibility based on the prophet's moral excellence (2.31.23f., 32.10ff. [E29f.; S74f.]). It follows — what Spinoza is chiefly concerned to establish in order to compel agreement among theologians — that the prophet's own theological or quasi-philosophical speculations are irrelevant to his credibility and can therefore be dispensed with as peripheral to the prophet's teaching. To cite only one of Spinoza's many examples: biblical theologians should therefore discount the details of, say, Micaiah's peculiar vision of the true and false Spirit of God and the heavenly host standing on either side of God, by which he announces the true outcome of the battle between King Ahab and the Arameans (1 Kings 22), and should concentrate mainly on the announcement and its moral appropriateness.[18]

Yet to revise biblical theology as Spinoza does, by looking first and foremost to what is incontrovertible or predictable about it in order to win agreement among dissenting theologians, is to politicize theology. It is to make of theology a matter of consent, if rarified consent, among public authorities or at any rate among public sermonizers and opinion makers. Lest he be thought to be merely imposing his own political project on the biblical text, Spinoza implies a biblical precedent for his politicizing activity: The prophets, too, politicize — including Moses, the most authoritative among them, whom Spinoza here considers simply alongside the others. Moses tells the Israelites that God has chosen them for Himself above all other nations (Deut. 10:15), that He is close to them and not to others (4:4, 7), that He has prescribed just laws only for them (4:8), and that He has become known to them alone while others are merely an afterthought (4:32). Moses is thus responsible for the biblical teaching of the "calling" or chosenness of the Hebrews.

But given that a prophet communicates what is in his imagination and persuades his addressees, if at all, because of his moral, not intellectual, excellence, it follows that he cannot help speaking "to their capacity" or limited preconceptions.[19] He says what will promote their obedience to law, whether or not it furthers their understanding of things as such. So Moses promises that obedience will bring the Israelites happiness as a nation and glory over other nations, as if true happiness consisted in one's superiority to others rather than in wisdom and knowledge of truth. But Moses' promise is empty, at least insofar as nature distributes human capacities for achieving happiness more or less evenly among all nations. Hence Moses' words cannot be construed except as political rhetoric, designed to ensure the Israelites' national survival by exhorting them with images that they are likely to grasp and take to heart. Even so, a passing remark by Spinoza suggests that the Israelites were, in addition, "often admonished . . . to true life and sublime speculations," though evidently to no avail (3.45.27f. [E44; S89]).[20] This remark carries the further implication that Moses, in accommodating himself to his people's capacities, must have come to see that any attempt to require of them wisdom and knowledge of truth would most likely fail, and that he therefore deliberately lowered the expectations that the law might otherwise have been intended to serve, in order that those expectations might be met more easily — an accommodation that Spinoza in his own way may be seen to imitate.

Spinoza's theological task is similar to, though not quite the same as, Moses'. Like Moses, he too faces the intellectual incompetence of his contemporaries, who fail to respond or to agree where what we might call sophisticated theological understanding — as opposed to mere "superstition"[21] — is called for. Spinoza's solution followed Moses' lead in seeking to ease public life of the burden of superstitious controversies. As we shall see more fully later on, Spinoza, like Moses, would remove from the law any insistence on theological conformity beyond a few simple dogmas. (These are the ones most frequently and evidently repeated in the biblical narratives, in the manner I have already shown in connection with Spinoza's discussion in chapter 7 of the *Treatise* concerning how to read the Bible.) Instead of theological sophistication, then, the law would require of fellow citizens only the practice of justice and charity, understood in the manner I have already indicated. About these elementary practical things, Spinoza assumes, all human beings can more or less agree.

Yet in his overall endeavor, Moses' law could guide him only part way. Not only does Moses himself not appear to have anticipated the rise of competing sectarian theologies, but also Moses' purely political solution has lost the force of its immediate authority with the demise of the ancient Jewish polity.[22] Spinoza, unlike Moses, must therefore confront the warring theologians directly, by arming himself with the compelling certainties of modern natural science. Spinoza's strategy here is evident in his sophisticated reinterpretation of the term *divine law*. In its sophisticated meaning, we learn, it refers to how human beings by their own powers can acquire a knowledge of God which is intellectually certain. Such certainty is made possible by acquaintance with the laws of physics and their implications, inasmuch as everything in nature may accordingly be seen to depend on God for its existence and intelligibility: "not only since without God nothing can be or be conceived, but also since we can doubt everything so long as we have no clear and distinct idea of God" (4.59.34–60.1 [E59; S103]). Still, those who are willing and able to live up to the intellectual demands of acquiring this kind of certainty are few and far between: to expect most human beings to follow the divine law in this sense of the term (which for emphasis Spinoza calls the "natural" divine law) is unrealistic, and therefore theologians must, like Moses, lower their expectations of human beings and forbear trying to convert them. There remains, then, the "divine law" in the more traditional sense of the term, namely the law of Moses, which, however, may only "be called . . . divine," since it is not "universal" or designed for all human beings but has been "accommodated fully to the character and the unique preservation of one people," although we nevertheless "believe it to have been sanctified by the prophetic light" (4.61.16–20 [E61; S104]).[23] Obviously, this last remark is to be understood in accord with Spinoza's critique of biblical prophecy — its reduction to simple justice and charity — which we have been considering all along.

The practical upshot of Spinoza's elaborate theological argument is thus to offer theologians a choice between two politically harmless alternatives. On the one hand, he outlines for them a sophisticated theology that is admittedly out of reach of the unintellectual many, yet whose promise of intellectual certainty offers a safe refuge for the few above the battlefields of sectarian theological wars. Readers who take this direction are less likely to be moved by the sectarian passions governing noisy pulpits and assemblies and more likely to become absorbed in the philosophical theorizing to be found in the quiet study of such books as Spinoza's own *Ethics Demonstrated in a Geometrical Order* or *Principles of René Descartes' Philosophy*. On the other hand, Spinoza purveys a streamlined biblical piety, purified of any need for speculation or occasion for controversy. It is all (as I have said) justice and charity. Consistent with this new piety, biblical "ceremonies" and "histories" are to be understood in terms of their original, if superannuated, political function, as means for inducing the people to obey the law from motives of spontaneous devotion rather than from fear of punishment. Spinoza even suggests a new pastoral or ministerial role for erstwhile theologians in place of their old conversion-seeking polemicizing: as popularizers of Spinoza's new way of understanding things for the unphilosophical many.[24]

The last direct link to the old, pre-Spinozist piety in Spinoza's argument is the notion of "miracles." It too must be severed, and the connection rerouted. Otherwise his carefully devised appeal to the certainties or regularities of nature as the solid basis from which all theologians might begin to see eye to eye could easily be set aside on the grounds that "prophecy," the "calling" of the Hebrews, "divine law," and so forth betoken unique divine interventions into human affairs and imply that the biblical accounts must be read in the old-fashioned way after all, putting the old sectarian wars in motion once more. Spinoza's argument here is fourfold: nothing can happen contrary to the external, fixed and immutable order of nature; miracles, even if they were to occur, do not tell us about the existence or essence or providence of God, whereas the orderliness of nature does; by God's decrees and volitions and providence, the Bible itself understands nothing more than the order of nature as it follows God's eternal laws; and finally, the notion of "miracle" is in origin only a Hebraism—a way of referring events immediately to God, given the aforementioned absence of "nature" in the Bible.

To Spinoza, then, *miracle* is virtually a psychological term, an indicator that the speaker does not know the causes of what he is talking about, as the very definition of the term implies: "a work that cannot be explained through a cause, that is, a work that exceeds human capacity" (6.85.17f. [E85; S128]). Still, this does not mean that one might not be more or less open to understanding the cause of the event in question. In line with his general Baconian approach, Spinoza implies that understanding the cause means looking to see the particular event in question as an instance of the universal laws of nature. At the same time, his appeal to laws of nature as the necessary and sufficient replacement for—all—reported miracles is, in the *Theologico-Political Treatise* at least, largely a promissory note, dependent in turn on the credit of his sources. Spinoza tacitly endorses the modern scientific project as announced by his quondam authority Descartes, who speaks of making mankind like the masters and owners of nature, as well as by Descartes's own trailblazer, Bacon, who speaks of the conquest of nature for the relief of man's estate.[25] But if so, then we might well wonder whether Spinoza in turn does not appeal to nature so much as to the desirability of the way of life that looks to the possibility of mankind's mastering nature, as we have already seen it set forth in Bacon's *New Atlantis*—to a project, therefore, rather than a *fait accompli*. Inasmuch as Spinoza's entire new piety thereby rests on a plan or program that is, for him as for us, as yet not fully tested or confirmed in practice (for we have not yet fully succeeded in mastering nature), we cannot make a proper judgment on the merits of that new piety before turning to examine the practical ins and outs of the political strand of Spinoza's argument in the concluding chapters of his *Treatise*.

꙳ **V** ꙳

Liberal democracy is, for Spinoza, the necessary complement to his philological and theological critique of the Bible. His critique, we recall, began in effect from the premise that to swallow the Bible whole, as the various competing sectarian theologians of Spinoza's day claimed to do, was to court political instability, so long as biblical religion formed the social bond. Only by means of a political argument proper could Spinoza then trace the broad outlines of the way of life that would replace the old conflict-ridden way and remove the old-fashioned theologians from centerstage to the margins of political life. Since Spinoza found the old way rooted in the moral authority of the Old Testament prophets, and ultimately in Moses, looked on as the greatest of the prophets, his critique is driven at bottom by the need to neutralize their authority so far as possible in the minds of his readers, in favor of modern science. Still, his readers' habit of deferring to them is long ingrained, and it is therefore not surprising that "prophets" — now redefined in terms of Spinoza's scientific critique — continue to figure in the argument of the *Treatise*'s final chapters. In the circumstances I have been pointing out concerning Spinoza's argument as a whole, it may therefore be said that prophets are for Spinoza the biblical equivalent of the sectarian theologians whose destabilizing influence on political life he has been trying to remove all along. Generally speaking, by encouraging false political hopes in their hearers, they obscure political life and so prevent the peace and harmony that political life might be counted on to provide if only our sights were narrowed so as to exclude them from unwarranted political influence. Spinoza's argument for liberal democracy and against biblical prophecy thus partakes of the new — if morally problematic — realism prefigured for him in Bacon as well as in Machiavelli, the political-philosophical authority whom both Bacon and he happen to share with Marlowe.[26]

Let us now see how Spinoza's final discrediting of "prophets" during the culmination of his specifically theological discussion in the *Treatise* (chaps. 13–15) prepares the way for his specifically political discussion (chaps. 16–20). There he draws two important theological conclusions. The first is summarized somewhat elliptically in the following passage:

> Just as faith was once revealed and written according to the capacity and opinions of the prophets and of the vulgar of that time, so even now anyone is bound to accommodate it to his own opinions. (14.178.35–179.2 [E188; S225])

Spinoza's words have a typically pious gloss to them but become doubt provoking on reflection. His argument is that, as the prophets once accommodated their "faith" — that is, as we have already learned from Spinoza, their common commitment to justice and charity — to their own capacity and opinions, so we are "bound" to imitate them by accommodating it likewise to our capacity and opinions. Remarkably, by the time we finish reading Spinoza's sentence, our being "bound" to the prophets' faith turns out to mean our being free to adapt it to whatever opinions we wish. How it is that we remain "bound" to them, then, is not entirely clear.

Spinoza has presumably solved this problem for us in a practical way by distilling that faith into seven easy-to-assimilate "dogmas" (14.177.4–178.10 [E186f.; S224f.]): (1) that a supremely just and merciful God exists; (2) that He alone requires our highest devotion, wonder, and love; (3) that He is everywhere; (4) that He is all-powerful; (5) that worshiping and obeying Him consist solely in justice and charity, or in love of neighbor; (6) that such worship alone brings salvation whereas submitting to pleasure brings perdition; and (7) that God pardons the sins of those who repent. Together these seven dogmas constitute a "catholic or universal faith," which is "binding" in the first instance by being necessarily acceptable to all sects because it is the common denominator of the biblical teaching as arrived at in the manner already described in Spinoza's discussion of method. And yet even this quasi-theological warrant may prove superfluous, inasmuch as subscribing to those dogmas would seem to be in the self-interest of any law-abiding citizen quite independently of their putative biblical basis. As we shall soon see, Spinoza will go on to argue that law-abidingness is most effectively based on self-interest alone. From this viewpoint, Spinoza's seven dogmas are perhaps better described as the minimal requirements of civic decency for anyone who has been in the habit of looking to the Bible for moral instruction. But if so, then one is "bound" to them no more than as one is bound — or tends — to one's own self-interest.

The second theological conclusion that Spinoza draws from the "prophets" weakens even further our need to defer to them. His argument here resembles the one just quoted and invites a similar interpretation:

> Since we see that the prophets commend charity and justice above all and do not intend anything else, we here conclude that they have taught not with malicious cunning but from a true spirit that human beings become blessèd by obedience and faith, and since moreover they have confirmed this by signs, we are here persuaded that they have not said it rashly, nor

were delirious when they prophesied; in which we are even more confirmed when we pay attention to the fact that they have taught nothing
[in the way of] moral[s] which would not agree most plainly with
reason; for it is not rashly that the word of God in the prophets would
agree altogether with the same word of God speaking in ourselves. But
these things, I say, we are equally certain of from the Bible, as the Jews
once concluded these same things from the live voice of the prophets.
(15.186.25–187.1 [E197; S234])

The context of this passage is the overall argument of chapter 15
concerning the need to keep theology separate from philosophy and
vice versa, so that neither one is used — or, in Spinoza's view, mis-
used — as handmaid to the other. It is this very theme that connects
Spinoza's professedly unphilosophical (or nonspeculative) treatment
of theology with his philosophical (or nontheological) treatment of
politics. It is in fact the stated theme of the *Theologico-Political Treatise*
as a whole.[27] Accordingly, to argue as this passage does that we are
just as "certain" as the prophets were concerning the basic teaching of
the Bible is to imply that we hardly need a philosophical or speculative defense of that teaching for our purposes, any more than they did
for theirs. We should simply follow the example of the prophets'
original audience, and let ourselves judge what is charitable and just
by our own capacities as best we can without necessarily consulting
them any further.

Following these ground-clearing theological considerations, Spinoza argues in the specifically political chapters of the *Treatise* that the
foundations of the best political society are to be established quite
independently of religion. He goes so far as to grant political authorities the sole right to decide in all matters concerning the public exercise of religion and denies in principle that they are "bound" by any
religious claims whatever. He appeals throughout to the "natural
right" of human beings (16.189.8–199.34 [E200–13; S237–48]). It
is, he says, the same as the natural right of all things, which is simply
to preserve themselves insofar as they have the power to do so. Hence
right is identical with might, and in their "natural state" human
beings are driven wholly by their private desires and are free in that

sense to do whatever they may deem conducive to their self-interest in satisfying those desires.[28] The burden of Spinoza's argument here is to show that a political society that takes its bearings by "natural" freedom or self-interest is more effective in promoting the ends it is intended to serve than is the biblical or biblically inspired alternative.

Political society, accordingly, is said to originate in a freely chosen agreement or covenant among individual human beings who have come to see the conflicts, frustrations, and general insecurity that result when all pursue their private desires on their own, and who therefore decide to transfer their right or power of self-preservation to a "sovereign power" of their choosing. Because the sovereign's purpose is to protect its subjects from themselves and others, while at the same time conceding back to them as much of their "natural" freedom as may be consistent with their living "harmoniously and peacefully," it will in the best case be a democracy—an elected assembly whose members regularly consult among themselves and with their constituents for that purpose (16.193.19–194.24 [E206f.; S243f.]). Spinoza's denial that the claims of religion have in principle any force over against the sovereign seems to be made not so much to restrict the "natural" freedom of its subjects, but to preserve its own effectiveness—as may be gathered from the fact that he allows for an exception. The exception is "a prophet who would be expressly sent by God and who would show it by indubitable signs" (16.199.7f. [E211; S247]). Apart from the theoretical implication just mentioned, however, Spinoza does not appear to consider this exception a serious practical possibility, for not only has he made a point of admitting in his opening chapter that "we have no prophets nowadays that I know of" (1.16.29f. [E14; S60]), but also the stipulated requirement of "indubitable signs" seems unlikely to be met in an age when sectarian discord is as great as the *Treatise* makes it out to be.

By now it might be expected that all mention of "prophets" would vanish from Spinoza's political chapters. But not so. "Prophets" come up repeatedly during his lengthy critique of the biblical polity in these chapters, the point of which would seem to be to confirm by way of contrast the merits of his account of the best (democratic) polity. Prophets are shown to be inherently seditious (chap. 17), largely ineffective (chap. 18), and presumably unnecessary in a properly organized polity (chap. 19). Chapter 17, for example, takes up the theme of the preceding chapter that the right of the sovereign remains unimpeded by any other right except that of a "prophet" by reassuring the reader that for all practical purposes the sovereign will nevertheless have to stop short of intruding altogether on the freedom of its subjects. Hence, especially in a democratic regime, there will be few if any popular complaints sufficiently radical to justify the protests of would-be prophets. The reason is that political rule, democratic or otherwise, depends not only on force but also on persuasion. It follows that any sovereign must leave subjects free enough to win consent to its decrees.

In contrast, because of its theological origins, the biblical polity soon deteriorated to a point where its failures to win popular consent made prophets inevitable. According to Spinoza, the biblical polity originated shortly after the Hebrews' exodus from Egypt when, no longer bound by Egyptian law, each individual freely transferred his natural right or power of self-preservation to God (see Exod. 24:7) in order to establish a "theocracy," that is, a regime where God was to be the sole ruler, where all had an equal right to consult Him, and consequently where there would be no difference between civil and religious law or between patriotism and piety. But the original theocracy had to be modified almost immediately, for the Hebrews grew terrified at the prospect of facing God directly and insisted that Moses himself be their go-between, and in so doing they outlawed all other prophets while Moses was alive (see Num. 11:28). Instead of choosing a single successor to himself, Moses arranged to divide his powers, on the one hand, among the Levites and the Aaronide priests, who were to administer the sacred ceremonies, and on the other hand, among the popularly elected "princes"[29] of each remaining tribe, who were to administer all matters of war and peace for their tribes — except during military emergencies, when a supreme commander was chosen, while the people themselves "swore faith not to the commander nor to the high priests but to the Religion or God" (17.209.7ff. [E223; S258]). Yet Moses' elaborate arrangement proved defective almost from the start, for the people began to resent the privileges of the Levites and priests — actually an afterthought in retaliation for the Israelites' forbidden worship of the golden calf (cf. Num. 8:17) — and although their resulting desert rebellions were quickly put down, a spirit of rebelliousness and stubbornness long remained (see Deut. 31:21) and led to generations of political disorder. The eventual establishment of kings for the sake of imposing order, moreover, supplied "huge material for new seditions, from which there followed at long last the ruin of the whole imperium" (17.219.33–35 [E235; S269]), aided and abetted, Spinoza adds, by increasing numbers of prophets, who with their powers of persuasion were now sought out and manipulated by kings and would-be kings alike in the ensuing discords and civil wars.

Add to the foregoing that the prophets' outspoken protests against the kings and others could not but contribute to the general confusion. Unlike the kings, who had official authority and means of coercion, the prophets were simply "private men," who "irritated rather than corrected men" when moralizing against them (18.223.23–25 [E239; S274]). This observation is first made in chapter 18. There Spinoza derives several "political dogmas" or pointers from his analysis of the biblical polity (18.221.14–225.11 [E237–41; S272–75]).[30] The observation is one of five such pointers, of which only the first two are said to be matters worth imitating: (1) the need to choose a supreme political authority (such as Moses while he was alive); and (2) the need to keep the theological interpreters of the law (the "ministers of the sacred," i.e., the priests) from judging or excommunicating citizens (a role that Moses left strictly to the popularly elected princes). Spinoza's three other pointers concern political errors that came from the failure to stick to the first two: (3) conflicting religious "sects" arose only when priests usurped the political authority of princes and mixed theological with political functions; (4) the prophets compounded confusion by mixing in as "private men"; and (5) kingship itself was a subsequent expedient for which the laws of Moses had not adequately prepared the people.

In general, for reasons both theological and political, Spinoza does not find the biblical polity worth imitating at all. Theologically, he argues, any attempt to reinstate it in its entirety would require a new covenant between God and those who wished to transfer their right of self-preservation to Him. But God has already indicated an unwillingness to accept that transfer by having revealed through the Apostles (i.e., so far as the Christian addressee of the *Treatise* is concerned) that His covenant is no longer written in ink or on stone tablets "but by God's spirit in the [human] heart" (18.221.24 [E237; S272]). Politically, moreover, Moses' laws "could perhaps only be useful" for a people who would dwell in isolation, "who wished to live to themselves alone without external commerce and close themselves within their own limits and be segregated from the rest of the globe, and hardly for those for whom it is necessary to have commerce with others" (18.221.25–28 [E237; S272]). On the contrary, "commerce"—both in the sense of trade and in the sense of a cosmopolitanism leading to the cultivation of the arts, natural science, and philosophy—would appear to be *the* political desideratum whereby Spinoza holds that the biblical law in its entirety is no longer suitable for the reader of the *Treatise*. Inasmuch as Spinoza's argument would thereby assume and encourage a predisposition to that "commerce" in his reader, I must conclude my comments on Spinoza by considering how it may be seen to underlie his two final references to "prophets" in chapter 19 of the *Treatise* and by implication all his previous references as well.

Chapter 19 argues that "prophets" are unnecessary in a properly organized political society. Here the sovereign, especially a democratic sovereign, has the exclusive right to set policy concerning religious worship. Much of Spinoza's argument here has already been anticipated in the foregoing, including his implicit assurance that, for the practical purpose of maintaining the consent of its subjects, the sovereign will be inclined to tolerate all sects that conform to the principles of Spinoza's all-purpose "catholic or universal faith." What is new, however, is the explicit suggestion that Spinoza's remarks about "prophets" are meant to be taken analogously for their bearing on "Christian imperiums" in the reader's own time. The suggestion occurs in connection with the first of his two remarks on "prophets" in this chapter, to which the second is a kind of reply. In the first remark, Spinoza repeats the observation made in chapter 18 that the prophets as "private men" were ineffective in moralizing to the people, whereas the kings backed by force were effective. Now he adds that the failures of the prophets and other religious leaders left only the kings to take religious matters in hand, even though technically it meant contravening the checks and balances inherent in Moses' law. Hence, "the kings themselves, merely from the fact that this right did not belong to them absolutely, most often broke with religion, and almost the whole people with them, which has obviously happened also in Christian imperiums from the same cause" (19.236.6–9 [E253; S287]).

Spinoza's argument amounts to a counsel of political prudence for a sectarian age, when the teaching of morality is in the hands of "prophet"-like spokesmen, who unfortunately tend to be theologically incompetent, politically disruptive, and arguably dispensable. Whereas one cannot always trust the "ministers of the sacred" to live up to their profession, he infers, one can usually trust sovereigns, whether biblical or Christian, to seek to preserve their own power as effectively as possible. Hence Spinoza's second remark about biblical "prophets" is at the same time advice to Christian sovereigns about how to increase their effectiveness. He reminds his reader that, given the complications of Moses' law, only the prophets' power of claiming a special revelation to pardon possible regicides stood in the way of the biblical kings' effectively taking control of the priests during those increasingly corrupt times when only the imposition of political power could restore order (19.238.20, 33 [E256; S290]). The lesson to be learned is that such artificial impediments may be avoided nowadays by keeping religious dogma simple — a right that, as we have already seen, Spinoza leaves entirely to the sovereign, albeit with the suggested "catholic or universal" guidelines. No longer constrained to listen to elaborate theological subtleties or crudities preached by incompetent spokesmen, then, citizens would be free to do something more productive with their time. Given the encouragement and tolerance of the sovereign, and without the ineffective castigations of the preachers, they could instead pursue "commerce" in both meanings of the term. And progress in that direction might gradually make citizens more receptive as well to the teachings of the artists, scientists, and philosophers who would also flourish under the increased political tolerance — if not to the teaching of the one philosopher who meanwhile aims to address their most urgent theological and political needs: Spinoza.

ᲙᲮ VI ᲙᲮ

We have at last reached the point of convergence between Spinoza's argument and the views of those scholars with whom we began in our attempt to come to terms with Shakespeare's Shylock. Where both meet is in Spinoza's all-too-brief description of the city of Amsterdam, which forms the epigraph to the present chapter (20.245.35–246.11 [E264; S298]). Amsterdam is the model of political and religious tolerance, according to Spinoza. It is a cosmopolitan and commercial city, whose inhabitants "of whatever nation and sect" live together "with the greatest harmony." Because commerce has all but displaced religion as the social bond in Spinoza's Amsterdam, human beings there are said to look on one another simply as potential business associates and to ask only whether someone is rich or poor and "is wont to act in good faith or by cunning." Religion is by and large irrelevant to their mutual assessments of themselves. Instead adherents of even the most "hateful" religious sect, "so long as they harm no one and pay each what is owed and live honestly," receive the full protection of the law. Surely such a city would allow political outsiders such as Shylock to flourish and would prevent would-be Antonios from hurling religious slanders against them: surely it would satisfy by and large the longings for political tolerance which guide the modern scholars represented in my first chapter.

Still, it is one thing to show, as I have tried to do, that the views of those scholars have a prehistory or genesis in Spinoza's work. It is another thing to show that Shakespeare's own views are superior to theirs, as I promised. To this end, let us reformulate the original question: Why does Shakespeare write *The Merchant of Venice* rather than, say, *The Merchant of Amsterdam?*

I have already indicated something of my answer to this question while remarking on the transitional character of political and religious life in Shakespeare's play. His Venice may be described as either a commercial city with a Christian heritage (or cultural lag, as a latter-day Spinozist might put it nowadays) or a Christian city with an up-and-coming commercial future. But Spinoza's Amsterdam, to judge by his brief description of it, has become a commercial city pure and simple, the *terminus ad quem* of his political argument. It follows that the conflict between the old theologico-political arrangements, which are the point of departure for Spinoza's argument, and the new Amsterdam, which is its goal, is a conflict that we have come to discover within Shakespeare's Venice itself. Here is a philosophical advantage that Shakespeare's play has over Spinoza's *Treatise.* In preparing us for the merits of his Amsterdam throughout the argument of the *Treatise,* Spinoza speaks as a partisan, reducing the broad theological and political issues that he raises to the narrower requirements of his practical solution. In the end, he is something of a political pamphleteer and publicist writing about his hometown. Shakespeare, on the other hand, cannot be said to write as, say, an ideological advocate of his Venice, for he writes in the first instance rather as a distant, English-speaking observer. Even so, he writes knowingly of a city whose deep religious and political crises are just now surfacing in its denizens' lives. Shakespeare as author makes himself the thoughtful beholder of those crises, so as to dramatize them for the benefit as well as the enjoyment of his English-speaking audience.

To see how Shakespeare displays for us the theologico-political principles subsequently found in Spinoza (and the modern critics) together with their larger implications, we must return to that moment during the trial scene where Shylock is most vociferous about his rights. Shylock makes two lengthy speeches in defense of his morally shocking lawsuit in quest of the pound of flesh to which the penalty clause in Antonio's note appears to entitle him. The two speeches are framed, on the one hand, by the Duke's exhortation to show mercy as befits Shylock's Jewish upbringing and, on the other hand, by the arrival of the disguised Portia whose "quality of mercy" speech is soon to follow. Shylock's twin speeches are theological as well as political in substance.

The first is his direct reply to the last line of the Duke's exhortation, which has urged a "gentle answer" to his public plea for mercy on Antonio's behalf:

> *I have possess'd your Grace of what I purpose,*
> *And by our holy Sabbath have I sworn*
> *To have the due and forfeit of my bond.*
> *If you deny it, let the danger light*
> *Upon your charter and your city's freedom!*
> *You ask me why I rather choose to have*
> *A weight of carrion flesh than to receive*
> *Three thousand ducats. I'll not answer that!*
> *But say it is my humour, is it answer'd?*
> *What if my house be troubled with a rat,*
> *And I be pleas'd to give ten thousand ducats*
> *To have it ban'd? What, are you answer'd yet?*
> *Some men there are love not a gaping pig,*
> *Some that are mad if they behold a cat,*
> *And others, when the bagpipe sings i' th' nose,*
> *Cannot contain their urine; for affection,*
> *Mistress of passion, sways it to the mood*
> *Of what it likes or loathes. Now for your answer:*
> *As there is no firm reason to be rend'red*
> *Why he cannot abide a gaping pig,*
> *Why he a harmless necessary cat,*
> *Why he a woollen bagpipe — but of force*
> *Must yield to such inevitable shame*
> *As to offend himself, being offended;*
> *So I can give no reason, nor will I not,*
> *More than a lodg'd hate and a certain loathing*
> *I bear Antonio, that I follow thus*
> *A losing suit against him. Are you answer'd?*   (*IV.i.35–63*)

Shylock's answer is congruent with what we already know of him from his "I am a Jew" speech and elsewhere. Here, as in his earlier disputation with Antonio on the Rialto, he starts from a theological premise. He has sworn an oath, he says, "by our holy Sabbath" to collect both principal and penalty on Antonio's note. Leaving aside Shylock's possible religious hypocrisy, it is a bit strange that he swears by the Jewish day of rest rather than, say, by his wife's grave or by the biblical God common to his hearers — though this last might well violate what remains of Shylock's Jewish scruples against profaning God's name, and his wife's grave might seem too inconsequential for his immediate purpose, whereas we already know that Shylock transacts business at his synagogue (see III.ii.109–14), and we may therefore infer that he is intending to flaunt this fact — the connection between his business and his Jewishness — now that it is safely protected from recriminations (so he thinks) by Venetian law.

At any rate, he takes his bearings by the "freedom" he finds afforded by the law. It is, as he sees it, the freedom simply to indulge his private preferences or whims. He equates his preference for a "weight of carrion flesh," as against the three thousand ducats of his principal, with four hypothetical alternatives: the decision to exterminate a rat from one's house, an idiosyncratic dislike of pigs, madness caused by seeing a cat, and urinary incontinence set off by hearing bagpipe music. All four alternatives are comparatively trivial, but we have seen something of each of them before in Shylock's behavior. Shylock spoke of "rats" (and punned on "pirates") as possible dangers to Antonio's ships, when assessing Antonio's credit rating aloud with Bassanio (I.iii.19–21). Shylock's considered willingness to eat pigs' meat at Bassanio's suggested, as he does here, that he considers the Jewish dietary laws a mere idiosyncracy (I.iii.28–33, with II.v.11–18, 35–37). And although we have not seen any maddening cats before in the play, we have seen Shylock's own creditor Tubal drive him crazy over the extravagances of his eloped daughter (III.i.70–114). Finally, I have already commented at length on the significance of Shylock's aversion to music (II.v.27–35). Together the four alternatives underscore the mercenary basis of Shylock's character — which we saw more fully during his disputation with Antonio, where his playfully equating ewes and rams with gold and silver has prepared us for his seriously blurring the difference here between (human) flesh and cash (see I.iii.63–91). Shylock's theology, if that is what his appeal to oaths amounts to, ends up conflating the trivial with the serious. But since he intends his theology to underwrite the "lodg'd hate" and "certain loathing" which he bears toward Antonio, he thereby conflates as well what is moral and what is immoral according to the very standards of Jewish law publicly admired, as I have shown, by the Duke and Portia. Shylock's personal theology partakes instead of the moral obtuseness of Marlowe's Barabas and Bacon's Joabin — and, as we shall see further in a moment, Spinoza's Amsterdam.

Shylock's second speech follows a further, one-sentence exhortation by the Duke: "How shalt thou hope for mercy, rend'ring none?" (IV.i.88) The Duke, nearing complete frustration and about to dismiss Shylock's suit on his own anyway, now waxes theological himself. Whereas Shylock's earlier speech had met the Duke's practical point (that Shylock should act in accord with the moral decency of Jewish law) by appealing to theology, his present speech meets the Duke's theological point (that Shylock should act so as to deserve God's mercy) by appealing to Venetian practice.

> *What judgement shall I dread, doing no wrong?*
> *You have among you many a purchas'd slave,*
> *Which, like your asses and your dogs and mules,*
> *You use in abject and in slavish parts,*
> *Because you bought them. Shall I say to you,*
> *"Let them be free, marry them to your heirs!*
> *Why sweat they under burdens? Let their beds*
> *Be made as soft as yours, and let their palates*
> *Be season'd with such viands"? You will answer,*
> *"The slaves are ours." So do I answer you.*
> *The pound of flesh which I demand of him*
> *Is dearly bought, 'tis mine, and I will have it.*
> *If you deny me, fie upon your law!*
> *There is no force in the decrees of Venice.*
> *I stand for judgement. Answer. Shall I have it?*   *(IV.i.89–103)*

Shylock's retort is that he does not fear any judgment that might induce him to pray for mercy, since by his own lights he is doing nothing wrong. His argument follows from his characteristic — and unbiblical — failure to distinguish between human beings and chattel goods, which we have been mindful of all along.[31] He refers to Venetians' practice of buying slaves, which, "like your asses and your dogs and mules," are then used in "abject and slavish" ways just because they now belong to the buyer.

Buyer's rights, Shylock implies, are the highest rights, and the use or abuse of private property is no one else's business. Venice's "decrees" exist simply to enforce buying and selling, that is, contracts, with no restrictions on what can be bought or contracted for. Shylock forgets for the moment that his original complaint in the play had to do with what he considered the abuse to which Antonio was putting his own private property by lending money gratis with the result that interest rates were depressed and Shylock's profits spoiled. A sign of Shylock's forgetfulness is his casual reference to "dogs" as mere property, whereas his original complaint had included the further fact that Antonio the Christian kept treating him as a dog (I.iii.106–26; III.iii.6–7). That Shylock himself does not put a simple ducat value on either Antonio's insults or his profit spoiling is shown by Shylock's continuing refusal in court to accept from Bassanio twice, thrice, or even six times his principal (IV.i.84–87, 225–28). The shortcoming of Shylock's theologico-political principles thus appears to be that they do not take into account how to rectify those private injustices that cannot quite be specified by means of publicly enforceable contracts — short of the surreptitious death penalty, which Shylock may or may not have had in mind for Antonio from the beginning.[32] Shakespeare's Duke may be baffled about how to meet Shylock's arguments on their own ground, which is why he has sent to Padua for legal help; but he is in no doubt at all about the moral unacceptability of those arguments, which is why he is about to dissolve the trial despite the bad publicity that would result for Venice's international commerce (IV.i.104–7, with III.iii.24–31). Here the Duke shows himself in moral agreement with the theologico-political principle soon to be articulated by Portia: that mercy must somehow season justice, regardless of how justice is understood.

Spinoza's Amsterdam, in contrast, is a city where religion is "of no avail at all in winning or losing a case before a judge." I may therefore conclude my argument as a whole by considering first what this phrase means for Spinoza (as well as for Shylock and, by implication, for the modern scholars whom we have cited) and afterward what it would mean for Shakespeare's Duke and Portia. As far as Spinoza is concerned, to say of his Amsterdamers, as he does, that in their business dealings they care to know only whether a fellow citizen or entrepreneur is rich or poor and is wont to act in good faith or by cunning, is not to imply simply that they prefer one who acts in good faith. Where riches and poverty are at stake above all, as Spinoza's description of Amsterdam suggests, those with ruthlessly mercenary motivations may well prefer to have others around them of similar motivation and cunning. To draw the extreme — but permitted — consequence from the state of affairs that Spinoza's argument means to encourage: the more biblical religion has been displaced by commerce as the bond of society, the more rich and poor alike will be encouraged to acquire riches and to stave off poverty by relying on their own cunning, and even to trample where necessary on those "of good faith" who merely "live honestly." In such a city, that is to say, the tolerance of which Spinoza speaks would amount to moral indifference. All this sounds very much like Shakespeare's Shylock as we have come to know him. What, we may then ask, is the fence against such cunning in Spinoza's Amsterdam? Especially if its judges lack that suprapolitical support for morality provided by the religious upbringing that Shakespeare's Duke, for one, praises, it is hard to see how they could avoid becoming either (as simple persons "of good faith") the dupes of the cunning, or (if cunning themselves) their corrupt collaborators. The practical difficulty here is indicated by Spinoza's own cunning expression, "religion or sect," which suggests that he continues by and large to understand biblical religion as at the start of his *Treatise,* namely as a politically corrupt and corrupting sectarianism. So, it seems, do the critics whom I cited at the beginning of my argument, at least insofar as they overlook the likelihood that I have taken pains to put forward, namely that Shakespeare's Duke and Portia equate mercy in the proper religious meaning of the term with political moderation.

It may surprise the critics to discover that Shakespeare's Duke and Portia would agree with Spinoza's implicit stipulation that religion ought to be irrelevant in court cases such as Shylock's. If I am correct, it should delight them as well. In no way, for example, does either the Duke or Portia recommend abrogating the laws on which Shylock's legal reasoning is based, which are laws favoring commerce together with a general acceptance of Venice's cosmopolitanism and endorsement of religious tolerance. Where Shakespeare's authority figures differ from Spinoza is in the spirit rather than in the letter of his stipulation. They seek to discover the limits of cosmopolitanism and tolerance, with a view to the moral bond that holds the political community together. Without Shakespeare's Duke, we might not be reminded that, contrary to Spinoza and his immediate political-philosophical forebears, the modern commercial city cannot thrive without the moderation encouraged by biblical morality or some reasonable facsimile of it as found in the sectarian religions that are its guardians and teachers. And without his Portia, we might not learn that the proper recovery of that morality in the perplexing circumstances of the modern city may well require the considerable help of traditional political philosophy.

Epilogue

ואל תדין את חברך עד שתגיע למקומו.

*Nor shall you judge your companion until you
stand in [lit. "reach"] his place.*

—*Mishnah, Avot* 2:4

———————————

THE FOREGOING ARGUMENT AMOUNTS TO A CALL to reexamine the
commonly accepted or tolerated opinion that Shakespeare is somehow morally obtuse toward Jews. Beyond that, an attentive reading of
The Merchant of Venice suggests that Shakespeare is not so pressingly
in need of our instruction on what it means to be a Jew in modern
times as we are of his. Yet because what I can only call hasty judgments
to the contrary seem so deeply ingrained nowadays, it may be helpful
to summarize how the evidence seen in Shakespeare's Shylock and his
half-look-alikes — Marlowe's Barabas, Bacon's Joabin, and the aver-
age businessman in Spinoza's Amsterdam — leads me to my twin
conclusion.

Admittedly, Shylock looks enough like Barabas at first glance to
invite the suspicion that Shakespeare merely follows Marlowe in the
latter's Jew-bashing. But that suspicion is hardly consistent with the
evident differences between the two. The harsh treatment of the Jew in

Marlowe's play turns out to be a measure of the unrelenting harshness of his Christian and Muslim adversaries toward each other as well. Marlowe's particular Jew-bashing is thus instrumental to his general religion-bashing. *The Merchant of Venice,* however, is more than the semideserved thwarting of Shylock. It is no less the thwarting of Antonio and, at the same time, Shakespeare's attempt to preserve what is noble in both Christian and Jew. Shakespeare qualifies Venice's harsh judgment against Shylock by indicating how Shylock might have avoided his legal catastrophe by simply sticking to the moral teachings of his own religion — its dietary laws, for example, along with the teaching of mercy that it shares with Christianity, to say nothing of the Torah's obvious prohibition against shedding innocent blood.[1] Meanwhile, Shakespeare also criticizes the excesses of Christian charity as found in Shylock's *agent provocateur* — in the arch-Christian Antonio's habit of exercising mercy without due concern for justice — so that the play cannot end without Portia's subtly reminding Antonio that he has overstepped the line between charitableness and meddlesomeness, at least as far as she is concerned, and therefore needs to step back. Shakespeare's critique here remains sotto voce, since unlike Marlowe he would not weaken the bond of society by further corroding the respect for Christian teaching, which, as things stand in his Venice, remains the city's chief ennobling element.

But doesn't Shakespeare then miss the opportunity, effectively seized by Bacon and Spinoza and others, to validate the Jew's claim to religious tolerance? Well, Shakespeare does vindicate Shylock — as he does Antonio — up to a point. By having Shylock press his claim past where it is salutary for society, however, Shakespeare means to show on reflection that while tolerance is a necessary consideration in the governing of a cosmopolitan modern city such as Venice, it cannot be the highest consideration. To say this another way, Shylock's solution, or what we have since come to call the liberal solution, does not by itself solve the problem of religious intolerance which it was, in part, first designed to meet. By removing religious discrimination from government and instead making religion a private choice to be protected by government, as Bacon and Spinoza would encourage and even require us to do, we also legitimize private choices *against* this or that religion — and so, for example, end up having to tolerate or legitimize Jew-hatred as well. It follows that although any liberal government has a vested interest in human decency which would presumably include the eradicating of Jew-hatred, no liberal government can take steps to eradicate it directly without at the same time risking encroachment on the private sphere, which according to liberal principles it is supposed to protect.[2] Any solution to this theologico-political difficulty would have to come, if at all, not by way of the mere subservience of government to private life however understood, but by way of the ennobling of private life as such. Yet whether liberal thought by itself can show the way to that ennobling is doubtful. It is beset, as I have shown in the case of Bacon and Spinoza, by its own moral obtuseness. The only practical alternative consistent with liberal principles would seem to be that we look again to our premodern roots in such a way that we keep in view, but are not obstructed by, the liberal premises that are our more recent inheritance. All this is to say that the question of the place of the Jew in modern life leads us, on the one hand, to biblical thought understood in its own terms and, on the other hand, to Socratic political philosophy understood in its own terms and to the ongoing tension or overlap between them as the original backdrop to modern liberalism. Closer to home, that question also leads us through Shakespeare's "Jewish" play, in whose purview all these themes are seen to find their proper place.

≈ ≈

Notes

≈ 1   The Mistreatment of Shakespeare's Shylock ≈

1. Harold Bloom, ed., *Shylock,* Major Literary Characters Series (New York: Chelsea House, 1991). Citations to this work and to those of other critics are given in the text.

2. I follow the text of the play as found in William Shakespeare, *The Merchant of Venice,* 2d ed., ed. George Lyman Kittredge, rev. Irving Ribner, Kittredge Shakespeares (New York: John Wiley & Sons, 1966). All citations are to that edition unless otherwise noted.

3. Cf. III.v.21–23, 30–33; IV.i.47, 54.

4. Cf. also IV.i.204, 221f., 226f., 233ff., 312.

5. John Lyon, *The Merchant of Venice,* Twayne's New Critical Introductions to Shakespeare (Boston: Twayne, 1988).

6. Harold C. Goddard, *The Meaning of Shakespeare,* 2 vols. (Chicago: University of Chicago Press, 1951), 1:109, as quoted in Lyon, *Merchant of Venice,* 105. Goddard's chapter is reproduced in H. Bloom, *Shylock,* 137–70; the sentence quoted is on 163; Goddard alludes in passing to III.i.32. Similarly, M. J. Landa, *The Jew in Drama* (reprint; Port Washington, N.Y.: Kennikat, 1968), 76f. On the other hand, Bernard Grebanier, *The Truth about Shylock* (New York: Random House, 1962), 282ff., correctly sees that Portia shows mercy to Shylock when exhorting him in effect to exculpate himself legally by showing mercy in turn to Antonio; but Grebanier misses the larger theological and political implications. Cf. chap. 3, sec. 5, and chap. 5, sec. 2, below.

7. Lawrence Danson, *The Harmonies of* The Merchant of Venice (New

Haven: Yale University Press, 1978). I omit from fuller consideration Grebanier, who defends the play on the too narrow grounds that Shakespeare understands his Shylock as a banker in conflict with a merchant prince rather than as a Jew in conflict with a Christian: "No one expects compassion from a bank" (*Truth about Shylock,* 213; cf. 95). See, however, I.iii.37, 41–43, with IV.i.17–34 and my remarks on Gross, below.

8. Danson here quotes S. K. Henninger, *Touches of Sweet Harmony: Pythagorean Cosmology and Renaissance Poetics* (San Marino, Calif.: Huntington Library, 1974), 5.

9. Edward Andrew, *Shylock's Rights: A Grammar of Lockean Claims* (Toronto: University of Toronto Press, 1988).

10. Harry Berger Jr., "Marriage and Mercifixion in *The Merchant of Venice:* The Casket Scene Revisited," *Shakespeare Quarterly* 32 (1981): 155–62.

11. Andrew acknowledges his debt for the term to C. B. Macpherson, *The Political Theory of Possessive Individualism: Hobbes to Locke* (Oxford: Clarendon Press, 1964).

12. Thomas Aquinas, *Summa Theologiae* II–II.10.8 (my trans.; my italics).

13. John Gross, *Shylock: A Legend and Its Legacy* (New York: Simon & Schuster, 1992).

14. For a useful discussion of Shakespeare's "verbal usury" in the play, that is, his habit of generating added meaning from given words, see Marc Shell, *Money, Language, and Thought: Literary and Philosophical Economics from the Medieval to the Modern Era* (Berkeley: University of California Press, 1982), 47–83.

15. Robert Alter, "Who Is Shylock?" *Commentary* 96, no. 1 (1993): 33.

16. James Shapiro, *Shakespeare and the Jews* (New York: Columbia University Press, 1996). Shapiro's larger argument disputes the suddenness and thoroughness of the expulsion of Jews under Edward II in 1290 and their readmission under Cromwell in 1656, partly because of the absence of hard documentary evidence in either case and partly because of Englishmen's ongoing fascination with, and abuse of, opinions about Jews in the meantime, as a foil for understanding what being English might mean for themselves.

17. Cf. ibid., 43, with 83, 110, 189 ("the play as a cultural safety-valve"), 228 ("*The Merchant's* capacity to illuminate a culture").

18. Premise 1 seems to be held by each of the five critics I have been considering who look at the play as a whole, except Danson (and perhaps Gross); premise 2, by Bloom, Lyon, Andrew, and Gross; premise 3, apparently by all (except perhaps Danson); premise 4, again apparently by all.

19. Leo Strauss, *Spinoza's Critique of Religion* (New York: Schocken, 1965), 35, 258–68; Hans W. Frei, *The Eclipse of Biblical Narrative: A Study in Eighteenth and Nineteenth Century Hermeneutics* (New Haven: Yale University Press, 1974), 42–46; Henry E. Allison, *Benedict de Spinoza* (Boston: Twayne, 1975), 188–208. For the traditional Jewish view that the Torah existed prior to God's creating the world and contains, as it were, the blueprint for creation, see *Genesis Rabbah* 1.1.

20. Lewis S. Feuer, *Spinoza and the Rise of Liberalism* (Boston: Beacon Press, 1958), 101–19; Stanley Rosen, "Benedict Spinoza," in *History of Political Philosophy,* 3d ed., ed. Leo Strauss and Joseph Cropsey (Chicago: University of Chicago Press, 1987), 465–75.

⨳ 2 Shylock and Marlowe's Barabas ⨳

1. Barabas's New Testament namesake is the criminal Barabbas, set for crucifixion alongside Jesus but released in preference to Jesus as an act of clemency by the Roman governor Pontius Pilate, after Pilate had asked the execution day crowd which prisoner it would prefer to have released (see Matt. 27:15–26; Mark 15:6–11; Luke 23:13–25; John 18:39–40; Acts 3:14). Traditional Christian apologetics connects Barabbas's name (which in Aramaic means "the father's son") with John 8:44 (where Jesus says to the Jews, "Ye are of your father the Devil") and so considers him a type of Antichrist; see G. K. Hunter, *Dramatic Identities and Cultural Tradition: Studies in Shakespeare and His Contemporaries* (New York: Barnes & Noble, 1978), 60–102, esp. 65, 91. Cf. n. 27, below. For these and other translations of the Bible into Elizabethan English, I have relied on *The Geneva Bible: A Facsimile of the 1560 Edition* (Madison: University of Wisconsin Press, 1969).

2. Christopher Marlowe, *The Complete Plays,* ed. J. B. Steane (Harmondsworth, Eng.: Penguin Books, 1969). Unless otherwise stated, all citations are to this edition.

3. Cf. Hunter, *Dramatic Identities,* 216ff. Bernard Spivack, *Shakespeare and the Allegory of Evil: The History of a Metaphor in Relation to His Major Villains* (New York: Columbia University Press, 1958), 346–53, 374ff.; and David Bevington, *From Mankind to Marlowe: Growth of Structure in the Popular Drama of Tudor England* (Cambridge: Harvard University Press, 1962), 218–33, liken Barabas to the Vice or stereotypical villain of popular morality plays, especially from the moment he begins his rampage of evil deeds (II.iii

and following). Joel B. Altman, *The Tudor Play of Mind: Rhetorical Inquiry and the Development of Elizabethan Drama* (Berkeley: University of California Press, 1978), 353–60, questions that description for its unwarranted consequence that inevitably, Barabas's "un-Vice-like behavior ends up being characterized as deception" (354): Altman finds Barabas's grievances in the taxation scene (I.ii), for example, morally proper (cf. 357). Cf., however, n. 30, below. See also n. 33, below, on the disputed question of the play's dramatic unity.

4. I.i. 58–68, 124–30, ii.89, 249–52; IV.i.66–77.

5. I.i.98–101, 149–69, 183–93, ii.1–50; II.ii.10–55.

6. Prol. 30. See n. 45, below. Cf. also chap. 3, sec. 4, below.

7. See especially Hunter, *Dramatic Identities,* 64ff., with Stephen J. Greenblatt, "Marlowe, Marx, and Anti-Semitism," *Critical Inquiry* 5 (1978–79): 291–307, esp. 292ff., and n. 3, above.

8. On the difficulty of determining Marlowe's firsthand acquaintance with Machiavelli's books, see, for example, Edward Meyer, *Machiavelli and Elizabethan Drama* (Weimar: Literarhistorische Forschungen, 1897; reprint, New York: Burt Franklin, n.d.), 22f., 39ff.; U. M. Ellis-Fermor, *Christopher Marlowe* (1927; reprint, Hamden, Conn.: Archon Books, 1967), 88ff.; Mario Praz, *Machiavelli and the Elizabethans* (London: British Academy Lecture, 1928), 27f.; Frederick S. Boas, *Christopher Marlowe: A Biographical and Critical Study* (Oxford: Clarendon Press, 1940), 134ff.; John Bakeless, *The Tragicall History of Christopher Marlowe,* 2 vols. (1942; reprint, Hamden, Conn.: Archon Books, 1964), 1:347–54; Michel Poirier, *Christopher Marlowe* (1951; reprint, Hamden, Conn.: Archon Books, 1968), 47ff.; Paul H. Kocher, *Christopher Marlowe: A Study of His Thought, Learning, and Character* (New York: Russell & Russell, 1962), 194–202; Douglas Cole, *Suffering and Evil in the Plays of Christopher Marlowe* (1962; reprint, New York: Gordian Press, 1972), 136ff.; N. W. Bawcutt, introduction to Christopher Marlowe, *The Jew of Malta,* Revels Plays (Manchester: Manchester University Press; Baltimore: Johns Hopkins University Press, 1978), 11–15, with Bawcutt, "Machiavelli and Marlowe's *The Jew of Malta,*" *Renaissance Drama,* n.s., 3 (1970): 3–49. Felix Raab, *The English Face of Machiavelli: A Changing Interpretation, 1500–1700* (London: Routledge & Kegan Paul; Toronto: University of Toronto Press, 1965), inexplicably omits all reference to Marlowe's play.

9. I.i.142, 184, ii.162, 163, 278; III.iii.12, 44; V.ii.28, 37, 66, 114, 123, v.25.

10. "Marlowe is evidently writing directly with the Bible before him," as H. S. Bennett observes in his edition of Marlowe, *The Jew of Malta* and *The*

Massacre at Paris (London: Methuen, 1931; reprint, New York: Gordian Press, 1966), 58 n and passim; Bakeless, *Marlowe*, 1:354f.; Cole, *Suffering and Evil*, 124f.; Hunter, *Dramatic Identities*, 218–20. Kocher, *Marlowe*, 122n, finds the parallels shocking to the point of speechlessness: "Marlowe's meaning in giving Barabas so many quotations from the book of Job . . . is not clear. It scarcely seems possible that he intends to suggest a prolonged parallel between the sufferings of the two men." See, however, sec. 4 of this chapter, below.

11. Cf. Wilbur Sanders, *The Dramatist and the Received Idea* (Cambridge: Cambridge University Press, 1968), 48f., 58f. See also Leo Strauss, *Thoughts on Machiavelli* (Glencoe, Ill.: Free Press, 1958; reprint, Chicago: University of Chicago Press, 1984), 292.

12. Prol. 29. Cf. Edward L. Rocklin, "Marlowe as Experimental Dramatist: The Role of the Audience in *The Jew of Malta*, in *"A Poet and a filthy Playmaker"*: New Essays on Christopher Marlowe, ed. Kenneth Friedenreich, Roma Gill, and Constance B. Kuriyama (New York: AMS Press, 1988), 129–42, esp. 132f.

13. See Aristotle, *Poetics* 1453a7–12 and context.

14. In this respect, Marlowe's prologue appears to be foreshadowed by Innocent Gentillet's *Discours sur les moyens de bien gouverner . . . contre Nicholas Machiavel florentin* (1576), whose purpose is to warn Englishmen of the Satanic or corrupting effect of Machiavelli's books on French politics and religion. According to Gentillet's Epistle Dedicatory, Machiavelli's entry into France was prepared by the morally dubious "Policie" of

rais[ing] up ieasters and fooles in Courts, which creeping in, by quipping and prettie conceits, first in words, and after by books, uttering their pleasant ieasts in the Courts and banquets of kings and princes, laboured to root up all the true principles of Religion and Policie. . . . For little and little, that which was taken in the beginning for ieasts, turned to earnest, & words into deeds. In the neck of these came new Poets, very eloquent for their own profit, which incensed into lust & lightness, such mindes as were already inclined to wantonnesse, by quickening their appetites with the delectable sauce of unchast hearing; and pricking them forward with the sharp spurres of pleasure. Who could then bridle vices and iniquities, which are fed with much wealth, and no lesse liberty? seeing them not onely in play, mirth and laughter entertained; but also earnestly accepted and commended, as being very excellent. . . . For then Sathan being a disguised person among the French, in the likeness of a merry ieaster, acted a Comaedie, but shortly ensued a wofull Tragoedie. When our countrie mens minds were sick, and corrupted with these pestilent diseases, and [their] disciples waxed stale; then came forth the books of *Machiavell,* a most pernitious writer, which began not in secret and stealing manner . . . but by open meanes, and as it were a continual assault, utterly destroyed, not this or that vertue, but even all vertues at once. . . . Truly it is a wonderfull thing to consider how fast that evill weede hath grown within these few yeares, seeing there is almost none that striveth to excell in vertue or knowledge: as though the onely way to obteine honour and riches were by this deceivers direction.

Innocent Gentillet, *Discours,* trans. Simon Patricke (London, 1602) as *A Discourse upon the Meanes of Wel Governing . . . Against Nicholas Machiavel the Florentine* (reprint; Amsterdam: Da Capo Press, 1969), n.p.

15. Marlowe's Duke of Guise dies as resolute and unrepentant as his Barabas; cf. V.v.82–94 with *The Massacre at Paris* V.ii.81–94. Cf. also Gentillet, *Discours,* III.31, 33 (trans. Patricke, 324, 348f.).

16. Cf. Marlowe, *Doctor Faustus* III.iii.183.

17. Cf. the argument of Prol. 18–26 with Gentillet, *Discours,* III.33 (trans. Patricke, 348).

18. Cf. Gentillet, *Discours,* III.1 (trans. Patricke, 145).

19. Cf. Barabas's death as described at V.v.26–94. Apparently the only source that tells of Phalaras's perishing in his own device is Ovid, *Ibis* 439–40; see Antonio D'Andrea, "Marlowe's Prologue to *The Jew of Malta,*" *Medieval and Renaissance Studies* 5 (1960): 220, 242. Cf., however, Gentillet, *Discours,* III.14 (trans. Patricke, 234):

And as for *Agathocles,* true it is (as *Suidas* and others write) hee usurped the tyrannie of Sicilie, by causing with treason and treacherie the chiefe rulers of *Siracuse* to be slaine: but what end made hee also? even such as he merited: For, being desirous to make great his domination over Italie, hee thought best to practise with intelligencers, which kept not their word with him, insomuch as his purpose being broken and anihilated, by the same meanes of treason and unfaithfulnesse, by which hee made himselfe great, hee died with griefe and heavinesse of minde. And still are not these the judgments of God, who ruinates tyrants by the same waies, which hee suffers them to get up and come to advancement?

20. For Draco, see Plutarch, "Solon," in *Lives of the Noble Grecians and Romans,* trans. John Dryden, rev. A. H. Clough (1864; reprint, New York: Modern Library, n.d.), 107.

21. V.i.54–88. Recall the discussion of Danson in chap. 1, sec. 1, above.

22. For example, Plato, *Timaeus* 39e–40d, with *Letter* XIII, 360b; Aristotle, *De Caelo* 290b12–291a28; *Metaphysics* 1073a14–1074b14 with 985b23–987a28 and 989b29–990a32; Thomas Aquinas, *In Aristotelis librum De caelo et mundo* 2.14.420–30; *Commentary on the Metaphysics of Aristotle* 12.9.2553–11.2599 with 1.7.119–9.150 and 1.13.201–7; *Literal Exposition on Job,* on Job 38:37; Maimonides, *Guide of the Perplexed* II.8.

23. See n. 21, above.

24. Apollonius Rhodius, *Argonautica* I.23–31 with I.494–518; II.161–63; IV.891–909. Cf. also *The Merchant of Venice* IV.i.75 ("pines"), 4 ("stony"), 72 ("flood") with chap. 3, sec. 3, below.

25. Cf. Maimonides, *Guide of the Perplexed* III.22–23; Thomas Aquinas, *Literal Exposition on Job,* prologue; Martin D. Yaffe, "Providence in Medieval Aristotelianism: Moses Maimonides and Thomas Aquinas on the Book of Job," in *The Voice from the Whirlwind: Interpreting the Book of Job,* ed. Leo G. Perdue and W. Clark Gilpin (Nashville, Tenn.: Abingdon, 1992), 111–28.

26. Cf. Gen. 12:1–3; 13:14–17; 15:1–16; 17:1–8; 18:18–19; 21:1–2; 22:15–18; 24:7.

27. Cf., for example, Isa. 54:11–14; 60:4–11, 17; 61:6, with 48:17. Hunter, *Dramatic Identities,* 218, places Barabas here in the traditional mold of Christian anti-Jewish apologetics. Bawcutt, introduction to Marlowe, *Jew of Malta,* 21, instead finds Marlowe alluding to Ovid, *Metamorphoses* I.127–62 (a description of the harshness of the age of iron). See also nn. 29, 37, below.

28. Cf., for example, Lev. 26:2–45; Deut. 11:26–32; 27:11–69. Cf. also Deut. 4:12–14; Isa. 47:13–15, with n. 41, below.

29. Cf. I.i.114–22 with II.iii.314–16.

30. Cf. I.i.141–48, 180–93 with ii.1–50.

31. Cf. Gentillet, *Discours,* II.Pref. (trans. Patricke, 76f.) on the "simplicitie" of the Christian religion.

32. Barabas's striking the earth may recall the gesture that God through Moses commands Aaron (or Aaron's rod) in bringing about the plague of lice against Egypt (Exod. 8:12). In the light of the Machevill's prologue, however, it also suggests Gentillet's Epistle Dedicatory (n. 30, above), which begins by recounting Solon's rebuke of Thespis for introducing drama to Athens: "After *Solon* . . . had seen Thespis his first edition and action of a

Tragoedie, and meeting with him before the play, demanded, If he were not ashamed to publish such feigned fables under so noble, yet a counterfeit personage: *Thespis* answered, That it was no disgrace upon a stage (merrily and in sport) to say and do any thing. Then *Solon* (striking hard upon the earth with his staffe) replied thus: Yea but shortly, we that now like and embrace this play, shall find it practised in our contracts and common affaires."

33. The expression is Hunter's (*Dramatic Identities,* 71f., 98). Critics have noted, with some perplexity, a subsequent falling-off in Barabas's dramatic characterization, especially in acts III–IV, with perhaps a recovery in act V (containing two soliloquies, V.ii.28–48, 112–25); see Bennett, introduction, 15ff.; Bakeless, *Tragicall History,* 1:331ff.; Poirer, *Marlowe,* 163ff.; J. B. Steane, *Marlowe: A Critical Study* (Cambridge: Cambridge University Press, 1964), 195ff. Some, including Ellis-Fermor, *Marlowe,* 95ff., and Boas, *Marlowe,* 140ff., 148–50, ascribe the apparent unevenness to a possible later editing or padding by Thomas Heywood for a court performance in 1633, more than forty years after the play was originally written. Others, including T. S. Eliot, *Elizabethan Essays* (New York: Haskell House, 1964), 28; Harry Levin, *The Overreacher: A Study of Christopher Marlowe* (Cambridge: Harvard University Press, 1952), 75f.; Spivack, *Shakespeare and the Allegory of Evil,* 352; Bevington, *From Mankind to Marlowe,* 225ff.; Sanders, *Dramatist,* 52ff.; Greenblatt, "Marlowe, Marx, and Anti-Semitism," 301ff.; and Rocklin, "Marlowe," 136, variously defend the play's textual integrity; see esp. nn. 3, above, and 37, 46, below.

34. Cf. Job 12:1–3; 13:1–13; 19:19, 21f.

35. Cf. Job 3:1–26.

36. Cf. Job 7:4, 13f.

37. Rocklin, "Marlowe," 133, rightly contrasts the dynamics of Marlowe's drama with that of the traditional Christian morality play: "The rhetoric of the prologue . . . uses, yet inverts, the morality-play frame, for while the members of the audience are assigned their traditional role as judges between the different ways of life presented, they must watch the play over the shoulder of a figure who has just challenged the world view in which they would ordinarily make that judgment." But to this statement must be added Hunter's apt reminder, *Dramatic Identities,* 61, 62f., that Marlowe wished to be "understood intellectually," not just appreciated aesthetically: "The use of [biblical] texts in this highly dramatic way not only reveals the skilled theological disputant in Marlowe himself; it implies an ideal audience that knows the suppressed halves of the quotations and can judge the hero by his understanding of the texts he uses. This judgment is supported by a tissue of ironies

throughout the play, and attention to these is a key which unlocks its whole meaning and structure." On the intellectual limitations of Marlowe's Machiavellianism in this regard, however, cf. Sanders, *Dramatist,* 38–60, and n. 47, below.

38. Cf. Greenblatt, "Marlowe, Marx, and Anti-Semitism," 302f.; Rocklin, "Marlowe," 140.

39. Cf. II.ii.264ff. with Hunter, *Dramatic Identities,* 73 and context.

40. Job 38:1–41:34. Cf. Robert D. Sacks, *A Commentary on the Book of Genesis* (Lewiston, N.Y.: Edwin Mellen Press, 1990), 118f. (on Gen. 16:12).

41. Cf. Job 1:8; 2:3; 42:7f., with Isa. 41:8f.; 44:1f., 21; 45:4; 49:3–6; 52:13–53:12.

42. Cf. Job 40:10–14, with Niccolò Machiavelli, *The Prince* trans. Harvey C. Mansfield Jr. (Chicago: University of Chicago Press, 1985), chap. 25, and nn. 11, above, and 49, below.

43. Cf. Plato, *Republic* 571a–592b; Xenophon, *Hiero;* Leo Strauss, *On Tyranny,* rev. and expanded ed., ed. Victor Gourevich and Michael S. Roth (New York: Free Press, 1991).

44. Cf. Prol. 24–26 and n. 18, above.

45. Cf. Aristotle, *Poetics* 1449b24–28; Laurence Berns, "Aristotle's *Poetics,*" in *Ancients and Moderns: Essays in the Tradition of Political Philosophy in Honor of Leo Strauss,* ed. Joseph Cropsey (New York: Basic Books, 1964), 70–87; Michael Davis, *Aristotle's* Poetics: *The Poetry of Philosophy* (Lanham, Md.: Rowman & Littlefield, 1992), 35–42. That Marlowe or his Machevill could call Barabas's drama a "tragedy" seems connected with his being the immediate heir to a tradition that had narrowed the meaning of the term to "the overturn from grandeur to misery" (the expression is H. Levin's, *Overreacher,* 102). Cf. Howard R. Patch, *The Goddess Fortuna in Mediaeval Literature* (Cambridge: Harvard University Press, 1927), 68–80; Frederick Reifer, *Fortune and Elizabethan Tragedy* (San Marino, Calif.: Huntington Library, 1983), 30–82; with, for example, Bevington, *From Mankind to Marlowe,* 161; and Cole, *Suffering and Evil,* 260–64.

46. Rocklin, "Marlowe," 138ff., conveniently summarizes the controversy among critics about how to read the governor's final overcoming of Barabas and the Turks. To take it simply as a Christian victory over a Barabas who is both Jew and Machiavel indifferently, as do Spivack, *Shakespeare,* 348–50, and Alfred Harbage, "Innocent Barabas," *Tulane Drama Review* 8, no. 4 (1964): 47–58, is to ignore the antitheological implications of the prologue and to see the dramatic action entirely in terms of the actors' labels. Likewise, to regard the governor instead as the play's most successful Machiavel while

seeking to accommodate the governor's hypocrisies and so on within the theology of a more idealized Christianity — as do Cole, *Suffering and Evil,* 123–44, Hunter, *Dramatic Identities,* esp. 95ff., W. L. Godshalk, *The Marlovian World Picture* (The Hague: Mouton, 1974), 203–22, and Don Beecher, "*The Jew of Malta* and the Ritual of the Inverted Moral Order," *Cahiers Elisabéthiens: Etudes sur la Pré-Renaissance et la Renaissance anglaises* 12 (October 1977): 45–48) — is to interpret the play more as a satire aimed at inducing its Christian audience to repent of the moral vices it sees onstage — but again it assumes that the Machiavellian argument of the prologue can be safely ignored for an interpretation of the play as a whole. Finally, Rocklin's own premise, that Marlowe's play invites its audience to understand the Christians' victory "in a subversive fashion," is also the view of H. Levin, *Overreacher,* 56–80; Steane, *Marlowe,* 166–203; J. L. Simmons, "Elizabethan Stage Practice and Marlowe's *The Jew of Malta,*" *Renaissance Drama,* n.s., 4 (1971): 93–104; Howard S. Babb, "Policy in Marlowe's *The Jew of Malta,*" *E.L.H.: A Journal of English Literary History* 24 (1957): 85–94, esp. 86–89; Nicholas Brook, "Marlowe the Dramatist," in *Elizabethan Theatre,* ed. John Russell Brown and Bernard Harris (New York: St. Martin's Press, 1967), 91 — and, with some differences, Sanders, *Dramatist,* 38–60; Greenblatt, "Marlowe, Marx, and Anti-Semitism," 292–305; and the argument of the present chapter.

47. Cf. Bevington, *From Mankind to Marlowe,* 232f.; Sanders, *Dramatist,* 53; with my argument in sec. 2, above.

48. Cf. I.ii.38f., 109–13, 132–34, 161–63.

49. Cf. Strauss, *Thoughts on Machiavelli,* 282. That Shakespeare is also capable of considering the problem posed by Machiavelli in its own terms is evident, for example, in his *Richard III;* cf. Richard's remark in *Henry VI,* pt. 3, III.ii.191–93 ("I can add colors to the chameleon, / Change shapes with Proteus for advantages, / And set the murderous Machiavel to school."), with Grant B. Mindle, "Shakespeare's Demonic Prince," *Interpretation* 20 (1993): 259–74.

⇜ 3   Shylock and Shakespeare's Antonio ⇜

1. Cf. I.iii.72–85, 89–91, with 37–46; III.ii.111f. Leslie Fiedler, *The Stranger in Shakespeare* (New York: Stein & Day, 1972), 97, speaks of "The common error which takes the 'Merchant' of the title to be Shylock." Cf. also James Shapiro, "'Which is *The Merchant* here, and which *The Jew?*' Shake-

speare and the Economics of Influence," *Shakespeare Studies* 20 (1988): 269–79.

2. For the following, cf. Benjamin Nelson, *The Idea of Usury: From Tribal Brotherhood to Universal Otherhood,* 2d ed. (Chicago: University of Chicago Press, 1969), esp. 73–89, 141–51. For the traditional arguments against usury, see, for example, Thomas Aquinas, *Summa Theologiae* II–II.78.1; *Commentary on Aristotle's Politics* I.8.134, with *Commentary on Aristotle's Nicomachean Ethics* V.9.979; Thomas Wilson, *A Discourse upon Usury* [1572], ed. R. H. Tawney (New York: Augustus M. Kelley, 1963), esp. "Ockerfoe, or the Preachers Oracion," 215–33; Francis Bacon, *Essays # 41* ("Of Usury"), in *The Works of Francis Bacon,* ed. James Spedding, Robert Leslie Ellis, and Douglas Denon Heath, 14 vols. (London: Longmans & Co., 1857–74), 6: 473–77; Shell, *Money, Language, and Thought,* esp. 48ff.; Michael Zuckert, "The New Medea: Portia's Comic Triumph in *The Merchant of Venice,*" in *Shakespeare's Political Pageant,* ed. Joseph Alulis and Vickie Sullivan (Lanham, Md.: Rowman & Littlefield, 1996), 18ff.

3. Cf. also III.ii.276–81; IV.i.7–13, 175–77.

4. Cf. IV.i.35–65, 85–103, 139–42, 204–5, 221–60, 297–314.

5. Cf. III.ii.275–81, with the stage directions to IV.i.

6. Shapiro, *Shakespeare and the Jews,* 188f., expresses puzzlement over the temporarily forgotten law (IV.i.345–60) under which Shylock eventually stands convicted: "while the city's charter guarantees equality before the law, a feature that has attracted foreigners to Venice, it retains legislation that renders this equality provisional, if not fictional." He thus finds the trial scene dramatically inconsistent—"a fantasy resolution to the conflicting and overlapping jurisdictions intrinsic to such trials," since the law in question "effectively supersedes the city's charter"—as if otherwise egalitarian civic charters should never give preferential treatment to citizens. Compare, however, Richard J. Arneson, "Shakespeare and the Jewish Question," *Political Theory* 13 (1985): 87: "At stake . . . is the issue of whether mere relations of contract can bind together the members of a society who may be hostile adversaries in matters of religion, culture, and community."

7. I.iii.101–24, 132–36; II.v.11–18; III.i.50–64, 70–114; IV.i.89–103, 293–95, 340, 372–75, 393–95; I.iii.66–85; II.v.35f.; IV.i.36f., 221f.

8. Cf. Lawrence W. Hyman, "The Rival Lovers in *The Merchant of Venice,*" *Shakespeare Quarterly* 21 (1970): 109–16; Barbara Tovey, "The Golden Casket: An Interpretation of *The Merchant of Venice,*" in *Shakespeare as Political Thinker,* ed. John Alvis and Thomas G. West (Durham, N.C.: Carolina Academic Press, 1981), 215–37; Zuckert, "New Medea," 3–36.

9. According to Thomas Aquinas, moroseness (*acedia*) is a "capital" vice, so called because, while forgivable in itself, it leads to other vices; see *Summa Theologiae* II–II.35.4, with I–II.84.3–4.

10. See Brown's note to I.i.1 in William Shakespeare, *The Merchant of Venice*, ed. John Russell Brown, Arden Shakespeare (London: Routledge, 1988), 4; Jan Hinely, "Bond Priorities in *The Merchant of Venice*," *Studies in English Literature* 20 (1980): 229ff.; Tovey, "Golden Casket," 221ff.; Richard Levin, *Love and Society in Shakespearean Comedy* (Newark, Del.: University of Delaware Press, 1985), 37f.; Zuckert, "New Medea," 4ff.

11. I.i.177–85, with III.i.38–40, ii.99–100, 313–15. Cf. David Lowenthal, "The New Shakespeareans," *Claremont Review of Books* 3, no. 2 (1984): 11f.

12. Cf. I.i.57–64, II.viii.35; III.ii.289–94.

13. Cf. I.i.65–118; also Paul Cantor, "Religion and the Limits of Community in *The Merchant of Venice*," *Soundings* 70 (1987): 245ff.

14. Allan Bloom, *Shakespeare's Politics* (New York: Basic Books, 1964), 32f.; Tovey, "Golden Casket," 220ff.; Shell, *Money, Language, and Thought*, 75–78; Cantor, "Religion," 241.

15. Cf. W. H. Auden, *The Dyer's Hand* (New York: Random House, 1948), 232: "we feel that Antonio's continual generosity has encouraged Bassanio in his spendthrift habits. Bassanio seems to be one of those people whose attitude towards money is that of a child; it will somehow always appear by magic when needed. Though Bassanio is aware of Shylock's malevolence, he makes no serious effort to dissuade Antonio from signing the bond because, thanks to the ever-open purse of his friend, he cannot believe that bankrupting is a real possibility."

16. If Shakespeare's Belmont is Montebelluna on the Piave River, then Bassanio's ship would have to sail northeast from Venice along the Adriatic coast to the river mouth, then inland. Given that Antonio's ninety-day note has meanwhile become overdue and his trial date set despite the hesitancy of the Duke et al. (see III.ii.275–81), the disproportionate length of the voyage becomes plausible only with the additional likelihood of shifting winds, contrary currents, and the need to circumnavigate a considerable number of shallows, flats, and rocks (see I.i.17–36; II.vi.64f., viii.27–30; III.i.2–7, 87f., 90–92, ii.53–57, 97f., 265–69; IV.i.71–72). Consider also I.i.168–72 and III.ii.239 with chap. 2, n. 24, above.

17. It is tempting to ascribe Bassanio's first informing Portia of his poverty to a conversation with her instead at his arrival in Belmont just before act III, scene ii, but this seems untenable in view of Bassanio's extravagant show

of wealth. Admittedly, my reading here is open to the possible objection that I am compelled to assume that Bassanio at III.ii.250–61 is conflating events that occur both before and after Antonio's contact with Shylock:

> *Gentle lady,*
> *When I did first impart my love to you,*
> *I freely told you all the wealth I had*
> *Ran in my veins — I was a gentleman;*
> *And then I told you true; and yet, dear lady,*
> *Rating myself at nothing, you shall see*
> *How much I was a braggart. When I told you*
> *My state was nothing, I should then have told you*
> *That I was worse than nothing; for indeed*
> *I have engag'd myself to a dear friend,*
> *Engag'd my dear friend to his mere enemy*
> *To feed my means.*

Nevertheless the conflation — if that is what it is (since the text permits us to see the two sets of events as separate in Bassanio's mind; see the transition at l. 258) — would be consistent with Bassanio's being "Giddy in spirit" (III.ii.144; see also 175–83) on winning Portia's hand. There is some evidence that Bassanio's giddiness begins to fade as soon as he learns that Antonio has defaulted on Shylock's note, just prior to his confession to Portia (see III.ii.242); but even so, Bassanio's clear-headedness has not necessarily returned entirely. As soon as he has Portia's leave to go to Venice immediately to attend Antonio's trial, for example, he promises to "make haste" in returning to Belmont without letting another day go by — though in so doing, he does not give a second thought to the possibility that Antonio's death on forfeiting his pound of flesh might affect his own ability to keep his promise (see III.ii.320–24).

18. Zuckert, "New Medea," 10, argues that had Portia's father "known and approved of Portia's liking [of Bassanio], then the whole rigmarole of the caskets would make no sense." See, however, my subsequent argument to the contrary.

19. In light of Portia's earlier insistence that she "will die as chaste as Diana unless [she] be obtained in the manner of [her] father's will," Allan Bloom's claim that she "cheats" seems a bit overstated; cf. A. Bloom, *Shakespeare's Politics,* 26, with III.ii.10–14 and n. 18, above. Zuckert, "New Medea," 8–13, in effect defends Bloom's view, but on the premise that Bassanio's

motives are more mercenary. See, however, my subsequent argument in support of the nobility of Bassanio's love for Portia.

20. See n. 3, above, with A. Bloom, *Shakespeare's Politics,* 18, 21, 24, 27, 29.

21. See n. 1, above.

22. Barbara K. Lewalski, "Biblical Allusion and Allegory in *The Merchant of Venice,*" *Shakespeare Quarterly* 13 (1962): 327–43.

23. See chap. 1, nn. 2, 3, above. A. Bloom, *Shakespeare Politics,* 20f., also sees that Shylock's willingness to violate *kashrut* is a "compromise with his principle . . . for relating to the Christian community in which he lives," but Bloom does not draw the inference, as I do, that it also compromises his Jewishness in Shakespeare's eyes.

24. Plato, *Republic* 553a–555b.

25. For example, Exod. 23:24–26, Lev. 25:35–55, Deut. 15:1–11 and 23:20–21, with n. 2, above.

26. Gen. 30:25–43.

27. Cf. I.iii.101–24, with 37–47 and III.iii.2.14–16.

28. A. Bloom, *Shakespeare's Politics,* 23f., comments on Shylock's "I am a Jew" speech: "The choice seems to be a hostile diversity on a high level or a common humanity on the level of the beasts—a common humanity grounded on an indifference to the opinion about the nature of the good. The four Jewish names in *The Merchant of Venice* seem to be drawn from two successive chapters, 10 and 11, of Genesis. Chapter 11 has as its theme the Tower of Babel; perhaps this is part of Shakespeare's meaning. 'Let us go down and there confound their language, that they may not understand one another's speech.' Men's separateness is an act of divine providence." Yet if my reading is correct, Bloom underestimates Portia's statesmanlike efforts to accommodate to these differences; see sec. 5, below.

29. Cf. I.iii.106–26, with III.iii.6–7, 18f.; IV.i.40ff., 128–38, 288–90.

30. II.ii.1–29, 96–105, 110–55, iii.1–6, v.1–5, 45–50.

31. II.iii.15–20, with I.i.69–71, 105; II.iii.5–12, iv.1–39, v.22–24, 55–56, vi.1–59; III.i.21–32.

32. Cf. chap. 2, n. 21, above, with John Hollander, *The Untuning of the Sky: Ideas of Music in English Poetry, 1500–1700* (Princeton: Princeton University Press, 1961); S. K. Henninger, *Touches of Sweet Harmony.*

33. V.i.1–22. Cf. Olivia Delgado de Torres, "Reflections on Patriarchy and the Rebellion of Daughters in Shakespeare's *Merchant of Venice* and *Othello,*" *Interpretation* 21 (1994): 348: "Both of [Lorenzo's] examples [Troilus and

Cressida, Dido and Aeneas] depict lovers betrayed by their beloveds, first a man, then a woman, but in Jessica's two examples [Pyramus and Thisbe, Jason and Medea], neither woman is faithless; on the contrary, both disobey and betray their parents, the better to keep faith with their loves. The closest mirror to Jessica is Medea, who disobeys her father's orders to save Jason's life, [and] who marries into a foreign circle and rejuvenates her father-in-law, but not before cutting his throat. There is just a trace of remorse, mingled with self-justification, in this image of a rebellious daughter cutting a patriarch's throat for his own good, much as Jessica rejuvenates her father by causing him to be born again as a Christian." Cf. Zuckert, "New Medea," 25f., with 8f., 10, 13.

34. Cf. II.vi.51–57 with iv.29–37; V.i.14–17, 288–94.

35. Consider III.v.62 with ii.235.

36. Cf. chap. 2., n. 24, above, and n. 42, below.

37. Cf. also Norman Rabkin, *Shakespeare and the Problem of Meaning* (Chicago: University of Chicago Press, 1981), 17: "Plainly Lorenzo and Jessica subvert any schematic reading of the play."

38. Cf. I.i.108–9, with chap. 1, n. 9, above.

39. Portia seems to rely on Jewish law's well-known prohibition (noted by Zuckert, "New Medea," 22) against consuming the blood along with the flesh of a slaughtered animal (Deut. 12:15–16, with Gen. 9:4–6; Lev. 17:13–14; 19:26) — a reliance that is appropriate insofar as Shylock sees himself as entitled to treat Antonio as "carrion flesh" (IV.i.41); cf. the beginning of sec. 4, above.

40. IV.i.362–65, 376, 396–98 (Gratiano), with 366–70, as against 389–90 and 395 (Duke).

41. It is hard to construe this "favour" otherwise, unless Antonio means that the beneficiary here is not himself but Lorenzo, whom he understands to have become part of Shylock's family. Still, Antonio benefits financially as Lorenzo's trustee.

42. Remarkably, this passage includes references or allusions to all three natural things said to be moved by means of Orpheus's music: trees (I.i.32, assuming that Antonio's "gentle vessel" is wooden), stones (I.i.30–31), and floods (I.i.33–34). See n. 38, and chap. 2, n. 24, above.

43. Cantor, "Religion," 244f.

44. Consider III.ii.290–94.

45. Cf. Matthew 6:7, 9–13. C. L. Barber, *Shakespeare's Festive Comedy* (Princeton: Princeton University Press, 1959), 185, argues that the "we" of

Portia's "quality of mercy" speech excludes Jews, on the grounds that "All through the play the word Christian has been repeated [by the Venetians], primarily in statements that enforce the fact that the Jew is outside the easy bonds of community"—but he ignores the likelihood that Portia's speech addresses just that predicament in the circumstances I have indicated.

46. For example, Plato, *Phaedo* 67e–69e, 81c–84b, 108d–115a; Aristotle, *Nicomachean Ethics* 1095b14–1103a10, 1106a14–1109b26.

47. Cf. I.ii.26f., with Plutarch, "Marcus Brutus," in *Lives*, 1187.

48. Consider also I.ii.31–111; II.vii.78–79 (assuming "complexion" here means, *inter alia*, "make-up"), ix.61f., 80–81; III.iv.10–18, 62–78.

49. Plato, *Republic* 517c–e, 519c–520d, with 347a–e, with Plutarch, "Marcus Brutus," 1193. Cf. Tovey, "Golden Casket," 234ff.

☞ 4 Shylock and Bacon's Joabin ☞

1. Bacon, *Works*, 3:125–66. I use the edition of Jerry Weinberger, *New Atlantis and The Great Instauration*, rev., ed. Crofts Classics (Arlington Heights, Ill.: Harlan Davidson, 1989), which I cite by page and paragraph number.

2. For a sustained argument to the effect that Baconian science is as such the replacement for or improvement on Christian charity as traditionally understood, see Jerry Weinberger, *Science, Faith, and Politics: Francis Bacon and the Utopian Roots of the Modern Age* (Ithaca: Cornell University Press, 1985), esp. 302–21. For the demurral that scientific technology is part and parcel of a larger political project of "Baconian individualism," which "culminates in a leader who seeks to be one alone by rising above human neediness, and who proceeds above all others, and even above oblivion, by providing for others in their neediness," see Robert K. Faulkner, *Francis Bacon and the Project of Progress* (Lanham, Md.: Rowman & Littlefield, 1993), esp. 87–141; the sentence quoted is on 127. On the custom tailoring of Christianity to suit the general requirements of scientific progress, see esp. David C. Innes, "Bacon's *New Atlantis:* The Christian Hope and the Modern Hope," in *Piety and Humanity: Religion and Early Modern Political Philosophy*, ed. Douglas Kries (Lanham, Md.: Roman & Littlefield, 1997), 49–77.

3. Francis Bacon, *De Sapientia Veterum*, in *Works*, 6:605–86; English translation by James Spedding in 6:687–764. Translations of the cited passages that follow are my own, and citations are first to the Latin original and

afterward to Spedding's translation. For the importance of Bacon's treatment of the Orpheus myth for his thought as a whole, see Howard B. White, *Peace among the Willows: The Political Philosophy of Francis Bacon* (The Hague: Martinus Nijhoff, 1968), 207–17; White, "Bacon's *Wisdom of the Ancients,*" *Interpretation* 2 (1970): 107–29, esp. 123–26; James Stephens, *Francis Bacon and the Style of Science* (Chicago: University of Chicago Press, 1975), 125–27; Timothy Paterson, "The Politics of Baconian Science: An Analysis of Bacon's *New Atlantis*" (Ph.D. diss., Yale University, 1982), 50–58, and Paterson, "Bacon's Myth of Orpheus: Power as a Goal of Science in *On the Wisdom of the Ancients,*" *Interpretation* 16 (1989): 427–44; John C. Briggs, *Francis Bacon and the Rhetoric of Nature* (Cambridge: Harvard University Press, 1989), 134–36; Heidi Studer, "'Grapes Ill-Trodden . . .': Francis Bacon and *The Wisdom of the Ancients*" (Ph.D. diss., University of Toronto, 1992), 124–37; Laurence Lampert, *Nietzsche and Modern Times: A Study of Bacon, Descartes, and Nietzsche* (New Haven: Yale University Press, 1993), 60.

4. See chap. 3, sec. 4, above.

5. On the resulting merger, or slurring, of theory and practice in Baconian science, see, for example, *Novum Organum* I.3, 5, 11, 81, 116–17, 121, 124, 129; II.1–4; in *Works,* 1:157, 158, 188, 211–13, 215f., 217f., 221–23, 227–30. Cf. F. H. Anderson, *The Philosophy of Francis Bacon* (Chicago: University of Chicago Press, 1948), 150f.; Lisa Jardine, *Francis Bacon: Discovery and the Art of Disclosure* (Cambridge: Cambridge University Press, 1974), 98ff.; Laurence Berns, "Francis Bacon and the Conquest of Nature," *Interpretation* 7 (1978): 1–26; James C. Morrison, "Philosophy and History in Bacon," *Journal of the History of Ideas* 38 (1977): 585–606, esp. 590–95; Michèle Malherbe, "Man and Nature in the Gardens of Science," in *Francis Bacon's Legacy of Texts,* ed. William A. Sessions (New York: AMS Press, 1990), 131 and context; Richard Kennington, "Bacon's Concept of Mastery of Nature," unpublished; Lampert, *Nietzsche,* 141.

6. White, *Peace among the Willows,* 104 n. 30, 121f.

7. Cf. Jerry Weinberger, "Science and Rule in Bacon's Utopia: An Introduction to the Reading of the *New Atlantis,*" *American Political Science Review* 70 (1976): 856–85; Faulkner, *Bacon,* 233–36.

8. Gen. 11:26–29; 22:20–24; 24:15, 24, 47; 29:5. Or "Nachoran" (as Joabin calls him) may refer to Abraham's grandfather, Gen. 11:24f.

9. In order to derive Joabin's dubious suggestion from, say, Lev. 19:17–18, which at first reading might appear to restrict the commands to love one's neighbor and to forgo hatred or grudges or vengeance toward fellow Israel-

ites only, one would have to overlook vv. 33–34, which explicitly extend those commands so as to include any resident "stranger" as well.

10. *New Atlantis* 48 (¶ 7) with 80 (¶ 44) and 77f. (¶ 38). Weinberger, "Science and Rule in Bacon's Utopia," 875f. Also, in general, Timothy Paterson, "On the Role of Christianity in the Political Philosophy of Francis Bacon," *Polity* 19 (1986–87): 19–42; Paterson, "The Secular Control of Scientific Power in the Political Philosophy of Francis Bacon," *Polity* 21 (1988–89): 457–80.

11. Cf. Plato, *Critias* 113a–121d with *Timaeus* 21e–25d.

12. Cf. Aristotle, *Poetics* 1451a37–b11. Whereas for Plato poetry imitates nature (*Republic* 393c–398b, 595a–603c; cf. Aristotle, *Poetics* 1447a14ff. and passim; and *Physics* 194a22), for Bacon poetry distorts history by exaggerating the heroic, the moral, and the rare in order to edify and enhance "the desires of the mind" over and against the constraints of nature (*Advancement of Learning* II, in *Works,* 3:343ff.); cf. Weinberger, *Science, Faith, and Politics,* 239–43; Faulkner, *Bacon,* 236–39. Cf. also the proffered corrective to Plato's account of Atlantis in Bacon's *Essays # 58* ("Of the Vicissitude of Things") in *Works,* 6:512f.

13. For illuminating comments here, see esp. White, *Peace among the Willows,* 112–26; Weinberger, *Science, Faith, and Politics,* 28–33. Also, Leo Strauss, *The City and Man* (Chicago: Rand McNally, 1964; reprint, Chicago: University of Chicago Press, 1978), esp. 93–128; Seth Benardete, "On Plato's *Timaeus* and Timaeus' Science Fiction," *Interpretation* 2 (1971–72):21–63, esp. 22–29, with Benardete, *Socrates' Second Sailing: On Plato's* Republic (Chicago: University of Chicago Press, 1989), 54–78, 109–23.

14. Plato, *Timaeus* 21a–25e.

15. Socrates in his summary outline of the perfectly just city had appealed repeatedly to "nature" (17c, 18a, 18c, 18d, 20b).

16. On Bacon's own recognition of the "great distinction" between progress in "matters of state" and progress in the arts and sciences, see esp. *Novum Organum* I.90, in *Works* 1:198; cf. also *De Sapientia Veterum # 19* ("Daedalus, or the Mechanic") in *Works,* 6: 659f., trans. 734–36, with Studer, "Grapes," 190–203, and Lampert, *Nietzsche,* 34–39.

17. Cf. Bacon, *De Sapientia Veterum # 13* ("Proteus, or Matter"), in *Works,* 6:651f., trans. 725f.; cf. Studer, "Grapes," 144–51. Morrison, "Philosophy and History in Bacon," 591ff., cites in this connection Bacon's *Cogitationes de Natura Rerum* (trans. *Works,* 5:424f.) Kennington, "Bacon's Concept," cites among other things *Valerius Terminus* (trans. *Works,* 3:222): "To

speak plainly and clearly, it is a discovery of all operations and possibilities of operations from immortality (if it be possible) to the meanest mechanical practice"—a discovery that leads Bacon, in Kennington's words, "to stake all on the victory of art over nature."

18. *New Atlantis,* 44 (¶ 3), 48 (¶ 6), with 50 (¶ 11), 60 (¶ 16), 78 (¶ 38, "means of seeing objects afar off," etc.); 49 (¶ 10), 68 (¶ 18). Consider also ibid., 65f. (¶ 17), where Joabin is described as "excellently seen" in the "laws and customs of that [Jewish? Bensalemite?] nation"—with the perfectly ambiguous suggestion that he is on display to others in authority and, being "wise," knows it and acts accordingly.

19. See Weinberger's note 171 to *New Atlantis,* 61.

20. If Salomon's House outranks Christianity in Bensalem, then while the connotations of "our Saviour" may be Christian, its denotation could be any one of the following: (a) Salomon's House, (b) Solamona, its founder, or (c) Bensalem itself. *Bensalem* in Hebrew is akin to *Jerusalem* and means "perfect son" or "son of peace." Cf. White, *Peace among the Willows,* 152f.

21. Cf. Bacon, *De Sapientia Veterum* # 24 ("Dionysus, or Desire") in *Works,* 6:664–67, trans. 6:740–43; Num. 13:20–27. See Mark A. LePain, "The Fruit of the Land: Biblical and Classical Allusions in Francis Bacon's *New Atlantis,*" unpublished. White, *Peace among the Willows,* 142f., 170–78, finds the overtones of the feast as a whole to be Egyptian, hence antibiblical and anticlassical; cf., for example, Plato, *Timaeus* 22bff.

22. What is said of prostitution seems meant, metonymically, for European marriages as well.

23. Cf. Gen. 19:1–11.

24. See 1 Kings 17:18 and context. Instead of the more usual English translation "Zarephath" for the Hebrew name of the biblical city, the narrator in his reply to Joabin uses the Greek term as found in the Septuagint. Similarly, for the prophet's name he uses the Greek "Elias," whereas Joabin's earlier use of "Eliah" is closer to the biblical Hebrew. LePain suggests that the narrator's preference for the Greek points to Joabin's role as one who is prophesying or moralizing to strangers rather than to his own people (who according to Luke 4:24 do not listen anyway). However that may be, the reader of 1 Kings 17 might well be expected to associate the putative sins of the widow's son with either filial disobedience (Lev. 20:13; Deut. 21:18–21) or homosexuality (Lev. 20:13, with 18:22, 24f.).

25. When explaining how the longstanding "interdicts and prohibitions which we have touching strangers" are meant "to join humanity and policy

together," the governor of Strangers' House adds in apparent innocence that "we have memory" of no ship ever returning from Bensalem and of only "thirteen" isolated individuals who "chose to return in our bottoms" (56f, [¶ 15]) — but consider that "bottoms" can mean sea bottoms as well as boats.

26. Thomas More, *Utopia*, trans. Paul Turner (Harmondsworth, Eng.: Penguin, 1961), 103f. Plato, *Laws* 771e–772a, speaks of the nakedness of young men and women "within the limits a moderate sense of shame sets for each" as afforded by publicly supervised choral dances; cf. also 924e–925a, where the Athenian Stranger's stricter wording seems to suggest that when there is no father to supervise the marriage arrangements, an even closer examination of the prospective bride and groom by the inspecting judges becomes necessary.

27. Cf. Aristotle, *Nicomachean Ethics* 1155a22–b6.

28. 2 Sam. 11:1–12:24. Cf. 2 Sam. 3:22–32; 10:8–12; 12:26–31; 14:1–20; 24:1–10; with 1 Kings 1:5–49; 2:1–6. On the dangers of gazing on naked women, see also Bacon, *De Sapientia Veterum* # 10 ("Actaeon and Pentheus"), # 11 ("Orpheus") in *Works*, 6:645–48, trans. 719–22.

29. *Joabin*, if Hebrew, would be the plural of *Joab* (i.e., "many Joabs") or, if Latin, would be the dual form (i.e., "double Joabs," as *Altabin* means "twice lofty"). On the Davidic character of the Bensalemite regime, that is, its need for Joab-like lieutenants, see Weinberger, "Science and Rule in Bacon's Utopia," 882, and his introduction to *New Atlantis*, xxviii–xxix. For the additional likelihood that individual Joabs may be troublesome or expendable, see 1 Kings 2:5–6 with 1:5–49; cf., on the biblical Joab, Sacks, *Commentary on Genesis*, 175–85 (on Gen. 23:2).

30. Hobbes, *De Cive*, chap. 1, secs. 4–15, in *Man and Citizen: Thomas Hobbes's De Homine and De Cive*, ed. Bernard Gert (Garden City, N.Y.: Anchor Books, 1972), 114–19; cf. Leo Strauss, *Natural Right and History* (Chicago: University of Chicago Press, 1953), 184 n. 23.

31. Consider n. 9, above.

32. Consider Aristotle, *Politics* 1252a24–b9, 1259a37–b17; Exod. 20:14; Lev. 18:1–30; 19:3, 29; 20:1–26; Deut. 5:16–18; 22:13–23:1; 24:1–5; 25:5–10; 27:16, 20–23.

33. Cf. *New Atlantis*, 80 (¶ 44: human sexuality may well be included among the "many things truly natural which induce admiration . . . in a world of particulars" and therefore, inasmuch as the Fathers of Salomon's House "hate all impostures and lies," is here shown "pure as it is"), 83 (¶ 59: the

narrative's concluding sentence says that "they give great largesses where they come upon all occasions").

34. See also Innes, "Bacon's *New Atlantis*," esp. 65–73.

ᘓ 5   Shylock and Spinoza's *Theologico-Political Treatise* ᘓ

1. Benedict Spinoza, *Tractatus Theologico-Politicus*, in *Opere*, ed. Carl Gebhardt, 4 vols. (Heidelberg: Carl Winters Universitätsbuchhandlung, 1925). All references are to this edition, cited by chapter, page, and line numbers. All translations are my own, though I add cross references to the translations by R. H. M. Elwes, in *Works of Spinoza*, 2 vols. (New York: Dover, 1955), vol. 1, and by Samuel Shirley, in Spinoza, *Tractatus Theologico-Politicus*, 2d ed. (Leiden: E. J. Brill, 1991) by E and S, respectively, followed by the page numbers in each case.

2. A literal translation of Spinoza's preface may be found in Martin D. Yaffe, "On Beginning to Translate Spinoza's *Tractatus Theologico-Politicus*," *Il cannocchiale* 94 (1994): 204–16; revised in the appendix to Yaffe, "Spinoza's *Theologico-Political Treatise*—A First Inside Look," in *Piety and Humanity*, 135–44. Elwes omits Spinoza's title page; Shirley translates it on S46–47.

3. *Praef.*8.1–9.1, 10.25–28, 11.1–8; 2.42.28–30; 5.80.24–30; 13.168.30–33, 170.32–172.29; 14.173.21–23, 176.16–18, 177.4–19, 33–35, 179.7–9, 180.4–6; 15.186.25–27; 18.225.17–226.6; 19.229.8–230.12; 20.241.29–242.3 (E6f., 9, 10, 40, 80, 177, 179–81, 182, 185, 186, 187, 188, 189, 196, 241f., 245–47, 258; S52f., 55, 86, 123, 215, 217–19, 220, 223, 224, 226, 233, 276, 281f., 292).

4. *Commercium*, 18.221.25–28 (E237: "relations," "dealings"; S272: "ties," "dealings").

5. 17.193.19–27, with 14.177.4–178.10 (E205, with 186f.; S241, with 224f.).

6. *Praef.* 12.12–19 (E11; S56). Cf. Leo Strauss, *Persecution and the Art of Writing* (Glencoe, Ill.: Free Press, 1952; reprint, Chicago: University of Chicago Press, 1988), 142–201, esp. 162ff.

7. Strauss, *Spinoza's Critique of Religion*, 6; or his *Liberalism Ancient and Modern* (New York: Basic Books, 1968; reprint, Chicago: University of Chicago Press, 1988), 230.

8. 1.19.26–33; 5.79.24–80.26; 7.113.7–116.11; 10.144.10–33; 15.180.33–

181.6, 184.18ff. (E17, 79f., 116–18, 149, 190f., 194; S63, 122f., 156–58, 189, 228, 232).

9. Cf. Spinoza, *Tractatus Politicus* 5.7; 10.1.

10. *Praef.*9.1–15; 13.167.32–168.24 (E7, 176; S53, 215).

11. See Chap. 3, n.2, above.

12. Cf. Thomas Aquinas, *Summa Theologiae* I.1.10.

13. *Praef.*9.1–15; 13.167.35–168.5 (E7, 176; S53, 215).

14. 7.98.22–23 (E99; S141). Cf. Bacon, *Novum Organum* II.10ff., in *Works,* 1:235ff.; also James C. Morrison, "Spinoza and History," in *The Philosophy of Baruch Spinoza,* ed. Richard Kennington (Washington, D.C.: Catholic University of America Press, 1980), 178 n. 13; Strauss, *Persecution and the Art of Writing,* 142ff.

15. *Sententiae,* 7.100.8ff. (E101: "contents"; S143f.: "pronouncements").

16. Deut. 4:24; 9:3; contrast Exod. 20:5; 34:14; Deut. 5:9; 6:15.

17. 3.44.12 (E43: "vocation"; S88: "vocation").

18. 2.31.10f., 19–23, 33.24–27, 43:6–8 (E28f., 31, 41; S74f., 77, 86). For a contrasting account of prophecy in general and of the instructiveness of Micaiah's prophecy in particular, cf. Sacks, *Commentary on Genesis,* 151f. and context; Martin D. Yaffe, "Biblical Religion and Liberal Democracy: Comments on Spinoza's *Theologico-Political Treatise* and Sacks' *Commentary on the Book of Genesis," Political Science Reviewer* 23 (1994): 315–18.

19. 3.44.33 (E43; S88), with *Praef.*10.28–30; 2.36.20, 27, 37.22, 29, 43.5–6, 17, 34; 3.45.19, 24, 27, 54.32; 4.65.28–29; 5.70.19–20, 77.15, 22, 31, 78.25; 6.84.5; 7.98.29–30; 11.156.1, 12; 12.172.5, 9; 14.178.30–31, 35f.; 15.180.25f. (E9, 33f., 34f., 41, 42, 44, 53, 65, 70, 77, 78, 84, 99, 161f., 180, 188, 190; S55, 79, 80f., 86, 87, 89, 97f., 108f., 113, 120, 121, 127, 141, 201f., 218, 225, 228). See Strauss, *Persecution and the Art of Writing,* 177f.

20. Consider, however, Maimonides, *Guide of the Perplexed III.* 27–28.

21. See 18.222.14–223.22; with *Praef.*9.32–10.4; 3.50.24ff., 56.19–57.20; 5.69.9–19; 19.230.31–232.8 (E238–39, with 9f., 49, 55f., 69, 248f.; S273f., with 54f., 94, 99f., 112, 282f.).

22. *Praef.*5–7, 10.22–27, 12.10f.; 2.29.29–30.4, 40.35ff.; 3.53.9–13; 7.97.31ff.; 9.129.9–11, 137.16.21; 11.158.13–15; 12.159.12–17; 16.199.29–32; 17.215.24–32; 18.222.12–223.23 (E3–6, 8f., 10f., 27, 38f., 52, 98f., 133, 141f., 164, 165, 212, 230, 238; S49–52, 54f., 56, 73, 84, 96, 140f., 173, 181f., 204, 205, 248, 265, 273). Cf. Martin D. Yaffe, "'The Histories and Successes of the Hebrews': The Demise of the Biblical Polity in Spinoza's *Theologico-Political Treatise," Jewish Political Studies Review* 7 (1995): 57–75.

23. For an illuminating consideration of the connection or rather elision

between the scientific and the political sense of *law* in Spinoza, see David R. Lachterman, "Laying down the Law: The Theologico-Political Matrix of Spinoza's Physics," in *Leo Strauss's Thought,* ed. Alan Udoff (Boulder, Colo.: Lynne Rienner, 1991), 123–53, esp. 131–36.

24. Consider 5.79.4–9 (E79; S122).

25. René Descartes, *Discours de la méthode/Discourse on the Method, A Bilingual Edition with an Interpretive Essay,* ed. and trans. George Heffernan (Notre Dame, Ind.: University of Notre Dame Press, 1994), pt 6, ¶ 2; Bacon, e.g., *Novum Organum* I.3, 129, in *Works* 1:157, 186f., with *Advancement of Learning* I, in *Works* 3:294.

26. Leo Strauss remarks pithily: "Spinoza lifts Machiavellianism to theological heights." *Spinoza's Critique of Religion,* 18; or his *Liberalism Ancient and Modern,* 242.

27. *Praef.*12.3–19; 15.180.14–33; 20.243.5–10 (E10f., 190, 261; S56, 228, 295).

28. 16.195.20f., 198.4–199.2 (E206f., 210; S243, 246f.).

29. 17.208.26f. and passim (E222ff.; S258ff.). On the Machiavellian overtones of Spinoza's Latin term *principes,* see Yaffe, "'The Histories and Successes of the Hebrews,'" 72f., n. 45.

30. Actually, Spinoza's chapter as a whole contains a list of nine such pointers. Besides the five mentioned here, Spinoza provides four modern-day caveats for the reader of the *Treatise:* don't give religious leaders political authority; don't make laws abridging freedom of thought; let political sovereigns alone decide right and wrong (within the foregoing limitations); and never let people not used to kings choose a king. See 18.225.12–228.14 (E241–44; S275–79); with Yaffe, "'The Histories and Successes of the Hebrews,'" 68f.

31. Lev. 24:17–22, for example, expressly distinguishes between capital punishment for murder and mere compensation for the destruction of livestock or the infliction of bodily injury. The formula "life for life" refers only to the compensatory payment of a replacement animal or, derivatively, its monetary cost; it does not refer to the execution of murderers. The biblical premise here seems to be that a human life that has been lost, unlike an animal's, is strictly speaking irreplaceable. Similarly, "fracture for fracture, eye for eye, tooth for tooth" refers to the monetary cost of a bodily injury for which another is culpable — given that replacement body parts are not available. The formulas quoted set limits to the legal damages recoverable in cases *other than* the loss of human life. See also Exod. 21:23–27.

32. To give Shylock the fullest benefit of the doubt, perhaps his consent

to supply Antonio with a loan may originally have been motivated by the wish to show publicly that even a religious crusader such as Antonio is sometimes in need of a usurer and hence to undermine the public respectability of Antonio's particular crusade. In any case, Jessica's sudden elopement complicated matters and intensified Shylock's longstanding wish for revenge against Antonio (I.iii.41–42, with III.i.20–43).

✣ Epilogue ✣

1. Gen. 9:5–6; Exod. 20:13; 21:12–14; 22:1–2; Lev. 20:1–5; 24:17, 21; Num. 35:6–24; Deut. 5:17; 21:1–9.

2. See chap. 5, n. 7, above.

Bibliography

Primary Sources

Bacon, Francis. *New Atlantis* and *The Great Instauration*. Rev. ed. Edited by Jerry Weinberger. Crofts Classics. Arlington Heights, Ill.: Harlan Davidson, 1989.

Bacon, Francis. *The Works of Francis Bacon*. 14 vols. Edited by James Spedding, Robert Leslie Ellis, and Douglas Denon Heath. London: Longmans & Co., 1857–74.

Marlowe, Christopher. *The Complete Plays*. Edited by J. B. Steane. Harmondsworth, England: Penguin Books, 1969.

Shakespeare, William. *The Complete Works*. Edited by Alfred Harbage. Pelican Text Revised. Reprint, New York: Viking Press, 1969.

Shakespeare, William. *The Merchant of Venice*. Edited by John Russell Brown. Arden Shakespeare. London: Routledge, 1988.

Shakespeare, William. *The Merchant of Venice*. New Variorum edition. Edited by Horace Howard Furness. New York: Dover, 1964.

Shakespeare, William. *The Merchant of Venice*. 2d ed. Edited by George Lyman Kittredge. Revised by Irving Ribner. Kittredge Shakespeares. New York: John Wiley & Sons, 1966.

Spinoza, Baruch. *Tractatus Theologico-Politicus*. 2d ed. Translated by Samuel Shirley. Leiden: E. J. Brill, 1991.

Spinoza, Benedict. *Works of Spinoza*. 2 vols. Translated by R. H. M. Elwes. New York: Dover, 1955.

Spinoza, Benedict de. *The Political Works: The* Tractatus Theologico-Politicus *in Part and the* Tractatus Politicus *in Full.* Edited and translated by A. G. Wernham. Oxford: Clarendon Press, 1958.

Spinoza, Benedictus. *Opere.* 4 vols. Edited by Carl Gebhardt. Heidelberg: Carl Winters Universitätsbuchhandlung, 1925.

ᘯ Secondary Sources ᘯ

Allison, Henry E. *Benedict de Spinoza.* Boston: Twayne, 1975.

Alter, Robert. "Who Is Shylock?" *Commentary* 96, no. 1 (1993): 29–34.

Altman, Joel B. *The Tudor Play of Mind: Rhetorical Inquiry and the Development of Elizabethan Drama.* Berkeley: University of California Press, 1978.

Anderson, F. H. *The Philosophy of Francis Bacon.* Chicago: University of Chicago Press, 1948.

Andrew, Edward. *Shylock's Rights: A Grammar of Lockean Claims.* Toronto: University of Toronto Press, 1988.

Apollonius Rhodius. *Argonautica.* Edited and translated by R. C. Seaton. Loeb Classical Library. London: Heinemann; Cambridge: Harvard University Press, 1988.

Aquinas, Thomas. *Commentary on Aristotle's* Nicomachean Ethics. 2 vols. Translated by C. I. Litzinger. Chicago: Henry Regnery, 1964.

Aquinas, Thomas. *Commentary on the* Metaphysics *of Aristotle.* Translated by John P. Rowan. Chicago: Henry Regnery, 1961.

Aquinas, Thomas. *In Aristotelis Librum De Caelo et Mundo, De Generatione et Corruptione, Meteorologicorum Expositio.* Edited by Raymundus M. Spiazzi. Turin: Marietti, 1952.

Aquinas, Thomas. *In Libros Politicorum Aristotelis Expositio.* 3d ed. Edited by Raymundus M. Spiazzi. Turin: Marietti, 1964.

Aquinas, Thomas. *The Literal Exposition on Job: A Scriptural Commentary Concerning Providence.* Translated by Anthony Damico. Interpretive essay and notes by Martin D. Yaffe. Atlanta: Scholars Press, 1989.

Aquinas, Thomas. *Summa Theologiae.* 3 vols. Edited by Petrus Caramello. Turin: Marietti, 1952.

Aristotle. *Metaphysics.* 2 vols. Edited by W. D. Ross. Oxford: Clarendon Press, 1924.

Aristotle. *The Nicomachean Ethics.* Edited and translated by H. Rackham.

Loeb Classical Library. London: Heinemann; Cambridge: Harvard University Press, 1962.

Aristotle. *On the Heavens.* Edited and translated by W. K. C. Guthrie. Loeb Classical Library. London: Heinemann; Cambridge: Harvard University Press, 1986.

Aristotle. *Politics.* Edited and translated by H. Rackham. Loeb Classical Library. London: Heinemann; Cambridge: Harvard University Press, 1959.

Arneson, Richard J. "Shakespeare and the Jewish Question." *Political Theory* 13 (1985): 85–111.

Auden, W. H. *The Dyer's Hand.* New York: Random House, 1948.

Babb, Howard S. "Policy in Marlowe's *The Jew of Malta.*" *E.L.H.: A Journal of English Literary History* 24 (1957): 85–94.

Bakeless, John. *The Tragicall History of Christopher Marlowe.* 2 vols. 1942. Reprint. Hamden, Conn.: Archon Books, 1964.

Barber, C. L. *Shakespeare's Festive Comedy.* Princeton: Princeton University Press, 1959.

Bawcutt, N. W. Introduction to Christopher Marlowe, *The Jew of Malta.* Revels Plays. Manchester: Manchester University Press; Baltimore: Johns Hopkins University Press, 1978.

Bawcutt, N. W. "Machiavelli and Marlowe's *The Jew of Malta.*" *Renaissance Drama,* n.s., 3 (1970): 3–49.

Beecher, Don. "*The Jew of Malta* and the Ritual of the Inverted Moral Order." *Cahiers Elisabéthiens: Etudes sur la Pré-Renaissance et la Renaissance anglaises* 12 (October 1977): 45–48.

Benardete, Seth. "On Plato's *Timaeus* and Timaeus' Science Fiction." *Interpretation* 2 (1971–72): 21–63.

Benardete, Seth. *Socrates' Second Sailing: On Plato's* Republic. Chicago: University of Chicago Press, 1989.

Bennett, H. S. Notes to Christopher Marlowe, *The Jew of Malta* and *The Massacre at Paris.* London: Methuen, 1931. Reprint, New York: Gordian Press, 1966.

Berger, Harry, Jr. "Marriage and Mercifixion in *The Merchant of Venice:* The Casket Scene Revisited." *Shakespeare Quarterly* 32 (1981): 155–62.

Berns, Laurence. "Aristotle's *Poetics.*" In *Ancients and Moderns: Essays on the Tradition of Political Philosophy in Honor of Leo Strauss.* Edited by Joseph Cropsey. New York: Basic Books, 1964.

Berns, Laurence. "An Introduction to the Political Philosophy of Francis

Bacon with Special Attention to the Principles of Foreign Policy." Ph.D. dissertation, University of Chicago, 1957.

Berns, Laurence. "Francis Bacon and the Conquest of Nature." *Interpretation* 7 (1978): 1–26.

Bevington, David. *From Mankind to Marlowe: Growth of Structure in the Popular Drama of Tudor England.* Cambridge: Harvard University Press, 1962.

Bloom, Allan. *Shakespeare's Politics.* New York: Basic Books, 1964.

Bloom, Harold, ed. *Shylock.* Major Literary Characters Series. New York: Chelsea House, 1991.

Boas, Frederick S. *Christopher Marlowe: A Biographical and Critical Study.* Oxford: Clarendon Press, 1940.

Briggs, John C. *Francis Bacon and the Rhetoric of Nature.* Cambridge: Harvard University Press, 1989.

Brook, Nicholas. "Marlowe the Dramatist." In *Elizabethan Theatre.* Edited by John Russell Brown and Bernard Harris. New York: St. Martin's Press, 1967.

Butcher, S. H. *Aristotle's Theory of Poetry and Fine Art, with a Critical Text and Translation of* The Poetics. 4th ed. New York: Dover, 1951.

Cantor, Paul. "Religion and the Limits of Community in *The Merchant of Venice.*" *Soundings* 70 (1987): 239–58.

Caton, Hiram. *The Politics of Progress: The Origins and Development of the Commercial Republic 1600–1835.* Gainesville: University of Florida Press, 1987.

Cole, Douglas. *Suffering and Evil in the Plays of Christopher Marlowe.* 1962. Reprint. New York: Gordian Press, 1972.

D'Andrea, Antonio. "Marlowe's Prologue to *The Jew of Malta.*" *Mediaeval and Renaissance Studies* 5 (1961): 214–48.

Danson, Lawrence. *The Harmonies of* The Merchant of Venice. New Haven: Yale University Press, 1978.

Davis, Michael. *Aristotle's Poetics: The Poetry of Philosophy.* Lanham, Md.: Rowman & Littlefield, 1992.

Delgado de Torres, Olivia. "Reflections on Patriarchy and the Rebellion of Daughters in Shakespeare's *Merchant of Venice* and *Othello.*" *Interpretation* 21 (1994): 333–51.

Descartes, René. *Discours de la méthode/Discourse on the Method: A Bilingual Edition with an Interpretive Essay.* Edited and Translated by George Heffernan. Notre Dame, Ind.: University of Notre Dame Press, 1994.

Eliot, T. S. *Elizabethan Essays.* New York: Haskell House, 1964.

Ellis-Fermor, U. M. *Christopher Marlowe.* 1927. Reprint. Hamden, Conn.: Archon Books, 1967.

Faulkner, Robert K. *Francis Bacon and the Project of Progress.* Lanham, Md.: Rowman & Littlefield, 1993.

Feuer, Lewis S. *Spinoza and the Rise of Liberalism.* Boston: Beacon Press, 1958.

Fiedler, Leslie. *The Stranger in Shakespeare.* New York: Stein & Day, 1972.

Frei, Hans W. *The Eclipse of Biblical Narrative: A Study in Eighteenth and Nineteenth Century Hermeneutics.* New Haven: Yale University Press, 1974.

Friedenreich, Kenneth, Roma Gill, and Constance B. Kuriyama, eds. *"A Poet and a filthy Playmaker": New Essays on Christopher Marlowe.* New York: AMS Press, 1988.

The Geneva Bible: A Facsimile of the 1560 Edition. Madison: University of Wisconsin Press, 1969.

Gentillet, Innocent. *A Discourse upon the Meanes of Wel Governing . . . Against Nicholas Machiavel the Florentine.* Translated by Simon Patricke. London, 1602. Reprint. Amsterdam: Da Capo Press, 1969.

Goddard, Harold C. *The Meaning of Shakespeare.* 2 vols. Chicago: University of Chicago Press, 1951.

Godshalk, W. L. *The Marlovian World Picture.* The Hague: Mouton, 1974.

Grebanier, Bernard. *The Truth about Shylock.* New York: Random House, 1962.

Greenblatt, Stephen J. "Marlowe, Marx, and Anti-Semitism." *Critical Inquiry* 5 (1978–79): 291–307.

Gross, John. *Shylock: A Legend and Its Legacy.* New York: Simon & Schuster, 1992.

Grudin, Robert. *Mighty Opposites: Shakespeare and Renaissance Contrariety.* Berkeley: University of California Press, 1979.

Harbage, Alfred. "Innocent Barabas." *Tulane Drama Review* 8, no. 4 (1964): 47–58.

Henninger, S. K. *Touches of Sweet Harmony: Pythagorean Cosmology and Renaissance Poetics.* San Marino, Calif.: Huntington Library, 1974.

Hinely, Jan. "Bond Priorities in *The Merchant of Venice.*" *Studies in English Literature* 20 (1980): 217–39.

Hobbes, Thomas. *Man and Citizen: Thomas Hobbes's.* De Homine *and* De Cive. Edited by Bernard Gert. Garden City, N.Y.: Anchor Books, 1972.

Hollander, John. *The Untuning of the Sky: Ideas of Music in English Poetry, 1500–1700.* Princeton: Princeton University Press, 1961.

Hunter, G. K. *Dramatic Identities and Cultural Tradition: Studies in Shakespeare and His Contemporaries.* New York: Barnes & Noble, 1978.

Hyman, Lawrence W. "The Rival Lovers in *The Merchant of Venice.*" *Shakespeare Quarterly* 21 (1970): 109–16.

Innes, David C. "Bacon's *New Atlantis:* The Christian Hope and the Modern Hope." In *Piety and Humanity: Religion and Early Modern Political Philosophy.* Edited by Douglas Kries. Foreword by Harvey C. Mansfield. Lanham, Md.: Rowman & Littlefield, 1997.

Jaffa, Harry V. "The Unity of Tragedy, Comedy, and History: An Interpretation of the Shakespearean Universe." In *Shakespeare as Political Thinker.* Edited by John Alvis and Thomas G. West. Durham, N.C.: Carolina Academic Press, 1981.

Jardine, Lisa. *Francis Bacon: Discovery and the Art of Disclosure.* Cambridge: Cambridge University Press, 1974.

Kennington, Richard. "Bacon's Concept of Mastery of Nature." Unpublished.

Kocher, Paul H. *Christopher Marlowe: A Study of His Thought, Learning, and Character.* New York: Russell & Russell, 1962.

Lachterman, David R. "Laying Down the Law: The Theologico-Political Matrix of Spinoza's Physics." In *Leo Strauss's Thought.* Edited by Alan Udoff. Boulder, Colo.: Lynne Rienner, 1991.

Lampert, Laurence. *Nietzsche and Modern Times: A Study of Bacon, Descartes, and Nietzsche.* New Haven: Yale University Press, 1993.

Landa, M. J. *The Jew in Drama.* Reprint. Port Washington, N.Y.: Kennikat, 1968.

LePain, Mark A. "The Fruit of the Land: Biblical and Classical Allusions in Francis Bacon's *New Atlantis.*" Unpublished.

Levin, Harry. *The Overreacher: A Study of Christopher Marlowe.* Cambridge: Harvard University Press, 1952.

Levin, Richard. *Love and Society in Shakespearean Comedy.* Newark, Del.: University of Delaware Press, 1985.

Lewalski, Barbara K. "Biblical Allusion and Allegory in *The Merchant of Venice.*" *Shakespeare Quarterly* 13 (1962): 327–43.

Locke, John. *Epistola de Tolerantia/A Letter on Toleration.* Edited by Raymond Klibansky. Translated by J. W. Gough. Oxford: Clarendon Press, 1968.

Lowenthal, David. "The New Shakespeareans." *Claremont Review of Books* 3, no. 2 (1984): 9–14.

Lyon, John. *The Merchant of Venice.* Twayne's New Critical Introductions to Shakespeare. Boston: Twayne, 1988.

Machiavelli, Niccolò. *Discourses on Livy.* Translated by Harvey C. Mansfield and Nathan Tarcov. Chicago: University of Chicago Press, 1996.

Machiavelli, Niccolò. *The Prince.* Translated by Harvey C. Mansfield Jr. Chicago: University of Chicago Press, 1985.

Macpherson, C. B. *The Political Theory of Possessive Individualism: Hobbes to Locke.* Oxford: Clarendon Press, 1964.

Maimonides, Moses. *The Guide of the Perplexed.* Translated by Shlomo Pines. Introductory essay by Leo Strauss. Chicago: University of Chicago Press, 1963.

Malherbe, Michèle. "Man and Nature in the Gardens of Science." In *Francis Bacon's Legacy of Texts.* Edited by William A. Sessions. New York: AMS Press, 1990.

Mansfield, Harvey C., Jr. *Taming the Prince: The Ambivalence of Modern Executive Power.* Baltimore: Johns Hopkins University Press, 1993.

Meyer, Edward. *Machiavelli and Elizabethan Drama.* Weimar: Literarhistorische Forschungen, 1897. Reprint. New York: Burt Franklin, n.d.

The Midrash Rabbah. 5 vols. Translated and edited under H. Freedman and Maurice Simon. New York: Soncino Press, 1977.

Mindle, Grant B. "Shakespeare's Demonic Prince." *Interpretation* 20 (1993): 259–74.

Mishnayoth. 7 vols. Edited and translated by Philip Blackman. Gateshead, England: Judaica Press, 1977.

More, Thomas. *Utopia.* Translated by Paul Turner. Harmondsworth, England: Penguin Books, 1961.

Morrison, James C. "Philosophy and History in Bacon." *Journal of the History of Ideas* 38 (1977): 585–606.

Morrison, James C. "Spinoza and History." In *The Philosophy of Baruch Spinoza.* Edited by Richard Kennington. Washington, D.C.: Catholic University of America Press, 1980.

Nelson, Benjamin. *The Idea of Usury: From Tribal Brotherhood to Universal Otherhood.* 2d ed. Chicago: University of Chicago Press, 1969.

Ovid. *The Art of Love and Other Poems.* Edited by J. H. Mosley. Revised by G. P. Goold. Loeb Classical Library. London: Heinemann; Cambridge: Harvard University Press, 1978.

Ovid. *Metamorphoses.* 3d ed. 2 vols. Edited and translated by Frank Justus Miller. Revised by G. P. Goold. Loeb Classical Library. London: Heinemann; Cambridge: Harvard University Press, 1984.

Patch, Howard R. *The Goddess Fortuna in Mediaeval Literature.* Cambridge: Harvard University Press, 1927.

Paterson, Timothy. "Bacon's Myth of Orpheus: Power as a Goal of Science in *On the Wisdom of the Ancients.*" *Interpretation* 16 (1989): 427–44.

Paterson, Timothy. "On the Role of Christianity in the Political Philosophy of Francis Bacon." *Polity* 19 (1986–87): 19–42.

Paterson, Timothy. "The Politics of Baconian Science: An Analysis of Bacon's *New Atlantis.*" Ph.D. dissertation, Yale University, 1982.

Paterson, Timothy. "The Secular Control of Scientific Power in the Political Philosophy of Francis Bacon." *Polity* 21 (1988–89): 457–80.

Plato. *Euthyphro, Apology, Crito, Phaedo, Phaedrus.* Edited and translated by H. N. Fowler. Loeb Classical Library. London: Heinemann; Cambridge: Harvard University Press, 1966.

Plato. *Laws.* 2 vols. Edited and translated by R. G. Bury. Loeb Classical Library. London: Heinemann; Cambridge: Harvard University Press, 1961.

Plato. *Laws.* Translated, with notes and an interpretive essay, by Thomas L. Pangle. New York: Basic Books, 1979.

Plato. *Republic.* 2d ed. Translated, with notes and an interpretive essay, by Allan Bloom. New York: Basic Books, 1991.

Plato. *Republic.* 2 vols. Edited and translated by Paul Shorey. Loeb Classical Library. London: Heinemann; Cambridge: Harvard University Press; 1937.

Plato. *Timaeus, Critias, Cleitophon, Menexenus, Epistles.* Edited and translated by R. G. Bury. Loeb Classical Library. London: Heinemann; Cambridge: Harvard University Press, 1966.

Plutarch. *Lives of the Noble Grecians and Romans.* Translated by John Dryden. Revised by A. H. Clough. 1864. Reprint, New York: Modern Library, n.d.

Poirer, Michel. *Christopher Marlowe.* 1951. Reprint, Hamden, Conn.: Archon Books , 1968.

Praz, Mario. *Machiavelli and the Elizabethans.* London: British Academy Lecture, 1928.

Raab, Felix. *The English Face of Machiavelli: A Changing Interpretation, 1500–1700.* London: Routledge & Kegan Paul; Toronto: University of Toronto Press, 1965.

Rabkin, Norman. *Shakespeare and the Problem of Meaning.* Chicago: University of Chicago Press, 1981.

Reifer, Frederick. *Fortune and Elizabethan Tragedy.* San Marino, Calif.: Huntington Library, 1983.

Rivkin, Ellis. *The Shaping of Jewish History: A Radical New Interpretation.* New York: Scribner's, 1971.

Rocklin, Edward L. "Marlowe as Experimental Dramatist: The Role of the Audience in *The Jew of Malta.*" In *"A Poet and a filthy Play-maker": New Essays on Christopher Marlowe.* Edited by Kenneth Friedenreich, Roma Gill, and Constance B. Kuriyama. New York: AMS Press, 1988.

Rosen, Stanley. "Benedict Spinoza." In *History of Political Philosophy.* 3d ed. Edited by Leo Strauss and Joseph Cropsey. Chicago: University of Chicago Press, 1987.

Sacks, Robert D. *A Commentary on the Book of Genesis.* Lewiston, N.Y.: Edwin Mellen Press, 1990.

Sanders, Wilbur. *The Dramatist and the Received Idea.* Cambridge: Cambridge University Press, 1968.

Schwartz, Joel. "Liberalism and the Jewish Connection: A Study of Spinoza and the Young Marx." *Political Theory* 13 (1985): 58–84.

Shapiro, James. *Shakespeare and the Jews.* New York: Columbia University Press, 1996.

Shapiro, James. "'Which is *The Merchant* here, and which *The Jew?*' Shakespeare and the Economics of Influence." *Shakespeare Studies* 20 (1988): 269–79.

Shell, Marc. *Money, Language, and Thought: Literary and Philosophical Economics from the Medieval to the Modern Era.* Berkeley: University of California Press, 1982.

Simmons, J. L. "Elizabethan Stage Practice and Marlowe's *The Jew of Malta.*" *Renaissance Drama,* n.s., 4 (1971): 93–104.

Smith, Steven B. "Spinoza's Paradox: Judaism and the Construction of Liberal Identity in the *Theologico-Political Treatise.*" *Journal of Jewish Thought and Philosophy* 4 (1995): 203–25.

Spivack, Bernard. *Shakespeare and the Allegory of Evil: The History of a Metaphor in Relation to His Major Villains.* New York: Columbia University Press, 1958.

Steane, J. B. *Marlowe: A Critical Study.* Cambridge: Cambridge University Press, 1964.

Stephens, James. *Francis Bacon and the Style of Science.* Chicago: University of Chicago Press, 1975.

Strauss, Leo. *The Argument and the Action of Plato's Laws.* Chicago: University of Chicago Press, 1975.

Strauss, Leo. *The City and Man*. Chicago: Rand McNally, 1964. Reprint. Chicago: University of Chicago Press, 1978.

Strauss, Leo. *Liberalism Ancient and Modern*. New York: Basic Books, 1968. Reprint. Chicago: University of Chicago Press, 1995.

Strauss, Leo. *Natural Right and History*. Chicago: University of Chicago Press, 1953.

Strauss, Leo. *On Tyranny*. Rev. and expanded ed. Edited by Victor Gourevich and Michael S. Roth. New York: Free Press, 1991.

Strauss, Leo. *Persecution and the Art of Writing*. Glencoe, Ill.: Free Press, 1952. Reprint. Chicago: University of Chicago Press, 1988.

Strauss, Leo. *Spinoza's Critique of Religion*. New York: Schocken, 1965. Reprint. Chicago: University of Chicago Press, 1996.

Strauss, Leo. *Studies in Platonic Political Philosophy*. Chicago: University of Chicago Press, 1983.

Strauss, Leo. *Thoughts on Machiavelli*. Glencoe, Ill.: Free Press, 1958. Reprint. Chicago: University of Chicago Press, 1984.

Studer, Heidi. "'Grapes Ill-Trodden . . .?: Francis Bacon and the Wisdom of the Ancients." Ph.D. dissertation, University of Toronto, 1992.

Tovey, Barbara. "The Golden Casket: An Interpretation of *The Merchant of Venice*." In *Shakespeare as Political Thinker*. Edited by John Alvis and Thomas G. West. Durham, N.C.: Carolina Academic Press, 1981.

Weinberger, Jerry. "Science and Rule in Bacon's Utopia: An Introduction to the Reading of the *New Atlantis*." *American Political Science Review* 70 (1996): 856–85.

Weinberger, Jerry. *Science, Faith, and Politics: Francis Bacon and the Utopian Roots of the Modern Age*. Ithaca: Cornell University Press, 1985.

White, Howard B. "Francis Bacon." In *History of Political Philosophy*. 3d ed. Edited by Leo Strauss and Joseph Cropsey. Chicago: University of Chicago Press, 1987.

White, Howard B. "Bacon's *Wisdom of the Ancients*." *Interpretation* 2 (1970): 107–29.

White, Howard B. *Peace among the Willows: The Political Philosophy of Francis Bacon*. The Hague: Martinus Nijhoff, 1968.

Wilson, Thomas. *A Discourse on Usury* [1572]. Edited by R. H. Tawney. New York: Augustus M. Kelley, 1963.

Wright, Eugene P. *Thomas Deloney*. Twayne's English Authors Series. Boston: Twayne, 1981.

Xenophon. *Scripta Minora*. Edited and translated by E. C. Marchant. Loeb Classical Library. London: Heinemann; Cambridge: Harvard University Press, 1971.

Yaffe, Martin D. "On Beginning to Translate Spinoza's *Tractatus Theologico-Politicus.*" *Il cannocchiale* 94 (1994): 240–16.

Yaffe, Martin D. "Biblical Religion and Liberal Democracy: Comments on Spinoza's *Theologico-Political Treatise* and Sacks' *Commentary on the Book of Genesis.*" *Political Science Reviewer* 23 (1994): 284–341.

Yaffe, Martin D. "'The Histories and Successes of the Hebrews': The Demise of the Biblical Polity in Spinoza's *Theologico-Political Treatise.*" *Jewish Political Studies Review* 7 (1995): 57–75.

Yaffe, Martin D. "Providence in Medieval Aristotelianism: Moses Maimonides and Thomas Aquinas on the Book of Job." In *The Voice from The Whirlwind: Interpreting the Book of Job.* Edited by Leo G. Perdue and W. Clark Gilpin. Nashville, Tenn.: Abingdon, 1992.

Yaffe, Martin D. "Spinoza's *Theologico-Political Treatise* — A First Inside Look." In *Piety and Humanity: Religion and Early Modern Political Philosophy.* Edited by Douglas Kries. Foreword by Harvey C. Mansfield. Lanham, Md.: Rowman & Littlefield, 1997.

Zagorin, Perez. *Ways of Lying: Dissimulation, Persecution, and Conformity in Early Modern Europe.* Cambridge: Harvard University Press, 1990.

Zuckert, Michael. "The New Medea: Portia's Comic Triumph in *The Merchant of Venice.*" In *Shakespeare's Political Pageant.* Edited by Joseph Alulis and Vickie Sullivan. Lanham, Md.: Rowman & Littlefield, 1996.

Index